Venture Capital Handbook

New and Revised

David Gladstone

Prentice Hall
Englewood Cliffs, New Jersey 07632

Library of Congress Catalog Card Number: 87-61607

Editorial/production supervision
  and interior design: **Sophie Papanikolaou**
Cover design: **Wanda Lubelska Design**
Manufacturing buyer: **Paula Benevento**

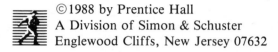
The publisher offers discounts on this book when ordered
in bulk quantities. For more information, write:

Special Sales/College Marketing
Prentice Hall
College Technical and Reference Division
Englewood Cliffs, NJ 07632

Printed in the United States of America

20   19   18   17   16   15

ISBN   0-13-941501-7   025

Prentice-Hall International (UK) Limited, *London*
Prentice-Hall of Australia Pty. Limited, *Sydney*
Prentice-Hall Canada Inc., *Toronto*
Prentice-Hall Hispanoamericana, S.A., *Mexico*
Prentice-Hall of India Private Limited, *New Delhi*
Prentice-Hall of Japan, Inc., *Tokyo*
Simon & Schuster Asia Pte. Ltd., *Singapore*
Editora Prentice-Hall do Brasil, Ltda., *Rio de Janeiro*

This book is dedicated to the women in my life.
It is dedicated to my wife, Lorna,
who has been my constant companion through everything.
It is dedicated to my mother, Lola,
who withstood the problems of raising me.
It is dedicated to my daughters, Kent, Jessica, and Laura,
and especially to Laura,
who wonders why anyone would write a book
when he could read a book, or watch television.
It is dedicated to our dog, Phoebe.
She wonders (I am sure)
why humans do anything except sleep and eat.
I am beginning to see life more in her terms.

Contents

v

3   The Proposal   39

Can You Put Together An Interesting Proposal?
A Complete Proposal Is One That Sells Your Company.

4   A Thousand Questions   71

Can You Answer A Thousand Questions?
Be Prepared By Answering All The Questions In This Chapter.

5   Meetings and Negotiations   97

Can You Have It Your Way?
What You Need To Know To Get The Best Deal.

6   Commitment Letter   121

Can It All Be Put Into Words?
Your Agreements Must Always Be Put In Writing.

7   Due Diligence   147

What Does The Venture Capitalist Want When He Visits?
What To Expect From Investigations Of Your Proposal.

8   The Closing   169

Will We Ever Learn To Live With Lawyers?
Getting It All Down In Legal Terms.

9   Working Together   189

How Can You Both Make Money?
Operating Your Company To Make The Most Money.

Preface and Acknowledgments

Why Did This Book Come Into Existence?
You Will Not Believe It.

This book came into being simply because I have reviewed a great many proposals for venture capital financing that were incomplete, inconsistent, and inane. I thought I was the only person in the venture capital industry receiving that many incomprehensible proposals. Then, during one of our annual conventions, I conducted a random survey of others working in the venture capital industry. Their cry was even louder than mine. Over and over, industry representatives told me how many poorly prepared business proposals they had received. They told me that entrepreneurs did not understand what venture capitalists want.

When I received an incomplete business proposal in the past, I sent back a two-page summary of the information needed in a sound business proposal. This tactic never seemed to work. I guess free advice is not worth very much. So I wrote this book to provide anyone who wants to spend the time and money with an insight into what venture capitalists really want.

Also, I wrote this book because of the overwhelming guilt I felt as I turned down proposal after proposal. I turned them down primarily because they were so poorly prepared that I couldn't understand the plan being presented. There is a saying in the venture capital field that if the entrepreneur or business owner cannot write a strong business proposal, then he is not worth investing in. That may sound cruel, but so many entrepreneurs are seeking venture capital that the venture capitalist cannot dedicate time and effort to helping the entrepreneur put together a business proposal. As I turned down all those business proposals, I saw the destruction of the dreams of entrepreneurs who wanted to be in business to make more money, and who wanted to have some control over their destinies.

After beginning the book I realized that the business proposal was only the beginning of a long relationship between the venture capitalist and the entrepreneur. For that reason, the book was expanded to include not just the business proposal, but the entire process from the presentation of the proposal, through the negotiations, the commitment letters, the legal closings, and the due diligence, to the exit by the venture capital company, when the entrepreneur is left to own it all. I saw a need for a complete book because often the entrepreneur does not understand the needs and desires of the venture capitalist when the entrepreneur comes looking for funds.

The book is written from the perspective of how I would act if I were an entrepreneur approaching a venture firm. In some respects it may be an idealized view because I approached the subject from the way I, as a venture capitalist, would like to be treated by an entrepreneur.

Since 1974 I have been an executive officer at Allied Capital Corporation, the largest publicly-owned venture capital firm in the United States. In 1959, Allied received the third license to be granted to a Small Business Investment Company by the U.S. Small Business Administration. Through one of its subsidiaries, Allied continues to operate as a Small Business Investment Company. In my position I have seen five to ten venture capital requests *daily* since 1974. I have spoken to thousands of entrepreneurs seeking financing.

Conceptually, the venture capital industry is at the center of capitalism, determining what new businesses will start, and what new ideas will receive financing. But like any "glamour" job, it has its daily routine. My daily routine includes many discussions with entrepreneurs about their businesses. Some conversations have been pleasant, and some lifelong friendships have formed. Other discussions have been outrageous and depressing.

Being in the venture capital business gives one a skewed outlook on life. One sees so many entrepreneurs that eventually one believes the whole business and industrial complex in the United States is entrepreneurial in character, when in fact only a small portion of the population is involved in entrepreneurial activities. Although there are many small businesses in this country, there are fewer entrepreneurs. I sometimes think their numbers are dwindling.

Philosophically the small business community harbors the remnants of the American pioneer spirit that made our country great. A small business is the last frontier where one can express an individual spirit and pioneer a dream. The entrepreneur is a modern version of the rugged individual who helped to build America.

I have tremendous respect for entrepreneurs. They are a hardy breed.

They go through hell to achieve their goals. They are ambitious dreamers. Many spend their entire lifetimes in the most stressful environments imaginable. A few create entire industries that change the way people live. Some entrepreneurs fail and the experience changes their lives forever. Most entrepreneurs merely survive. All entrepreneurs work very hard.

Entrepreneurship is the driving force of every economy. Its growth orientation creates approximately 85 percent of all *new* jobs in the free world. The thousand larger firms in the world create very few new jobs. The effect of the entrepreneur on the economy has never been measured or evaluated in a successful manner. This is a vast unstudied area in business and economics, as well as in psychology, sociology, and history. I hope someday someone will make a complete study of the entrepreneur.

Acknowledgments

Many people made this book possible. Most of them are in the venture capital industry. It is important that some of them be given credit here. The mistakes and problems of this book are not theirs, but mine. I hope that those who helped and whose names I didn't mention will forgive my oversight.

Many employees of Allied Capital Corporation played a decisive role in this book. George C. Williams is directly responsible for this book because he has been teaching me about venture capital since 1973. Brooks Browne, Jon Ledecky, David Parker, Harry Brill, and other employees of Allied unknowingly made contributions to this book. Joan Barra of Allied had a special role in creating this book, for which I owe everlasting indebtedness.

The Board of Directors of Allied Capital Corporation, all entrepreneurs in their own right, also unwittingly contributed to this book. Curtis Steuart made the greatest impression on me and therefore made the greatest contribution to this book. Other board members, such as Henry Kaufman, Walter Green, Paul Courtney, Murray Toomey, Bob Long, and Wally Holladay all shared their entrepreneurial knowledge and personal investment history with me on many occasions. As newer members of the board, Willem deVogel and Ray Lee brought their own current experience as venture capitalists to bear on many of my thoughts.

Many people in the industry helped to shape my thinking about this book. None of them, of course, should be held responsible for the final product. A list of these individuals and their corporations follows:

Robert Allsop	R. W. Allsop Capital Corp.
S. W. Austin	Metropolitan Capital Corp.
Richard Bannon	Cardinal Development Fund
Thomas Barry	North Riverside Capital Corp.
Frank Bonsal	New Enterprise Associates

Frederick Beste	Mountain Ventures
John Blackburn	Orange Nassau Capital Corp.
David Blair	White River Capital Corp.
Robert Braswell	MCA New Ventures
Earl Brian	Biotech Capital
Greg Bultman	R. W. Allsop Capital Corp.
Ian Bund	Doan Resources Corp.
Donald Burton	South Atlantic Venture Fund
William Cannon	Capital For Business, Inc.
Frank Chambers	Continental Capital Ventures
Don Christensen	Greater Washington Investors
Patricia Cloherty	Fifty-Third Street Ventures, L.P.
Morton Choen	Clarion Capital Corp.
Floyd Collins	First Southern Capital Corp.
William Comfort	Citicorp Venture Capital
Joseph Conway	Michigan Capital & Service
John Crabtree	First Southern Capital Corp.
David Croll	T. A. Associates
Michael Cronin	First SBIC of California
Robert Davidoff	CMNY Capital Co.
Barry Davis	Alliance Business Investment
Kenneth DeAngelis	Rust Capital Ltd.
David C. Delaney	First SBIC of Alabama
J. B. Doherty	TDH Capital Corp.
Cyril Draffin	Greater Washington Investors, Inc.
David Dullum	Frontenac Capital Corp.
Thomas du Pont	First Tampa Capital Corp.
Bruce Duty	Capital Southwest Venture Corp.
Daniel Dye	First SBIC of California
David Engelson	First Connecticut SBIC
Philip English	Broventure Co.
A. Hugh Ewing	Hillcrest Group
Raichard Farrell	The Venture Capital Fund of New England
H. Wayne Foreman	Marine Venture Capital, Inc.
John Foster	J. H. Foster & Co.
Bondurant French	First Chicago Investment Advisors
Richard Frisbie	Battery Ventures
Jeffrey Garvey	Rust Capital Ltd.
Stanley Golder	Golder, Thoma & Cressey
Gary Granoff	Elk Associates Funding Corp.
Andy Greenshields	Pathfinder Venture Capital Fund
Robert D. Gries	Gries Investment Co.
Jeffrey Griffin	Greater Washington Investors, Inc.

Samuel Guren	William Blair Venture Partners
William Gust	Broventure Co.
Daniel Haggerty	Norwest Growth Fund, Inc.
Patrick Hamner	Capital Southwest Venture Corp.
David Harkins	Massachusetts Capital
Thomas Harvey	Carolina Venture Capital Corp.
Timothy Hay	First SBIC of California
James Hebenstreit	Capital For Business, Inc.
Victor Hecht	Croyden Capital Corp.
James Hellmuth	BT Capital Corp.
E. F. Heizer	Heizer Corp.
John Hines	Continental Illinois Venture
John Hoey	Beneficial Capital Corp.
C. L. Hoffman	Southeast Venture Capital
David Howe	Peachtree Capital
Brian Jones	First SBIC of California
David Jones	InterVen Partners
Joseph Kenary	First Mayland Capital, Inc.
Mark Kimmel	Columbine Venture Mgmt., Inc.
David King	Sovran Funding Corp.
Wayne Kingsley	InterVen Partners
Eugene Landy	Monmouth Capital Corp.
William Lanphear	The Early Stages Co.
Charles Lee	Abacus Ventures
Janice Leeming	Fund of New England
Arthur Little	Narragansett Capital Corp.
Troy McCrory	NCNB SBIC Corp.
James McGrath	Hutton Venture Investment Partners
Herman McManaway	Heritage Capital Corp.
James McManus	Market Corp. Venture Associates
Robert Manchester	Narragansett Capital Corp.
Andrew McWethy	Irving Capital Corp.
Brian Mercer	American Security Capital Corp.
Steven Merrill	Merrill, Pickard, Anderson & Eyre I
Jane Morris	Venture Economics, Inc.
Irwin Nelson	Nelson Capital Corp.
Charles Newhall	New Enterprise Associates
Thomas Noojin	Invesat Corporation
Martin Orland	AMEV Capital Corp.
John Oxendine	Broadcast Capital, Inc.
John Padgett	First SBIC of California
Charles Palmer	North American Company
Alan Patricof	Alan Patricof Associates

Milton Picard	Financial Resources, Inc.
Martin Pinson	Greater Washington Investors
P. S. Prasad	Falcon Capital Corp.
Robert Pratt	Atlantic Venture Partners
Stanley Pratt	Venture Economics, Inc.
Brent Rider	Union Venture Corp.
Kinsey Roper	Heritage Capital Corp.
Donald Ross	Rand SBIC, Inc.
Alan Ruvelson	First Midwest Capital Corp.
Stephen Schewe	Norwest Growth Fund, Inc.
David Schroder	MorAmerica Capital Corp.
David Silver	Santa Fe Private Equity Fund
Sanford Simon	Ferranti High Technology, Inc.
Max Simpson	Crosspoint Investment Corp.
Harold Small	M & T Capital Corp.
Barry Solomon	Irving Capital Corp.
Edwin Spina	North American Company
William Starnes	Heritage Capital Corp.
John Sterling	Reedy River Ventures
Tony Stevens	First SBIC of California
Richard Tadler	Orange Nassau Capital Corp.
G. Jackson Tankersley	The Centennial Fund
Don Taylor	MorAmerica Capital Corp.
Carl Thoma	Golder, Thoma & Cressey
William Thomas	Capital Southwest Venture Corp.
Noel Urben	BT Capital Corp.
Franklin Van Kasper	VK Capital Corp.
Peter Van Oosterhout	River Capital Corp.
Patrick Welsh	Welsh, Carson & Anderson
Harvery Wertheim	Harvest Ventures, Inc.
Alex Wilkins	Delta Capital, Inc.
Walter Wilkinson	Kitty Hawk Capital, Ltd.
Martin Witte	Marwit Capital Corp.
Robert Zicarelli	Norwest Growth Fund

For those that I missed, please forgive me.

A special apology is extended to the women who read this book. Common usage of the English language provides for the use of masculine pronouns. The use of masculine pronouns is not meant to diminish the contribution of female entrepreneurs , or to discourage female readers from becoming entrepreneurs.

Special Offer

For all of those entrepreneurs who read this book and *use its format,* I will personally review your business proposal and determine if it has a prayer of getting financing in the Venture Capital Community. It is important that you use the format of this book or this offer is not good. If you do not include a summary, then no review will be possible. Please send your proposals to:

David Gladstone
Allied Capital Corporation
1666 K. Street
Suite 901
Washington, D.C. 20006

1

I'll Back
Your Venture

Can You Get the Venture Capital Needed to Finance
Your Business? A Summary of What It Is All About.

E very small business needs venture capital. Venture capital is risk money. It permits a small business to grow and prosper. When an entrepreneur has a new idea he wants to try out or owns a small business that is growing, he usually approaches a bank for a loan. He soon discovers that banks make loans where the risk of loss is negligible. After being turned down by a bank, the small business owner or the entrepreneur with a new idea often asks a wealthy individual or several friends to back the business venture. Approaching an individual for capital can be dangerous. For one thing, the individual's method of venture capital investing may be highly unprofessional. For another, the investor's objective may be to own the business. Wherever possible, an entrepreneur should deal with professionals. This book tells you how to raise money from professionally run venture capital companies and how to make the relationship work for you.

Venture capital investing is a difficult business. The decision to finance a small business is itself a complex process. Many questions must first be answered. Certain critical elements must be present in a business proposal before it will receive venture capital backing. This book explains those elements and in so doing answers the question, "How can you raise venture capital to start a

1

business, to buy a business, or to grow an existing business?" It explains how you can work with the venture capitalist to maximize your personal profit.

I'll Back You

I'll back you if you have a good idea that will make money for both of us. That simple sentence contains all the ingredients necessary to obtain funds from a venture capital company. Analysis of the parts of the sentence will give you an understanding of venture capital.

In the middle of the sentence is the clause, "that will make money." It is pretty obvious what that means. Venture capitalists are not interested in investments based on motives of faith, hope, or charity. A venture capital company is run exclusively for profit. Even though some investments made by venture capital companies perform so poorly that they may look like charitable contributions, rest assured that the original intent was profit. If you are offering anything except profit, you should not approach the venture capital investor. Many times an entrepreneur thinks that if he offers the venture capitalist some additional benefit, it will induce the venture capitalist to make the investment. For example, the venture capitalist who is considering financing a broadway play may be offered an opportunity to meet some famous stars who are to act in the play. One venture capitalist was told that if he invested in a particular company and it succeeded, he would be remembered forever in history as having financed one of the greatest inventions in this century. While the venture capitalist is not above a little glamour, greed and avarice, not glamour, are his primary motivations in making an investment in your company.

Now, let's turn to the part of the sentence that says, "for both of us." Surprisingly enough, venture capitalists are *not* interested in a project that will make money solely for them *or* for you. They look at *every* situation as if it were a partnership. Your interests and those of the venture capitalist must be congruent or the venture capitalist will not make an investment. As a result, any investment opportunity in which only the venture capitalist will make money or only the entrepreneur will profit is not considered a good investment from a venture capital standpoint. Both parties should be able to make money.

Now turn to the hard part: "a good idea." Good ideas are *easy* to find. Thousands of good ideas are floating around everywhere. The problem with all good ideas is that very few are profitable. Finding an idea that will make money is not easy. Finding a good idea that has a large profit opportunity is extremely unusual. Explaining how profitable a good idea can be for an investor is also a difficult assignment. It will be easier for you to communicate your ideas to a venture capital company if you follow the procedure in this book. If you follow the directions, any venture capitalist will understand what your company is about and how your idea will make money.

Finally, look at the beginning of the sentence, "I'll back you." It is the most important part of the sentence. The venture capitalist must be convinced that you and your management team can make the idea happen and make money doing it. This will be your most difficult task—explaining why you and your team are the ones who can make it all happen.

What Is Venture Capital?

It is easier to begin the description of venture capital by explaining what venture capital is not. The loan that a bank makes to a business is not venture capital. The stocks and bonds an investment company buys on the New York Stock Exchange do not involve venture capital. A real estate investment company buying apartment buildings, shopping centers, and so on is not investing venture capital. A subsidiary of a bank that makes investments in small business could be using venture capital. Some investment companies that buy new issues of public traded companies might also be considered investors of venture capital. If you and a group of friends get together and put some money into a small business to get it off the ground, your investment may be a type of venture capital. If you loan some money to your brother who is opening a new type of store, that money may be considered venture capital. If you buy stock in a private company that is starting to manufacture a new type of machine, the money you invest is traditionally known as high technology venture capital. The equity money put up to buy a business is considered venture capital. The money invested in a new company that shows a potential for fast growth is venture capital.

As you are now beginning to understand, a venture capital investment is characterized by high risk. It doesn't matter how the investment is structured, whether it is an equity investment that generates long-term capital gains, or a high risk loan that gives the venture capitalist a 25 percent return on his investment. If high risk loans qualify, then you might ask yourself, "What is the difference between a finance company and a venture capital company? After all, a finance company makes loans at a high rate of interest." The difference between the two is management assistance. You will find the venture capitalist more involved in your business than a finance company. He frequently reviews your operations and constantly makes suggestions. He is, in essence, your business partner. He tries to make your company grow so it will be more profitable and be able to give him a higher return. When you approach the venture capitalist you should not approach him with the thought that you are seeking only money. When you acquire venture capital you are acquiring additional brain power to help your corporation achieve the goals that you have established.

In the past one could say that institutional money was not venture capital and that venture capital funds came from noninstitutional sources. That distinction disappeared in the last twenty years. Now there are institutions with the sole function of investing in venture situations. With the passage of the Small Business Investment Act of 1958, the U.S. government began assisting venture capitalists. Venture companies that qualify with the U.S. Small Business Administration (SBA) are able to borrow money from the SBA at lower rates as long as they invest their funds in small businesses. Over 350 venture capital companies are now licensed by SBA. Among the larger institutions, many stockbrokerage firms have assembled clients' money and placed it into large venture capital pools for investing in venturing situations. In the last fifteen years there has evolved a group of professional managers of pools of venture capital funds such as might be found managing any mutual fund. These venture funds obtain their money from pension funds, insurance companies, and in the case of public venture capital companies, from individual stockholders. The managers are a highly trained and educated group, unlike their "gun-slinging" predecessors of twenty years ago. Approximately one hundred of these venture capital pools are not affiliated with the SBA. In total, there are approximately five hundred professionally managed venture capital companies in the United States.

Where Can You Find Venture Capital?

Two published lists are available to help you to find the right venture capital company for your situation. The first contains the names of firms licensed by SBA, which are known as Small Business Investment Companies (SBICs). A list of the members is included in Appendix 2 of this book. The members are the most active venture capital companies. If you want to obtain a new listing write to their trade association at:

National Association of Small Business
Investment Companies (NASBIC)
1156 15th St
Suite 1101
Washington, D.C. 20005
(202) 833-8230

The second list is another trade association of venture capitalists largely made up of companies that are not affiliated with government. Their names are also included in Appendix 2. A more current list can be obtained from that trade association by writing to:

The National Venture Capital Association
1655 North Fort Myer Dr., Suite 700
Arlington, VA 22209
(703) 528-4370

What Kinds of Venture Capital Companies are There?

Venture capital companies can be defined in a number of ways. There are two general types of venture capital companies: those that are leveraged, meaning they have borrowed a great deal of money from either the government or private sources; and those that are equity venture capital companies. The equity companies, as their name implies, have not borrowed any of their funds. The equity from their stockholders is used to buy equity securities in small businesses. On the other hand, leveraged venture capital companies borrow most of their funds. As a result, their investments in small businesses have to be loans or convertible debentures. They must have interest income from the small business in order to pay the interest on their own borrowings. You should review each of your potential venture capital investors and determine whether they are leveraged or unleveraged. If you are seeking equity, you probably should not approach a leveraged venture capital fund. Small businessmen often ask why SBICs do not invest equity in their small businesses. It is easy to illustrate why they do not. No individual should go to the bank and borrow money at high interest rates to buy equity in a small company. The individual will have to make the interest payments of the debt at the bank. Also, it may be a long time before the money invested in a small business matures so that the individual can repay the bank debt. When you approach a Small Business Investment Company, think of it as an ice cream store. It has only one flavor of ice cream, chocolate (debt). If you are looking for vanilla (equity), you are out of luck.

Family and Institutional Equity Venture Capital

There is a general division in the equity venture capital community. On one side are the private wealthy individuals or families that often back venture capital situations. Some have grown to be quite large. Some of these family organizations are spin-offs from large family industries, and the family or individual venture capital investors are the remnants of the original venture capital industry. Most of the large ones are run by professional managers.

The second great category of equity venture capital organizations consists of institutions. It wasn't until the late 1950s and early 1960s that the venture capital community became institutionalized. There are now approximately five hundred institutional venture capital investors. These corporations or partnerships are run by professional managers just as any other corporation would be run. Some family groups have hired nonfamily professional managers to run their venture capital activities. From an entrepreneur's standpoint, if given a choice you should deal with the institutions or professionally run family venture firms rather than the nonprofessional family groups. Sometimes a nonprofessional family venture fund can become quite possessive and limit the potential of a small growing business. Often the family wants to own and control the business.

What is the Corporate Structure in the Venture Capital Industry?

Venture capital companies can be defined according to their ownership or affiliation.

Public Companies

A small number of publicly owned venture capital companies are traded on various stock exchanges. These publicly owned venture funds may be leveraged or unleveraged and they invest in a wide variety of companies. The public companies tend to be larger than the average venture funds. If you need a large amount of money, you may wish to seek a public venture capital company. Also, the reputation of public companies is easier to determine.

Private Companies

By far the greatest number of venture capital companies are private ones, and they include some larger companies. Most of these private firms have been formed by a small number of institutions such as pension funds and insurance companies that have placed money in a venture capital limited partnership to be invested in venture situations. The company may be partially leveraged, but generally it is equity oriented if the fund is larger than $10,000,000. The smaller private funds tend to be SBICs and most are debt oriented. Many small SBICs only make high interest rate loans.

It is harder to obtain information on private venture capital firms. Their managers rarely talk about internal activities. The size and age of the venture fund may add to the difficulty of checking out the company. Since the larger and older firms are better known, it will be easier for you to determine if they are ethical businesses.

Bank-Related Companies

Many banks have set up venture capital companies so they may own equity in small businesses. In this way, they are able to circumvent some of the banking laws that prevent them from owning stock in a small business. The large money center banks have large venture capital subsidiaries. You might think that a bank's lending department works closely with the bank's venture department. However, in most banks that is not the case. The departments function as two separate entities. If you need a bank loan and also venture capital, you need not select a venture capital company affiliated with a bank. The two do not always work together.

Large Corporate Venture Companies

A number of the major corporations in the United States have established venture capital subsidiaries or have invested in one or more venture capital pools. Generally speaking, the corporate-owned venture capital company has been on the decline in the past few years. It is more common for large corporations to invest in venture capital through participation in venture capital limited partnerships. They become a limited partner along with others in a professionally managed venture capital fund. Some entrepreneurs become skittish about having a big company's venture capital company invest in their small business. If the entrepreneur is successful he might think the big company will want to acquire him at a time that may not be optimum for the entrepreneur to sell out.

An entrepreneur should spend a few minutes discussing the activities of any venture capital company that he is considering in order to determine the types of investments it is seeking as well as the type of company it is. Entrepreneurs should determine the reputation of the venture capitalist before trying to raise money from him. This subject is covered in detail in Chapter 7.

What Type of Business Are You Trying to Finance?

Somewhere along the way, the venture capitalist will try to define your business situation according to a set of categories used by the venture capital community to stereotype each business situation. These categories are as follows.

"Start-Up" Stage or First-Round Financings

These are the most difficult situations to finance because few people are willing to believe in an idea. The fact is that not many new ideas have the potential to make money. It is especially hard to communicate a new money-making idea to a venture capitalist because he is constantly bombarded with ideas— some of them good, some ludicrous. Rather than obtaining funds from a venture capitalist, you may have to beg, borrow, and steal from friends and relatives in order to obtain the initial seed money to get your idea off the ground. Remember, a start-up is only an idea with no prototype product. It usually takes two to three years before the company attains a cash flow break-even point. Anyone investing in a start-up is taking a huge risk and will be looking for a tremendous reward. In recent years more venture capital companies have been making more investments in start-ups. About one-third of venture investments are now start-ups, whereas only a few years ago the figure was 10 percent. There is a good chance that your start-up can be financed by a venture capital company.

Development Stage or Second Round

Once you have proved the idea can work by means of a prototype, an economic study, marketing analysis, or some other means, you are in a position to have a good shot at obtaining financing from the venture capital community. However, your selling ability still needs to be extremely sharp in order to convince people that the idea that works in a prototype can be brought to the marketplace at a profit. By this time, your company is usually one to two years away from cash flow break-even. As a result, the venture capital company will want a considerable return on its investment for taking a high risk. After all, some companies never reach cash flow break-even after this stage of their development.

Expansion Stage or Third Round

At this stage of development the company has created a product or service and is marketing it with some degree of success. The company needs additional funds to finance expansion of the business. In most of these cases venture capital is abundant. The entrepreneur will be in a good negotiating position to obtain the best price from the venture capital community. A company in the expansion stage is usually near the break-even point or perhaps no more than one year away from breaking even. You will not have to give up as much of the equity in your company if your venture has reached this stage in its life cycle.

Growth Stage or Fourth Round

When the company is running well and is generating a profit but needs additional capital in order to continue its strong growth, you will have the venture capital community eating out of your hands as long as you do not structure the deal so that they cannot make any money. A company at this stage of development is beyond breaking even and is making money. It needs money to grow quickly. Strong profits are just around the corner. In this situation you may have to give up only a small amount of equity unless you are raising a large sum of money. You may consider "going public" at this stage.

Some other special categories that you may be slotted into should be kept in mind when you are speaking to the venture capital community.

Leverage Buy-Outs

In some cases an existing company may be purchased by an entrepreneurial team. The entrepreneurs come to a venture capital company in order to obtain additional equity to purchase the business. Sometimes the entrepreneurial group that is managing a division of a large conglomerate can buy the division away from the conglomerate by using the venture capitalist's funds. In independently owned small businesses a leverage buy-out occurs when the non-owner management team buys the company from the original owners who are ready to retire. Any of these situations is called a leverage buy-out because most of the money is invested into the company as debt. Many venture capital companies are seeking these types of investments.

Turnaround Situations

Some venture capitalists finance turnarounds; that is, companies in trouble or even in bankruptcy. These turnarounds need money and management assistance. Turnarounds are hard to finance, and only a few venture companies specialize in this activity. Most people in the venturing industry agree that there are a hundred ways to fail in a turnaround. The difficulty is that you can think of and plan for only twenty of them. The other eighty are waiting to pop up at the most unexpected moment. You have to have lots of luck to handle turnarounds. The business presentation to the venture capitalist for a turnaround situation must emphasize the new management team—how they can make the company profitable and what they will do to make the company become profitable quickly.

Public Offerings

Some venture capital companies and venturesome mutual funds will buy equity in a new issue or second-round public offering for a business on a path of high growth. This only happens from time to time. What interests the venture capitalist in a public offering is strong growth and a hot stock market.

What Industries Do Venture Capitalists Prefer?

Most venture capitalists will tell you that they want to invest most of their funds in high technology products. That usually means that they are oriented toward industrial products rather than retail products such as new toasters or new cameras. A new robot designed to be used in auto production is an example of a high technology industrial product.

Most venture capitalists do not finance retail operations such as dress shops or muffler stores that are open to the public. Generally, if you have a new concept for a retail store, you will find your innovation falling on deaf ears at the venture capital level. A number of venture capitalists in the Small Business Investment Company community will finance retail operations. One such group specializes in retail grocery stores. There are several new venture capital funds that specialize in retailing and there are some new ones in medical products. In the wholesale-distribution area there are no venture capital firms except for a few SBICs that specialize in this area. You will again find it difficult to finance an innovation in distribution. A few venture firms specialize in financing projects concerned with natural resources such as coal mining or oil well drilling. Again, this is a difficult area to finance within the venture capital community. Entertainment projects are also difficult to finance. A group of specially licensed Small Business Investment Companies financed entertainment ventures for a while, but these seem not to have prospered and no new ones are being licensed. Service companies are not as easy to finance as product companies. The easiest companies to finance are ones with high technology products. A number of venture capital firms have financed real estate ventures. Only a few venture funds have as much as 20 percent of their assets in real estate. Others are precluded by their charter from investing in real estate. A small number of SBICs have special licenses to invest only in real estate. No new SBIC licenses are being issued to companies specializing in real estate.

As you look through the full category of business ventures, you will find only those venture capital companies specializing in "leverage buy-outs" and "tunarounds" willing to look at the full spectrum of the business. Several venture firms invest only in leverage buy-outs and therefore rarely invest in high technology ventures. In a nutshell, an electronic gadget that has uses in an industrial market will be easier to finance. If the electronic gadget is oriented toward the retail market, it will be more difficult to finance. All other products and services will have varied success in receiving financial support from the venture capital community.

What Type of Products Do Venture Capitalists Prefer?

Since it seems obvious from the foregoing that venture capitalists like products rather than services, what type of products do they prefer? There are four such categories: revolutionary, innovative, evolutionary, and substitute products. *Revolutionary* products are extremely difficult to finance anywhere. The light bulb, the television, the telephone, the camera, the phonograph, and the early automobile are examples of revolutionary products that changed life dramatically. The current computer industry developed from the financing of a revolutionary product: the computer. Another industry that could be considered revolutionary is the one derived from genetic engineering. All revolutionary products absorb enormous amounts of capital. They have a very long development time before one can realize a substantial profit.

Venture capitalists prefer *innovative* products. By innovative one means that a product is the next generation in a series. For example, the instant camera, the personal minicomputer, the color television, and the fluorescent light are all next generation stages after their predecessors. The change was large enough to generate demand but small enough not to create a need for extensive education. Many venture capital firms prefer *evolutionary* products such as a cheaper instant camera. These firms want to be one year ahead of the competition rather than five or ten years ahead of the competition. With an *evolutionary* product and an aggressive management team, venture capitalists believe they can stay one or two years ahead of the competition and make significant profits.

Still another group of venture capitalists do not finance any of the above categories, but instead prefer *substitutions*. These are the people who finance a fast food place that substitutes chicken for burgers. They are the leverage buyout specialists that back an aggressive new group to buy a stodgy old firm and substitute a repackaged product for the current one.

All venture capitalists are looking for sizable markets. If your product is competing in a marketplace that is very large, you will have a better chance of receiving financing. However, if your product is in a marketplace that is growing 10 to 15 percent a year and total gross sales are only $20 million or $30 million, the venture capitalist will not see the beauty in being the market leader in such a small market.

How Much Venture Capital Is Available?

Dramatic things have happened to increase the size of the venture capital industry. First, when the tax laws were changed so that the capital gains tax was reduced substantially more people were willing to invest money in venture capital firms. The investors were seeking outstanding long-term capital gains because the tax on these capital gains is much lower. This brought a great deal of money into the venture capital industry. With the tax increase in capital gains less money will be available in the future for venture capital investments. The second great change that has helped create more venture capital occurred in the pension fund area. The U.S. government decided that pension funds may invest a small percentage of their total assets in high risk ventures such as venture capital companies. In practice this means that approximately 2 percent of a pension fund's assets may be invested in the venture capital community. Two percent may sound small, but it is large when multiplied by the hundreds of billions in Amercian pension funds. Because of these two changes, the venture capital industry is receiving substantial attention from institutional investors. Venture capital firms are able to raise money quite easily. For the entrepreneur there is a great deal of money available to back his ventures.

Opportunities Available for Entrepreneurs

At this point in time a great opportunity is open to entrepreneurs. Staggering changes in the U.S. economy have created numerous opportunities for small businesses to spring up. The United States is changing from an industrial nation to an electronic-information nation. Fewer and fewer people are being employed in industrialized businesses such as steel, the automotive industry, and the like. On the other hand, our electronic and information processing industry has shown sharp growth. Where there is growth, there is opportunity.

The restructuring of many large corporations and the mega-takeovers has brought opportunities. Big corporations are spinning off some of their small subsidiaries in order to generate cash to pay off the mountains of debt they have created. Because of low interest rates, entrepreneurs are willing to pay high prices for business. Because of these high purchase prices, more small businessmen have decided to retire early and sell their businesses. For every seller today there are five trying to buy. It is an excellent opportunity for entrepreneurs who want to buy and own their own businesses, but they must be careful not to pay too much.

Can You Raise Venture Capital?

With so much money available, you would think that money would be easy to obtain. However, there continues to be intense competition for money among entrepreneurs and small businesses. The reason: many people are seeking financing for their new ventures or their growing small businesses. The baby boom that worked its way through our colleges in the 1960s and early 1970s is now at work in business. These young men and women have been working for the past five to fifteen years. They have reached an age and maturity in the work place that leads them to reconsider their long-term objectives. There are only so many vice-presidential slots and presidential slots in the one thousand largest U.S. companies. There are only so many opportunities to make a great deal of money inside large businesses. Many young people in their thirties are realizing that they have to start their own businesses now if they are ever going to do it at all. Because this generation has reached that stage of life, more entrepreneurs than ever before are looking for money. This book will give you an edge over others seeking funds from the venture capital community because you will understand the process better.

Another impediment to your progress in obtaining venture capital financing is the lack of senior venture capital officers to review your proposal. Because of the extreme growth in the venture capital community, there are fewer seasoned executives to manage the billions of dollars that have been invested into the venture capital business. As a result, you will probably work with a junior officer until a critical decision can be made as to whether the venture capital firm will invest or not. You may hear yes, yes, yes, from the junior executive, only to receive a resounding no from the senior management after your deal is discussed at their management meetings. Currently there is no way to avoid this problem. The best thing to do is to work as quickly as possible toward obtaining a decision from the senior management.

How Much Money Should You Seek?

How much money you should seek is always difficult to determine, particularly in the early stages of development. A useful equation to remember is that the more money you raise, the more equity ownership you must give up to the investor. Of the four stages of development we covered above (start-up, development, expansion, and growth), the start-up stage is the most difficult to raise funds for. It is also difficult to raise enough money in the initial start-up phase to carry the company through to the growth stage. Each time you have to go back to the venture capitalist or other investors in order to raise additional money, you have to give up an additional piece of equity ownership.

In seeking money you must seek enough to do the immediate job at hand. That is, you must seek enough money to make significant progress so that the next round of financing will cost you much less than the initial financing. If you sold 30 percent of your company in the first round of financing, you would have to make enough progress so that in the second round you would give up only 10 to 15 percent of the ownership. There are horror stories about entrepreneurs who have approached venture capitalists and asked for the money they needed to take them through the start-up phase. The venture capitalist, acting in an unethical manner, states that he wants the entrepreneur to cut back on the amount of cash he needs by trimming his budget. The entrepreneur trims his budget to the bone. With less money from the venture capitalist, he still tries to make a go of it. When he runs out of money before reaching a significant milestone, he returns to the venture capitalist and asks for additional funding. Since the milestone has not been reached, the only way the entrepreneur can raise the necessary cash in order to make the milestone happen is to give up a large amount of equity. Often he gives up control of his company for the amount of money he first asked for. Besides selecting an ethical venture capital firm, you should make sure that you raise enough money in your first financing to make it through to the next stages of development. If you have achieved your stated goals, you will find it easier to switch to a different venture firm or outside investors in order to raise additional capital.

What Type of Funds Are You Seeking?

There are only four basic ways to obtain venture capital financing. Each has its advantages and disadvantages. Usually an advantage for you is a disadvantage for the venture capitalist. Each of the four alternatives is discussed in turn.

Common Stock

Most people would like to sell common stock in their company. The price is always the question. The venture capital firm cannot gain control through common stock unless it owns 51 percent. Therefore there are fewer opportunities to sell common stock in a company without making additional concessions. You may be able to sell stock, but the venture capital firm may require that all stock be placed in a voting trust that the firm will control if your projections are not met. Also, the firm will want representation on your board of directors. You will have to keep this in mind when trying to sell stock. The venture firm may seek other means to control the company if you get in trouble. This problem is discussed later in Chapters 5 and 6.

Preferred Stock

Venture capitalists may agree to purchase preferred stock in your company under certain conditions. First, they may want dividends paid on the preferred stock, probably in the range of 6 to 8 percent. Second, they may want your company to repurchase the preferred stock after a specified period of time. This arrangement will assure the return of their money in case your company does not grow quickly. Finally, they may want the preferred stock to be convertible into common stock so that they can share in the equity ownership if your company performs well.

Convertible Debenture

Most Small Business Investment Companies in the venture capital community will be willing to buy a convertible debenture from your company. The debenture is a loan to your company that is convertible into common stock. The conversion price, the interest rate, and the covenants of the loan agreement are all the items you will have to negotiate with the venture capitalist. These terms are discussed in Chapters 5 and 6.

Loan With Warrants

Many SBICs in the venture capital community will make loans to your company if you agree to let them have detachable stock options, known as warrants, to buy stock in your company. In this way, if their loan is paid off, they will still have the option to buy stock in your company. Warrants are discussed in later chapters.

How Will the Venture Capitalist Be Involved?

When it comes to the venture capitalist's involvement in your business, there are two types of venture capitalists: passive advisers and active directors. Most venture capital companies are passive advisers. They may sit on your board of directors and they may come to monthly management meetings, but they merely *advise* your company on the direction they believe it should take. Most venture capitalists limit their advice to areas in which they have strong expertise, such as the financing of your company, growth of the company, and matters involving projections and employees. Usually the passive adviser does not become involved in your business unless you have operating trouble. If you do have trouble, he will become very active in trying to manage your company in order to save his investment.

On the other hand, the active director will want to help you run the business. Usually he does not help on a day-to-day basis, but may be at the business once or twice a week. Some venture capital firms even supply part of the management team to companies they have invested in. If, for example, you have outstanding finance and good production people on your management team but no marketing experts, the venture capitalist may provide the skills necessary to help you in marketing. Some venture capital companies have consultants on their staff who will help you with the marketing plan and help you hire a marketing person. They will charge a fee for this consulting arrangement. You should usually take advantage of any such benefit.

Some venture capital companies play a more active part than just direction. They actually seek to control the company, either directly by having their company manage the small company, or by controlling the board of directors or the voting stock. This may not be entirely bad for you. If you have an idea that is tough to finance and that needs a great deal of ingenuity to bring it to the marketplace, try to find a venture capital company that provides this type of complete assistance. If the venture capitalist truly has people that can help achieve your goals, then it may be in your interest to accept assistance as part of the financing for your idea.

How to Select a Venture Capital Company

Before you approach any venture capital company, you should determine the type of company that best fits your situation. First, using the list of the venture capital companies in Appendix 2, determine which firms are closest to your location. Venture capital companies prefer to invest in companies located nearby. You will save yourself a large amount of time if you choose a venture capital company that is located close to your business. Many venture capitalists on the east coast of the United States are surprised when they receive a proposal from a small business on the west coast. They ask, "Why didn't this small business receive financing from a west coast venture capital firm?" It seems unlikely that a small business would come that far in order to find venture capital. If you are unable to raise the capital from your local venture group, then you need to explain why you are seeking capital outside your area. One reason may be that the local venture capitalists do not wish to invest in your industry. Another reason may be that the distant venture capital firm is a specialist in a certain type of business. You should explain that you have gone 3,000 miles to find a specialist, rather than just to find capital.

Once you have selected a few venture capital firms that are close, you can begin the second phase of selection. You should ask around town about thier business ethics. Do these firms live up to their commitments? Are they involved in a great deal of litigation? Are they profitable companies? Do they have money to lend? These are all questions you should be asking others about the venture capital companies you are considering. You might run a credit report on the firms just to find out what is in their credit file. You may check the courthouse records to see if they have suits against them. After all, once you have obtained money from a venture fund, you will have to live with the venture capitalist for a very long time. Find out as much as possible about the one you finally choose before you obtain the funds.

In talking with the venture capitalist you should ask him to tell you about some of the firm's investments. You should call the companies mentioned to ask how they are being treated by the venture capitalist. When you talk with a venture capital company, you may ask for a bank reference or other references. Again, it is important for you to select a venture capital company as a partner, not just as an investor. Be careful in selecting the venture capital company that you will take money from. The company doesn't go away after it invests its money. Investigating the venture firm is discussed in detail in Chapter 7.

Should You Phone the Venture Firm?

Now that you understand what you are trying to finance and what type of venture capital firm you may wish to seek out, the question arises, "Should you phone the venture capital company to determine if they are in the business of financing your type of venture?" You should telephone if you follow the guidelines set out below.

When calling a venture capital company, remember that it probably receives 50 to 100 phone calls per day plus many unsolicited letters. Your phone call should be to the point. Explain the type of deal you are trying to finance, ask if the venture capital company has funds available, and finally, ask if it will be able to review your business proposal during the next week. If the answer to all three of these questions is yes, then do not take up additional time; send in a summary and business proposal as set out in Chapters 2 and 3 of this book. Of course, if the venture capitalist wants to discuss your situation, begin selling your concept.

Venture capitalists are not important people who are unapproachable, but they are very busy people. They receive hundreds of telephone calls from entrepreneurs as well as crackpots with crazy ideas. Be sensitive to the time pressures of the venture capitalist and he will appreciate your tact. The telephone call below is considered by venture capitalists to be a helpful opening telephone conversation:

Secretary: Mr. Capitalist, Joe Entrepreneur is on the phone and he wants to talk about venture capital.

Venture Capitalist: Hello, this is A.V. Capitalist.

Entrepreneur: Mr. Capitalist, this is Joseph Entrepreneur. Just call me Joe. I am calling to find out if you have an interest in a business that needs financing.

Venture Capitalist: Can you tell me about the business?

Entrepreneur: Well, Mr. Capitalist, my best friend and I started a small electronics company about two years ago. We now have the prototype completed and we have received preliminary orders from a number of major corporations that believe this will solve a number of computer security problems. We have applied for a patent on this machine and we believe it will be granted. What we are looking for is about $800,000 in order to begin production so that we can fill some of our back orders that we have received on a preliminary basis. Do you have money available for this kind of investment?

Venture Capitalist: Yes, we do have funds available, but what kind of funds are you looking for? By this I mean are you seeking common stock or loans?

Entrepreneur: Well, we are completely flexible on this issue. We would, of course, like to sell common stock. However, we realize that some venture companies don't buy common stock and we would be open to discussion as to whether it is a convertible debenture or preferred stock.

Venture Capitalist: Fine. Do you have a proposal put together outlining what you are trying to accomplish? Does it have projections, resumes, and those kinds of things?

Entrepreneur: Yes, we have a business proposal with a summary and I would like to send it out to you. I would like to know how long you think it would take for you to have an opportunity to review it so that we could come by and discuss how we might work together on this project.

Venture Capitalist: Well, I am tied up this week but beginning next week on Monday or Tuesday I should get to your proposal and should be back to you by the middle or end of next week. If you really want me to rush, I may be able to squeeze it into this week's work.

Entrepreneur: Oh no, I think that timetable fits with what we are trying to do. We hope to have something, at least a preliminary commitment from a venture capital source, within thirty days and we would like to work with your group because we have heard so much about you.

Venture Capitalist: Fine. Send it to my attention. I assume you have our address.

Entrepreneur: I have the address as listed in the Directory of Venture Capital? Is that correct?

Venture Capitalist: Yes, that is correct.

Entrepreneur: Thank you very much for your time. I will get this in the mail today and I look forward to speaking with you next week.

Venture Capitalist: Thank you and goodbye.

The conversation above is ideal from the venture capitalist's point of view because the entrepreneur gave the venture capitalist an inkling of the business that sparked his interest. The entrepreneur was flexible as to the type of investment capital he was seeking, and did not ask for an overnight determination of the venture capitalist's interest. The conversation was short and to the point. The venture capitalist could have asked more questions about the project if he had wished to, but he decided to wait for the proposal. Some entrepreneurs want to explain their business on the telephone and ask if the venture capitalist is interested in financing the business. No venture capitalist can give a positive response on the telephone. He must have a well-documented proposal before he can give the entrepreneur encouragement.

Certain venture capital firms make it a policy not to talk to the entrepreneur. Instead the secretary will ask the entrepreneur to mail in the written proposal and will explain that the venture capital manager will not talk to anyone until he has reviewed the proposal. When these venture capital firms receive the proposal, they log it in with a number and begin their processing. This is not an unusual procedure and you should not be taken aback by such treatment. However, if you are treated poorly and not given an opportunity to discuss your proposal with anyone, even after you have sent it in, then it is best to move on to another venture capital company.

Other Questions for the Venture Capitalist

The conversation just mentioned covered some but not all the facts that you may want to know about the venture capitalist before you proceed. The first, and most important question is, "Are you investing money in companies?" If the answer is not yes, then you do not want to spend any time talking to this venture capitalist. The second most important question is, "Do you have time to review my proposal?" Most venture capitalist are pressed for time. They may have several companies in trouble and may be trying to work themselves out of a loss situation. They may have made commitments to another company and may be involved in due diligence in that situation. If the venture capitalist is too busy to *review* your proposal within a week to ten days, you may want to consider discussing your proposal with other venture capitalists. In the above conversation the venture capitalist indicated he would review the entrepeneur's proposal at the beginning of next week. Such a date should not be interpreted in absolute terms. If you don't hear by the date indicated, then give the venture capitalist a few more days before you call.

A third area you must question the venture capital about is your industry. Does the venture capitalist have an interest in your company's industry? If you are in a rather mundane industry, the venture capitalist may not be interested. On the other hand, it may be just the industry he has been seeking as an investment. A related question is, "Have you ever invested in this industry?" If he has already invested in the industry or looked at potential investments in the industry, he understands the economics involved. If you can find a venture capitalist who has such experience and understands your industry, you are weeks ahead of the schedule for receiving your money. A venture capitalist with experience in your industry will not have to go through the learning period necessary before investing in an industry.

A fourth subject to discuss with the venture capitalist is that of contracting other venture capitalists. Most venture capitalists would rather review your proposal without having others review it at the same time. It is better for you, however, if you select several venture firms and send them your proposal. To do this tactfully, do not ask if he minds if you contact other venture capitalists, but perhaps phrase your question as follows: "Do you have any friends in the venture capital business who might also be interested in reviewing my proposal?" Or, if he says he is interested in your industry, you might ask him whether he would like to work with any other venture companies that also know the industry.

You should let the venture capitalist know that you are sending your business proposal to several other venture capital firms. He should not expect an exclusive. On the other hand, do not push on him the idea that he has to move quickly or he will miss this golden opportunity to invest in your firm. Remember, venture capitalists have dozens of places to put their money, and if you become pushy, your company will definitely not be one of them.

Other items you need to determine about your venture capital partner is the matter of due diligence. Chapter 7 covers how you can determine whether a venture capital firm is the one that you want to deal with. Most venture capital firms are run by honest professionals. However, some are not. Don't neglect your due diligence in investigating your potential venture capital partner.

How Long Does It Take to Get the Money?

A final key question concerns the time it will take to obtain funds. The amount of time from your initial contact until the time of a legal closing—when you receive the money—can be as short as three weeks or as long as six months. The time involved depends on many factors. In general, the procedure takes six to eight weeks. You must remember that there is more to the business of venture capital investing than listening to a sales pitch from an entrepreneur.

First the venture capitalist must review a written business proposal if he is to understand your business, your industry, and your management team. The length is not a critical factor, but every venture capitalist wants a *written* proposal. It is vital to understand that the venture capitalist wants to know something about your business before he meets with you. Therefore he needs a written business proposal. After reviewing the business proposal, he will decide whether to have a meeting with you. The next step is to hold an initial meeting and discussion of the business proposal, which cannot always take place immediately. As mentioned before, venture capitalists work under extreme time pressures. They have hundreds of business propositions sent to them on a monthly basis. Taking half a day to discuss your business idea is a large time commitment on the part of the venture capitalist. Once the initial meeting has taken place the venture capitalist will want to check out all the things you have claimed in your proposal.

If your proposal is successful, the final step is to obtain a commitment on the part of the venture capitalist, which normally involves a meeting of his board of directors and a review of the situation by his partners and associates. Also, the legal documents have to be drawn and signatures have to be obtained on these documents before the formal legal closing on the commitment takes place. This book discusses these stages in detail so that you will understand what a venture capitalist must go through before he can invest in your venture.

By far the largest amount of time in this process will be devoted to the investigation of your industry by the venture capitalist. You can minimize that time by picking a venture capitalist who has already invested in your industry or a similar industry. The process can also be simplified if the venture capitalist has reviewed, but not necessarily invested in, several deals in your industry. Such contact will reduce the time needed to understand the industry and your situation. You can shorten the time further by writing a complete business proposal as set out in this book.

Myths About Venture Capital

A number of myths should be dispelled at the outset. They are as follows.

Myth 1: Venture capital firms want to own control of your company and tell you how to run the business.   Nothing could be further from the truth. No venture capital firm intentionally sets out to own control of a small business. The venture capitalist seeks more than 50 percent of a company only when he needs to have that much of the company in order to justify the amount of money he is putting into the business.

Venture capitalists have no desire to run your business. They do not want to tell you how to make day-to-day decisions and have you report to them on a daily basis. As you will see later in this book, venture capitalists are busy keeping up with their investments and seeking new investments. They want you and your management team to run your company profitably. They do want to be consulted on any major decisions, but they want no day-to-day say in your business operations.

Myth 2: You must have an introduction to the venture capitalist from one of his friends in order to obtain financing.   You do not need an introduction to the venture capital management from anyone. A business proposal that is well prepared is the best introduction you can have. Gone are the days when you needed an intermediary to introduce you to a rich investor before he would invest money into your venture. Most venture capital firms are run by middle-class, non-elite individuals. They are interested in good investments. They are not interested in your social contacts or introductions. Later on in your relationship, if you have mutual friends or know people of similar background, such contacts will enhance your credibility; but there is no need to have an intermediary to get your idea across to the venture capitalist or to gain financing.

Myth 3: Venture capital firms are interested only in new technological discoveries.   Most venture capital companies are not interested in revolutionary ideas that change the way people live. These kinds of ideas take ten to twenty years to develop. I doubt that any professional venture capitalist would have backed the electric light bulb. It took a farsighted person to see that someday everyone would replace their oil lamps with light bulbs. Revolutionary ideas are very difficult to finance because the return on investment takes so long to realize. The venture capitalist is more interested in an add-on technology. He is interested in a new type of computer, a new silicone chip, a new marketing technique, or something that will involve moderate change. It is true that venture capitalists tend to be oriented toward high technology, but a better way of viewing their orientation is to say that they are interested in companies that promise high growth. If you have a company that has a potential for high growth, then you can attract venture capital money.

Myth 4: Venture capitalists are satisfied with a reasonable return on investments.   No venture capitalist expects a reasonable return on his investment. The truth is, these people expect very high, exorbitant, unreasonable returns. They can obtain reasonable return from hundreds of publicly traded companies. They can obtain a reasonable return from many types of investments not having the degree of risk involved in financing a small business. Because every venture capital investment involves a high degree of risk, there must be a corresponding high return on investment. Expect the venture capitalist to require a very high rate of return.

You may believe that your business is a special situation, and that the strong potential and high demand for the product assures the investor of a very low risk of failure. You may believe that if you could only accomplish certain events in your business plan, everyone would be rich. Your optimism and inability to see a potential failure are expected of you as an entrepreneur, but ask yourself, "If this is such a riskless investment why can't I get a loan from a bank in order to finance the company?" If you come seeking funds from a venture capital firm, it expects to take a risk and to receive a very high rate of return on its investment.

Myth 5: Venture capitalists are quick to invest.   On the contrary, it takes a long time to raise venture capital. On the average, it will take six to eight weeks from the initial contact to raise your venture capital. If you have a well-prepared business proposal such as that discussed later in this book, you will be able to raise money in that time frame. A venture capitalist will see 50 to 100 proposals a month. Out of that number, ten will be of some interest. The venture capitalist will read those ten business proposals. Out of those ten, two or three will receive a fair amount of analysis, negotiation, and investigation. Of the two or three, one may be funded. This funneling process of selecting one out of a hundred takes a great deal of time. Once the venture capitalist has found that "one," he will spend a significant amount of time investigating possible outcomes before he will fund it. Your proposal will be weighed against the many alternate investment opportunities available. Make sure it stands out and is well prepared so you can receive your funds quickly.

Myth 6: Venture capitalists are interested in backing new ideas or high technology inventions. Management is secondary consideration.   Venture capitalists only back good management. If you have a bright idea but have a poor managerial background and no experience in the industry, try to find someone in the industry to bring into your team. The venture capitalist will have a hard time believing that you, with no experience in that industry and no managerial ability in your background, can follow through on your business proposal. You do not necessarily need a complete management team the day you write your proposal. Many venture capitalists have staff members who can help you with certain areas of your business. However, most of them would prefer that you have your management team pulled together before you get the venture off the ground. A good idea is important, but a good management team is even more important.

Myth 7: Venture capitalists only need basic summary information before they make an investment.   A detailed and well-organized business proposal is the only way to gain a venture capital investor's attention and obtain funding. If you think that you can hastily write a two-page summary and have a venture capitalist fund your investment, you are sadly mistaken. Venture capitalists want a good summary as a start, not a substitute for a sound plan. Every venture capitalist, before he becomes involved, wants the entrepreneur to have thought out the entire business plan and to have written it down in detail.

A well-prepared business proposal serves two functions. First, it informs the venture capitalist about your idea. Second, it shows that you have thought out your intended business. It shows you know the industry and have thought through all the potential problems.

Objective

The objective of this chapter has been to give you the skills to identify the proper venture capital firm and decide if it has an interest in reviewing your business proposal. This is usually a simple task, since most venture capital firms will review almost any proposal. You must identify the best venture firm to review your business proposal. You must also be sure that this venture firm has money and the time to review your proposal.

Now that we have presented the basics of the venture capital community and you understand how to determine which firm may be best for your business situation, you are ready to prepare the two documents that you will be sending to the venture capital company: the summary and the business proposal.

2

Summary
Presentation

Can You Summarize What You Intend to Do?
A Good Summary Has Less Than a Thousand Words.

Any venture capital fund with money to invest is under constant assault by entrepreneurs seeking money to back their ideas or their businesses. Virtually hundreds of people and ideas are vying for the opportunity to be reviewed by a venture capital company. Therefore, it is absolutely imperative that the presentation being made to the venture capital company be excellent. The presentation must be of a high quality in order to have a competitive edge over all the other proposals arriving on the venture capitalist's desk. The only response a poorly presented business proposal will receive is a toss into the trash can. The most crucial part of the presentation is the summary because this is what sparks the interest of the venture capitalist. It must *not* be more than three pages long. You may attach to the summary a complete business proposal, but venture capitalists prefer *not* to plow through the details of a business proposal until they understand the business from a summary proposal. Three out of four venture capitalists will read only the summary and will not take the time to review a full proposal. A venture capitalist will see as many as twenty proposals a day. Out of about a hundred proposals per week, maybe ten proposals are read. The others are usually so poorly prepared that they are only cursorily glanced at. Your goal is to be in that top 10 percent and have your proposal read. The summary will make the difference.

What Does a Summary Look Like?

What follows is an effective summary format. This format is a composite of many I have seen. I have used this format for seeking additional financing for many of the companies we have invested in. What follows is a disguised financing request based on an actual company in which funds were invested. The numbers and people have been changed completely. The investment made a tremendous amount of money for everyone.

Company: Electronic Press, Inc.
8888 Avenue of the Americas
New York, New York 10005
Telephone: (212) 555-1212
September 1982

Contact: Joseph Entrepreneur, President

Type of Business: Electronic preparation of camera-ready copy and printing of materials requiring quick turnaround.

Company Summary: A new company has been formed to purchase the assets of an ailing printing company. The company uses the method of setting type known as "hot type." The company will write computer programs to drive a special machine that will produce camera-ready copy for printing. This method will make "hot type" obsolete. All existing customers will be serviced with "hot type" until the new system is ready.

Management: Joe Entrepreneur, President, has been in printing for twelve years. He has worked in all phases of the business. He has been working with computer programs to set type for the past year. He has a B.A. from a New York university in accounting. He is thirty-two years old.

Jim Black, Vice-president, has been in the computer field for eight years. He has been a programmer, systems analyst, and management consultant on computer applications. He has been working on a computer program to set type for one year. He has an engineering degree from a large Boston college.

Product/Service and Competition: Electronic Press will begin by continuing to offer conventional typesets and printing. Once the computer can be used to set type, the company will offer the customer twenty-four hour or quicker turnaround typesetting and printing. Customers can use the actual camera-ready copy for corrections and can make corrections quickly.

Funds Requested: $800,000 in common stock for a 40 percent ownership.

Collateral: None

Use Proceeds: $400,000 as down payment of the business; $200,000 accounts payable; and $200,000 to carry the company's research and development budget to develop the computer program. The purchase price is $600,000, $200,000 in cash, and $400,000 in a five-year 8 percent note.

Financial History:	Actual 2 Yrs. Ago	Actual Prior Yr.	Actual Last Yr.
Revenues	$2,109,000	$2,289,400	$2,460,500
Net income (loss)	79,900	(43,100)	(11,600)
Assets	2,279,500	2,700,100	2,870,000
Liabilities	1,956,400	2,420,100	2,601,600
Net worth	323,100	280,000	268,400

Financial Projections:	Projected This Yr.	Projected Next Yr.	Projected In 2 Yrs.
Revenues	$2,900,000	$3,800,000	$6,000,000
Net income	10,000	160,600	800,000
Assets	3,970,000	4,770,000	5,570,000
Liabilities	3,601,600	3,731,000	3,372,000
Net worth	878,400	1,039,000	1,839,000

Exit: The company will go public in three years. If the company does not go public in five years, then the investors can exchange their ownership for three times their investment and be paid out over three years.

Why Is the Venture Capitalist Interested?

The venture capitalist has interest in this situation from a number of perspectives. First, he sees a management that has experience in both printing and in computers and he sees the benefits of combining the two talents in order to initiate a new approach to an old industry. Second, he sees profit opportunities, for this company has the potential to grow beyond the projected $6 million to as high as $60 million or $100 million. The third aspect that the venture capitalist sees is uniqueness. It is not unique that computers can set type but it is unique to use computer typesetting to fill a niche in the printing industry where quick turnaround is needed. Finally, the venture capitalist is interested because he sees a public company. Should the company be able to hit the projections it has set out to achieve, it should be able to have a public stock offering and give the venture capitalist an opportunity to liquidate his position at a considerable profit.

How to Complete a Summary

Now let us look at each category used in the above summary to see what is needed, because you should understand how each section is to be prepared and what the venture capitalist is looking for.

Company

You would be surprised to learn how many people fail to include a name, address, or telephone number on their proposals. It sounds stupid, but it happens. In one instance, we received an extremely interesting proposal but could not find a return address. Unfortunately, I did not read it until the day after it came into the office and by then the envelope had been thrown away. Too bad, whoever you are!

Most of the time the name and address are in the package but not in a conspicuous location. One must wade through page after page looking for this basic information. Do not let this happen to you. Put the company's name, address, and telephone number up front on the first page of the proposal and also make it the first item on the summary sheet.

Contact

Many proposals list a number of people in this section but do not indicate the person to contact. The venture capitalist is not sure if he is supposed to talk to the president, the vice-president of finance, or someone else. You should indicate on the front of the proposal the person within your company who is responsible for raising the money along with the special telephone number at which that person can be reached. Usually it is the president of the company, but sometimes another person is the ongoing contact.

Leave a number where you can be reached. A number that is attended only part of the time is useless. Have an answering service answer for you if you do not have a permanent number. A venture capitalist will try to reach you only so many times before he gives up.

Type of Business

Here you need no more than ten words, just enough to let the venture capitalist zero in on the industry. Because there are a number of industries in which many venture capitalists will not invest, identifying your type of business saves a lot of time and agony.

You may also wish to identify the stage of your business, such as "start-up," development, and so on, as discussed in Chapter 1. This information will permit the venture capitalist to respond more quickly. If the venture firm has a policy of not investing in turnaround situations, for example, it's better to receive a quick no, than a delayed no.

Business Summary

Here you are trying to give a thumbnail sketch of the company's history to date. Give a little background on the company and emphasize some of its strong points. The objective is to get the venture capitalist interested in your company. If you have more than half a page in this section, it is not a summary. Be brief!

Management

Although this is the most important section of the entire presentation, the information does not need to be covered in detail in the summary. The more you can emphasize the entrepreneur's experience in the industry, the better the presentation will be. List the top two or three people and give a two-sentence background statement for each. The venture capitalist will want to investigate management in detail, but the summary is not the place to itemize all the accomplishments of management.

Product/Service and Competition

In this section, first give a short description of the product or service. Second, show why that product or service is unique. If it is not unique, then explain why this product or service will succeed over all the other products and services that are offered in the marketplace. You need to discuss the competition briefly in order to show the niche that it occupies in the industry. Do not write more than a half page here.

Funds Requested

Briefly state how much money you want to raise. And, for goodness sake, do not give a range! For example, do not say $200,000 to $400,000. Pick a number and show why you need that amount. Also, state the type of funds you are raising. Is it equity? Is it debt? Remember, not only is it easier to raise debt financing, but you will give up less equity in your company with debt financing. It is important to state what type of funds you are seeking because some investment companies do not make equity investments. They make only convertible subordinated debentures or loans with options to buy stock. This is particularly true of the 350 active Small Business Investment Companies (SBICs). If you are flexible, then don't worry about structuring the deal; just state your preference and add that you are flexible. If the venture capitalist likes your proposal, he will come back and suggest a restructured deal.

Collateral

If you are seeking debt, you should state whether any collateral security is available for the loan request. Loans with collateral are easier to obtain than those without collateral. If there is collateral, you have a greater chance of obtaining the financing from SBICs. If there is none, state "none." The more collateral you have, the less equity you will have to give up.

Use of Proceeds

One need not be extremely specific on the use of proceeds in the summary. That will come later in the full business proposal. Here you should indicate how the funds will be used. Avoid broad terms like "working capital" or "to pay expenses"; it is better to be more specific and to indicate whether the funds will be used to pay salaries (and put in a dollar amount), build inventory (and put in a dollar amount), pay accounts payable, and so on. This gives the venture capitalist an idea of how the funds will be used.

Financial History

This section seems to be fairly self-explanatory, but remember that it is important to put down the actual figures in columnar form alongside the list of items to be included. If the company is a new one, obviously the historical section will be dropped.

Financial Projections

Most venture capitalists would like to see five years of projections even though they realize the fifth year is based on wild speculation. It gives them a clearer idea of how much money they could make if everything goes right. Again, use a columnar format.

Exit

As has been mentioned before, the venture capital company does not want to be a minority stockholder in your company forever. It would prefer to realize a capital gain soon after investing its money. In practical terms, its horizon is three to seven years. That is, somewhere after the third year, the company would like to begin receiving a capital gain on its investment. This means a public offering of stock in which you and the venture capitalist can sell some shares. This means selling part of the equity position owned by the venture capitalist, or all of its equity position, to a third party or perhaps back to the company. You need to keep this problem in mind, because the venture capital company will not invest if there does not appear to be a way out somewhere down the road. Chapter 10 will discuss this in detail.

Structure

This section needs to be included after the items stated above if it is a complex investment structure. For example, you may be investing in common stock and you may have an investor friend who is investing in preferred stock. You are now trying to raise debt financing from a venture capital company. There will also be a loan from a bank. In that case, the structure might look like this:

Bank	$3,000,000
Venture Capital	$1,000,000
Preferred Stock	$ 500,000
Common Stock	$ 100,000
TOTAL	$4,600,000

Many venture capital companies have indicated that they eventually put each of their investments into a summary format similar to the one above. They do this for their own record keeping, for presentation to their board of directors, or for discussion purposes. To give your deal a head start, prepare an effective summary.

What Kind of Cover Letter Is Needed?

Many investment companies want only a summary and do not want a full business proposal. Along with the summary, entrepreneurs want to submit a covering letter that sets out some basic introductory information. Here is a typical covering letter:

Mr. A. V. Capitalist, President
Venture Capital Corporation
123 Main Street
Washington, D.C. 20006
Re: XYZ Corp. Financing
Dear Mr. Capitalist:

Attached is a summary of the financing I am seeking for my company. If you have an interest in providing this or similar financing, I would be pleased to send you a full business proposal. Please call me if you have any immediate questions.

Sincerely,

Joseph "Joe" Entrepreneur
123 Main Street
McLean, Virginia 22102
(703) 555-1212

Some venture capital companies are taken aback when such a query letter is attached to the summary. They perceive it as part of a mass mailing. That is, it may suggest that the person seeking the money is sending the summary to hundreds of venture capital companies to determine if any of them is interested in the business. If your query letter has that look, you may be doing yourself a disservice by discouraging the venture capital company from taking the time to review the summary. The company's theory is that you must be desperate if you have to send out that many letters. Other venture firms routinely respond to a query letter by saying, "We are interested. Please send me your business proposal." This response may merely mean the venture capitalist has a cursory interest. He may turn down the funding requested after looking at your full proposal for only two minutes.

In order to avoid the look of a mass mailing and to ensure a speedy response, you should select several venture capital companies located close to you, of the type you believe to be interested in your company, and mail them a query letter, a summary, and a business proposal as set out in Chapter 3. By giving them the full treatment, you will dispel any suspicions about your being in a mail-order operation.

Personally, I like to see the complete package; that is, the summary with the business proposal attached to it. With that material in hand, I can continue to review the company after examining the summary. In other words, providing the potential investor with the business proposal as well as the summary speeds up the process tremendously because the venture capitalist does not have to write or call you to ask for the business proposal. If time is a critical factor in obtaining support money, you should send the business proposal along with the summary. If the venture capital company turns you down, you can always ask the venture capitalist to mail the business proposal back to you.

Strategic Use of Summary

It is obvious that the purpose of the summary is to entice the venture capitalist to read the entire business proposal and "fall in love" with your company. The summary then becomes an advertisement for your company, much like the advertisements placed in a singles magazine. You hope to entice someone into making a considerable effort to contact you.

You should treat the summary as an advertising document. It is a sales pitch for your company, your idea, and you. Never send out a summary or a business proposal that is a rough draft or anything less than a complete, professional piece of work. To do so is to make a halfhearted attempt at selling your idea and company. Instead of a rough draft, you should have a polished copy with dynamic words and an effective selling orientation. After all, you are the one who has to sell this idea. Thousands of ideas out there are competing for the same funds that you are seeking from the venture capital company. Without a strong selling document you will never meet the venture capitalist and have a chance to discuss your idea. When you have finished writing your summary presentation, sit back for a few minutes and think about it. Try to determine if it really stands out, if it makes an exciting statement, and if it suggests that your situation is an opportunity the venture capitalist cannot miss. If your summary accomplishes these things, then you have satisfied the basic requirement of the summary. Remember, the basic idea is to sell your idea to the venture capitalist.

Rather than talk about how wonderful your management is, you should mention the actual achievements that management has accomplished to date. By eliminating superlatives you will avoid giving the impression that you are a salesman first and an achiever second.

Another Kind of Venture Capital

The summary for Small Business Investment Companies (SBICs) is quite different from the summary for "pure" venture capital just covered in the preceding section. SBICs lend money and have an option to buy stock in your company, whereas venture capitalists make equity investments by means of common or preferred stock. The summary above would be used to request an equity investment. In contrast, the following summary is oriented toward as Small Business Investment Company. The summary is a disguised version of one that was presented to us some years ago. The numbers and people as well as the stage of development have been changed completely. We made the investment along with others, but it had a poor return.

Company: TT5 Corporation
123 Main Street
McLean, Virginia 22101
Telephone: (703) 555-1212

Contact: Joe Entrepreneur, President

Type of Business: Manufacturer of switching gear for telephone equipment.

Company Summary: TT5 Corporation was founded two years ago by Joe Entrepreneur, an individual with seven years' experience in the communication and switching-gear industry. The company's first product was a multipurpose switching unit attached to PBX systems permitting the buyer of the unit to use several low-cost telephone services. The company has reached profitability after its second year of business, and estimates show that it will be very profitable in three years.

Management: Joe Entrepreneur, with seven years' experience in manufacturing PBX and related equipment, founded the company in 1980 and has served as President since that time. He previously worked for a large communications network conglomerate and several other communications corporations. He is a graduate of a Boston technology university with a degree in electrical engineering.

John Smith, Executive Vice-president, has been with the company for one year. Previously he had seventeen years of experience in the field of PBX and related equipment. He has written two books on the subject and has been granted six patents for work in telecommunications. Currently he guides the company in all of its marketing operations. He has an M.B.A. degree from a large university in Maryland.

Product/Service and Competition: TT5 Corporation manufactures a unique electrical switching box that can be adapted to all forms of PBX and telephone equipment. At present no companies other than TT5 Corporation are in the business of manufacturing these add-on communication boxes. It is doubtful that anyone will enter the business in the next two years. If competitiors do enter, TT5's patents should give it a monopoly on certain types of PBX installations.

Funds Requested: $500,000 convertible subordinated debentures at 15 percent interest and convertible into 20 percent ownership of the company.

Collateral: Second secured interest in the assets of the business subordinated to a local bank debt of $1,750,000.

Use of Proceeds: The company has currently outstripped its line of working capital at the bank ($750,000) and its low equity base prevents the bank from increasing the line of credit beyond the current status. The company will use the $500,000 initially to pay down the bank loan and negotiate a larger line of credit ($1,750,000) with the bank so that more working capital will be available to the company.

Financial History:	Actual 2 Years Ago	Actual Prior Year	Actual Last Year
Revenues	$100,000	$450,000	$979,000
Net income	(226,000)	(443,000)	62,000
Assets	443,000	1,002,000	1,200,000
Liabilities	232,000	1,402,000	876,000
Net worth	211,000	(232,000)	(170,000)

Financial Projections:	Projected This Year	Projected Next Year	Projected In 2 Years
Revenues	$1,425,000	$3,260,000	$8,350,000
Net income	90,000	224,000	1,790,000
Assets	1,500,000	2,000,000	2,900,000
Liabilities	900,000	1,230,000	1,800,000
Net worth	(80,000)	144,000	934,000

Exit: The company will attempt a public offering in three years. If there is no public market and no prospect for a public market in the near future, then the company will offer to buy back the stock owned by the venture capitalist. A predetermined price could be set ahead of time, if desired by the venture capitalist.

What Makes It Exciting?

There are three reasons why the above summary is exciting to a venture capitalist. First, the product is unique. As discussed under "Product/Service and Competition," the product is manufactured only by this company, and there appears to be no potential competition on the horizon. The second bit of information that is music to the venture capitalist's ears is the fact that both individuals have had previous experience in this area and have been working in this company for almost three years. This background usually makes the venture capitalist more comfortable about the operation and about the prospects for the future. The crowning touch to this exciting summary is the financial projections. Not only has the company turned the corner from its actual financial statements, but it is now projected to have strong earnings. Obviously the venture capitalist will be led to believe that in the years ahead the company will go public or be sold to a large company. When the public offering occurs, the venture capital company (as well as the entrepreneurs) will reap huge capital gains. The projections would probably not excite a true-blue venture capitalist, but they suggest a good return on investment to an SBIC that lends money.

Perspective for Your Summary

Both of the summaries discussed in this chapter have followed a specific format. This format has worked well for people seeking money in the venture capital field. It may not be the best format for you to use because it may not present your company in its best light. You should use the format that you believe does this. However, be aware that the venture capitalist is seeking the four basic items we have described. You may cover some of the items in greater detail than others, but you should mention all four.

Management

You should indicate that you have a competent and experienced management team.

Profits

You should indicate that there are substantial profits available for your company.

Uniqueness

You should mention the uniqueness of your product or why this situation is special.

Exit

You need to take into account the venture capitalist's desire to have an exit.

These are the four basic items that venture capitalists look for immediately. You need to cover all four in your summary. You should cover them in sufficient detail. If you fail to cover these four items, the venture capitalist may merely put your proposal on the "back burner" while he reads some other proposal.

The summary document will be the most important piece of paper that you will create. The summary must interest the venture capitalist. It must act as a hook and pull him toward reading the entire business proposal.

Write your summary proposal before you write your full business proposal. In doing so, you should place in the summary only the essence of your entire business proposal. Then when you write your business proposal, make sure you substantiate and expand on everything in the summary proposal. Once you have finished your business proposal, return to the summary and rewrite it to make sure the summary is consistent with your business proposal.

Once you have finished the summary and the business proposal, you will want to have a friend read the entire product. Your friend should be asked to keep in mind certain questions during this reading. First, did it grab the reader's attention? Did it say, "This is a tremendous investment opportunity?" Second, was it easily understood? If your summary is not easy to understand, you can be sure that the business proposal will not be easy to understand either. The third question should be, "How can the summary proposal be improved?" Remember, constructive criticism can be of great assistance.

What Do Venture Capitalists Think About Summaries?

Venture capitalists believe that summaries should be exciting, that they should turn the reader on. Writing a summary is not like writing a novel. It doesn't take a talent for creative writing. And it doesn't take a talent for clever writing, as composing a jingle or a catchy phrase does. But, the summary should be exciting. What excites you about the situation should come through in the proposal summary, not in the form of superlatives, but in the form of a strong sales pitch backed up by facts.

You may have seen the prospectuses printed to sell stock in small businesses. These prospectuses must conform to the requirements of securities laws as enforced by the Securities and Exchange Commission (SEC). Usually, the writing is "dry." The prospectus merely outlines how the investor can lose his money. There is rarely a sense of excitement. In making a presentation to a venture capital investor, you are not bound by the SEC requirements to make your proposal drab. You can make it exciting. It can be a sales document as long as you reveal the facts, and all of the facts.

Confidentiality of Your Great Idea

From time to time, an entrepreneur will call a venture capitalist and discuss an idea in vague terms. After the venture capitalist has asked several questions, the entrepreneur will ask how he can be assured the venture capitalist will not steal his idea. In an effort to prevent piracy, many entrepreneurs ask the venture capitalist to sign a nondisclosure agreement. The agreement provides that the venture capitalist will maintain confidentiality with regard to the business situation presented by the entrepreneur. Most venture capitalists will refuse to sign such nondisclosure agreements. They will give you every assurance that they will maintain the confidentiality of your special situation and, in most cases, this is true. Any venture capitalist who steals ideas faces the risk of a law suit and a bad reputation. A venture capital firm that deliberately divulges confidential information in a proposal could be considered liable if the act proved to be detrimental to the entrepreneur. However, the greatest repercussion for disclosure of confidential information would be the damage caused to the venture capital firm's reputation, since many people would find out about it and entrepreneurs would not send the firm business opportunities. In most cases, you can rely on professional integrity of the venture capital firm not to use or distribute the information you have given him.

Many times a broker will ask a venture capital firm to sign an agreement to pay his fee if the firm is financed. Virtually all venture capital firms will refuse to sign these agreements, simply because they do not want to obligate themselves to pay any brokerage fees. Most venture capital firms will honor any directive given by the small business being financed. That is, if the small business tells the venture capital firm to pay the broker out of the proceeds of the investment proceeds, then it will be paid by the venture capital firm out of the proceeds.

As in any business, if you are dealing with a professional venture capital group, then you do not have to worry about confidentiality, and brokers do not have to worry about losing the opportunity to make a fee. Venture capitalists are in the business of making money for themselves, but they do not mind other people making money.

Objective

In your own summary, you need to develop strong ideas that will make the venture capitalist wish to be an investor in your company. The summary should make him want to read and study the business proposal. As we discuss the items in the business proposal in Chapter 3, you will understand more clearly the desires of the venture capitalist company as well as the things you need to do to keep his interest going once he has been sold by the summary.

3

The Proposal

Can You Put Together an Interesting Proposal?
A Complete Proposal Is One That Sells Your Company.

Many people telephone an investment officer of a venture capital company and try to set up an appointment so they can explain their financial needs and the potential of their company. Most venture capitalists will resist such visits until after they have received the business proposal. Without the proposal, or at least a summary proposal, the venture capitalist has no idea of the details of the business. If you do meet he is not prepared to ask intelligent questions. Some people show up at the office of the venture capitalist with an inadequate business proposal in hand, and want to talk about their business. Sitting in a meeting with them, the venture capitalist fumbles with the papers and stumbles through the business proposal before he can understand the situation. Such visits make it difficult to have a productive meeting. On the other hand, after reading a sound business proposal, the venture capitalist usually knows if he wants to invest in the company. If he does not wish to invest, he can save the entrepreneur a trip to the venture capital company. If the venture capitalist wants to invest, he is prepared to discuss the company in detail when the meeting occurs.

Some entrepreneurs believe that if they can only meet with the venture capitalist, they can "sell" him on their idea. This attitude is especially common in cases where the venture capitalist has read the business proposal and notifies the entrepreneur that he does not have an interest in investing. I have never seen a "sale" happen in such circumstances. Entrepreneurs often believe they can meet the venture capitalist, present their idea orally, and receive financing. A meeting with the venture capitalist cannot substitute for a well-prepared business proposal. After reading a strong business proposal, he knows precisely the type of investment he wants to make, as well as what questions still remain unanswered. For most venture capitalists, then the business proposal is the turning point in the decision to go forward, to invest time and energy in trying to analyze the situation, and to work out a deal with the entrepreneur. If the entrepreneur is invited to the office of the venture capitalist to discuss the business proposal, the venture capitalist is probably seeking a way to make the investment. The entrepreneur is 50 percent on the way to obtaining funds if he is invited to meet with the venture capitalist. Because of the emphasis placed on the business proposal by the venture capital community, every entrepreneur must understand the vital importance of having an excellent business proposal.

The business proposal is similar to the business plan, except that it is shorter and contains fewer details. A full-blown business *plan* could be several hundred pages long. It would have sections on the financial plan, the marketing plan, the production plan, and personnel needed to carry out the plans. It would discuss the strengths and weaknesses of the company in all business segments. It would discuss strategies, long-range objectives, and short-run objectives. There are hundreds of books on business plans.

A business *proposal* is much like any other proposal in that it proposes something to someone. In the case of a venture capital proposal, it suggests how the venture capitalist and you can both make money. A business proposal is an abbreviated business plan with an emphasis on showing an outsider how the company will succeed. In many ways the business proposal is a promotional document meant to sell your company to an investor, in this case the venture capitalist. When you write your business proposal, remember that it's a promotional document. It is the sales literature for your company.

Should You Use a Broker or Consultant?

Many "consultants" and "financial brokers" prepare business proposals. The business proposals prepared by these people are known by their generic name, "packages." Brokers usually charge a great deal to assemble packages. Unfortunately, this fee is normally required in advance, and when the consultant is finished with the package it is usually a poor imitation of a business proposal. Many financial brokers merely send out sketchy information supplied to them by the entrepreneur. This usually insures that the venture capital management will turn down the proposal. The reason a financial broker cannot prepare an effective business proposal is simple. He rarely knows your business as well as you do. He cannot write a proposal without the help of the entrepreneur. By using Chapters 2-4 of this book, you can create a business proposal that will present your business in its best light. The proposal will be submitted to a venture capital company, not a bank. Bank proposals are different and there are many good books on preparing them. By using this book you will be able to deal directly with the venture capital source. Of course, it is wise to have your banker, your accountant, and friends review the proposal. They may be able to suggest another point of view for you to consider. If you must use a business broker or consultant, please read Chapter 11 before you pay out a single cent to one of them.

Most Important Quality of a Business Proposal

The most important quality of your business proposal is succinctness. A business proposal that is longer than thirty pages, excluding the financial exhibits, is probably too long. One that runs over fifty pages is definitely too long. The idea behind a business proposal is to impart the main ideas important to the venture capitalist. Chapter 4 covers the additional information you will need to prepare.

The business proposal format set forth on the following pages has been organized for a traditional, straightforward company. A business proposal can be organized in any manner. Most of the components listed in the following pages should be included in every business proposal; however, some items should be deleted if they are not applicable to your situation. You should not cover those that are not significant. For example, a service company would delete many sections dealing with production. The organization and presentation of the components can be rearranged to place important items first. Some items can be combined under a single heading.

What follows is the description of a complete business proposal. When you read it you might ask why you should do all this work for the venture capitalist. The fact is that if you do not, he will have to do it himself before he invests in your company. By doing the work for him, you speed up the process. Also, remember there are many business proposals arriving on the desk of the venture capitalist. If yours is to win out, the proposal should eliminate as much work as possible for the venture capitalist. Make it easy for the venture capitalist to invest in your company and you will be ahead of the pack.

Many venture capitalists will not invest in a company that does not have a strong business proposal. They believe that if the entrepreneur cannot prepare an effective business proposal, he cannot possibly be a competent entrepreneur. Other venture capitalists will not lean that far, but every venture capitalist agrees that a well-prepared business proposal is a sign of an intelligent person of the type they want to back.

Legally, you want to prepare a complete business proposal. If you do not or if you leave out material information, then the venture capital investor may have recourse against you personally if the venture fails. Everyone understands that the venture capitalist is an adult. He has the ability to review proposals and make a professional judgment. He is, by every standard, a sophisticated investor. But you should remember that security laws dictate how a private placement of securities must be carried out. Of course, you cannot include fraudulent or misleading information in your proposal; moreover, you are supposed to fully disclose any material item about your business. The disclosure must be in writing to the purchaser of the securities. If you fail to disclose a material item, the venture capitalist may be able to demand all of his money back; or worse, if the business fails, he could have a legal basis to sue you personally. Therefore, as you prepare your business proposal, begin by including too much information. Later, when you begin to pare it down to size, remember not to delete those items that will be material to a reasonable investor.

In general, the major sections you should cover in your business proposal are:

1. Summary
2. Business and its future
3. Management
4. Description of the financing
5. Risk factors
6. Return on investment and exit
7. Analysis of operations and projections
8. Financial statements
9. Projections
10. Illustrative information

Let's discuss each item in turn.

Part 1:   Summary

The summary should be the first item a venture capitalist sees. The summary was discussed in Chapter 2. It gives the venture capitalist an initial impression of you and your proposal so it should be typed perfectly and presented clearly.

Part 2:   Business and Its Future

This section covers a number of key topics that will help the venture capitalist understand your business. Each item is important in its own right, but throughout this section there must also be a general, if not specific, attempt to show how your business is unique. Show the reader what makes your business special in the world of business. While reading this section, the venture capitalist will try to determine the "keys to success" for this industry. In other words, he will try to identify these two or three things that must be executed very well in order to be successful in your business situation. Note the numbering system has headings with a single number and sub-headings have decimals such as 2.01.

2.01   General

Begin with a paragraph that starts with the sentence, "The company's principal offices are located . . . ," and put in the address, the telephone number, and the individual who should be contacted, as well as the standard industrial classification (SIC Code) for your industry, if you know it. The SIC's codes are established by the National Bureau of Standards and its code book is available in most libraries.

2.02   Nature of the Business

In this part give a general synopsis of the business that you are in. For example, you might say, "The company designs, manufactures, markets, and services minicomputer-base software-controlled medical diagnostic equipment used in outpatient monitoring." A pithy sentence describing what your company does is probably the best beginning. Next, you should describe the product or service in general terms. You want to make sure the venture capitalist understands your product or service in as few words as possible.

2.03   Business History

In this section you should tell when the company was incorporated, specify when it introduced its first product or service, and list the most important milestones (with dates) through which the company has passed. The business history section of the report must be brief and to the point. If it is more than a page, or at the most, two pages, you have included too many historical asides. There may be a special reason for including a long historical section if the company has had a colorful past, but by all means be brief. The venture capitalist will talk to you about the business history section in order to understand your business. At that time, you can go into many details.

2.04   Business of the Future

Spell out in chronological sequence the plan for the company and indicate critical milestones. In essence, the venture capitalist wants to know how you move from where you are today to where you intend to be in five years. The form of this section of the proposal is open to a great deal of freedom even though it must be brief. You may simply state that you intend to continue producing your two basic products for the next five years and that in year three you will introduce another similar product. In that case, your business of the future would be brief and to the point. On the other hand, if you expect to go through innumerable changes before you reach your final point of stability, you should indicate what changes will take place. The venture capitalist wants to know precisely what the company will have to do to be a success.

2.05   Uniqueness

Every business proposition to a venture capitalist should have some unique property. Is the management team unique? Is the product or service unique? Is the production process unique? Is it based on unique financing? All these items could be included. The important point is that something should make this company stand out from all the other investment opportunities available to the venture capitalist. Venture capitalists do not like to invest in "me too" companies. They want a company that has a unique business position. In a separate section such as this, or in various sections throughout the business plan, you should stress the uniqueness of your company. If your business involves a new product, a patent on a process, or some other particularly unusual feature, then it should be covered in a separate section such as this. Besides including this section, the entrepreneur should interlace the business proposal with the strengths of the company.

2.06   Product or Service

In this section you must describe the product or service precisely, in terms that will leave no doubt in the mind of the reader as to what you produce or plan to produce. If you have several products or services, describe each in a separate paragraph. You should describe the price of the product, how the price was determined, and the amount of gross profit. Entrepreneurs tend to treat pricing of their product too hastily. Spend enough time to think through all the factors affecting your pricing of the product and make sure that you can explain in straightforward, logical terms, the rationale behind the pricing. Is it priced because competition has forced prices in that direction? Is it priced high because you can get away with it? You must be prepared to answer these questions.

2.07   Customers or Purchasers of the Product

Describe in detail the customers of the product: who uses it, what they use it for, and why they buy your product or service. Do they buy your product because of price alone, or are there other considerations? What need does the product or service satisfy for the customer? In this section you also need to list the top three purchasers of your product, along with the dollar volume and unit volume of their purchases. You can do this in columnar form, the first column containing the company, the second the dollar volume, and the third column the number of units purchased. You will be furnishing the venture capitalist with a complete purchaser's list if he becomes very interested in your company. This section of your proposal will give the venture capitalist an idea of the business at an early stage in your dealings with him.

2.08   Industry or Market

Here you should describe the general marketplace for your product: the total dollar volume, the rate it has grown, and the overall demand for this product or service. A projection for the future size of the marketplace is necessary. You may use a tabular format such as:

Year	Industry Sales	% Increase
Prior Year Actual	$100,000,000	—
Last Year Actual	120,000,000	20
This Year Projected	150,000,000	25
Next Year Projected	200,000,000	33
Two Years Projected	280,000,000	40

In stating industy sales, make sure you don't fall into the trap of stating industry sales for the entire marketplace when, in effect, your product will be sold to only a very small part of that industry. The classic example is the company that is going to manufacture computer disk drives. In its business proposal it lists the entire computer disk drive market as its marketplace. Actually, the computer disk that it is going to manufacture is compatible with only one manufacturer. That manufacturer only has a 10 percent share of the market. Venture capitalists are eager to know the details of industry sales and the penetration of the industry with your product. You will need to be an expert in this area.

2.09   Competition

Here you must describe all the competing products and the various companies that produce them. Pay particular attention to the dollar volume that they are selling, the percentage of the market that they have, and the financial strength of the company that is your competitor. You should also describe precisely how your product is different from their products. A typical description of a competitor might be:

> *AJAX MFG.* Ajax Mfg. is a $300,000,000 company with one division selling widgets to this industry. The division had sales of approximately $14,000,000 last year, which indicates it has 12 percent of the market. Ajax's other business has suffered and currently Ajax seems to be draining this division of capital because Ajax has not introduced a new product in four years. Its product is obsolete and lacks many of the features of our machine. Our machine has a three-dimensional matrix, whereas theirs is two-dimensional. Our machine is microcomputer driven; theirs is manual. Ours is only 10 percent more expensive.

If you have no competition, then describe why you do not have competition. A reason for no competition might be your patent position. If you think there might be competition in the future, then you should indicate each probable competitor and when he might enter the market. Most entrepreneurs do not know enough about their competition. A venture capitalist will be leery of your analysis if you do not understand your competition. Be aware, too, that most venture capitalists believe every product has some type of competition.

2.10   Marketing

This section must contain information about your marketing process and the channels of distribution. That is, how does the product leave your plant and arrive in the hands of the ultimate user? Will you have a direct sales force or use distributors? What brokers or intermediaries are involved in selling your product? What is the relationship of your company to these intermediaries? You must describe any special arrangements you have entered into in order to market your product.

Most venture capitalists are poor market analyzers. They fancy themselves as marketing men, but they are not. In explaining the marketing of your product, you will have to take one step at a time so they can understand the marketing process. If you are marketing to state, local, or federal government almost exclusively, most venture capitalists will be nervous because your company will be subject to the whim of governmental appropriations. You will need a convincing explanation to overcome the objections to the marketing of most of your products to the government. Further, if you have a sole customer, it may be difficult for the venture capitalist to accept your marketing dependence on one customer. The risks are too high.

2.11   Production

Here you need to describe all stages of the production process and whatever affects production. A key point here is production costs. How did you arrive at the cost of goods sold?

2.12   Production Characteristics

This section should focus on the production characteristics. Is it a difficult or a sophisticated production process? Are there many components or just a few? How much value does the company actually add to the product? How much is purchased in subassembly format? What components are crucial to the production process? The venture capitalist wants to determine the difficulty of the production process. Is it a standard production process or does it have many difficult tasks? If it is a complicated process, will people with special skills be needed to carry it out?

2.13   Labor Force and Employees

In this section you need to describe the number of employees you have, your relationship with the work force, and whether it is union or nonunion. Also, categorize members of the work force in terms of white collar, blue collar, and so on. If the work force is unionized, you should describe the union contract, the relationship with the union, and when the contract will expire. The venture capitalist will want to determine how difficult it will be to acquire and maintain your employees. If your employees are hard to find, you will have to explain how you intend to attract and keep good employees.

2.14   Suppliers

In this section describe the companies that supply your company with raw materials or other necessary items. At this point in the proposal, you need to list the three or four top suppliers and the items they supply. You will want to do this in columnar form, the first column listing the suppliers, the second column listing the dollar volume of the supplies, and the third column showing the product supplied to your company. Later, you will be required to provide the venture capitalist with a complete list of suppliers of major components. The venture capitalist will use the list to call suppliers and verify your list.

2.15   Subcontractors

If subcontractors or other people complete part of the work in bringing the product to the marketplace, describe them and the relationship with them. In this section you should list several of the subcontractors and the dollar volume of work you are contracting with them. Later you will need to supply the venture capitalist with a complete list of subcontractors, names, addresses, telephone numbers, and volumes so the venture capitalist can contact these subcontractors.

2.16   Equipment

Describe in some detail the equipment that you have or intend to buy. Give a general idea of the fixed assets and their value of resale. Describe the total dollar volume and number of units that you can produce using the existing equipment. Identify any long lead time in acquiring machinery. In this section, the venture capitalist wants to know if your equipment is difficult to obtain. If it is and you reach capacity, the company will have to wait for a long period of time before it can acquire additional equipment in order to increase capacity. The venture capitalist will want to know if the equipment is complicated and requires a special skill to operate. If so, you will need a special work force in order to operate the machines. The question is, "How difficult is it to find such a special employee to operate the machine?" Finally, if the machinery is used for a special purpose, it will be difficult to sell. Therefore, its collateral value is worth much less. All these points are important to the venture capitalist.

2.17   Property and Facilities

Describe the real estate that the company owns, or the lease that it has for its offices and plant. Describe the size of the plant in square feet, and the price per square foot. You must describe the equipment that you have or intend to buy; describe the fixed assets in detail. Here the venture capitalist wants to know that the plant is sufficient to take care of the growth of the company. If you will have to move out of the plant in a year, the company will have difficulty continuing to expand at a rapid rate. Some venture capitalists don't like to invest in companies that have to move within a short period of time. They believe such moves are disruptive and destroy the company's growth.

2.18   Patents and Trademarks

You must describe in detail any patents or trademarks held by the company or ones it intends to apply for. You may wish to describe why a patent has been granted in order to emphasize the product's uniqueness. At some point in the process you may want to give the venture capitalist a copy of your patent so he can read it and determine for himself why you have a unique patent or trademark. You should not put a copy of the trademark in the business plan unless it is key to describing the uniqueness.

2.19   Research and Development

Here you should indicate the amount of money being spent on research and development, the amount that has been spent in the past, and the amount that you intend to spend in the future. You should describe precisely what you intend to accomplish with the funds spent on research and development. It is every venture capitalist's nightmare that he will somehow misjudge the entrepreneur and invest in a consummate researcher, rather than an entrepreneur who wants to develop a product. The research entrepreneur will spend millions researching and developing new product variations of the existing product. The venture capitalist wants an entrepreneur who can make the transition into a marketing and production company that is trying to make money.

2.20 Litigation

Describe any litigation the company may be involved in now, including suits against the company and those the company has filed against others. Be sure to mention any potential litigation that may be contemplated. Venture capitalists are litigation shy. If they find that a company has been involved in a great deal of litigation, they are apt to turn down the request for funds. After all, if everybody is suing you, there must be something wrong with the way you operate your company. On the other hand, if you are the type who sues others at the drop of a hat, there must also be something wrong. The venture capitalist will have every reason to wonder if you won't end up suing him very soon after he has made is investment. A company with a history of litigation will have to explain the details to the venture capitalist in order to help the venture capitalist overcome his natural reservations about companies with such a background.

2.21 Government Regulations

Describe the governmental agency that regulates the company and describe the relationship with the government. In this section describe how you plan to comply with regulations set down by the Occupational Safety and Health Administration. Most venture capitalists can tell stories about excruciating experiences with a federal or state agency that had one of their portfolio companies tied in red tape for months or even years, and that in some cases, destroyed the company. If your business comes under a great deal of governmental regulation—for example, by the Food and Drug Administration—you will have to use extra persuasion to convince the venture capitalist that you know how to operate in a regulated environment.

2.22 Conflicts of Interest

Describe any potential conflicts of interest, such as a director who is also the owner of one of your suppliers. Describe any transactions with management in which management has sold something to the company for a price that may or may not be reasonable. If you do not reveal conflicts of interest and the venture capitalist uncovers them, you lose credibility instantly. It is better to meet this problem head on and reveal it to the venture capitalist at the outset. Show

how the company is better off by being involved in a potentially conflicting situation than it would be otherwise.

2.23   Backlog

In this section you should indicate the amount of backlog outstanding for the company's products. List the items requested and the size of the order. You can also give the venture capitalist a good idea of the backlog by listing the top three or four customers and their backlog of orders. Do this in columnar form. The first column should contain the name of the company that has placed the order, the second column the dollar volume of the orders, and the third column the number of units ordered. Later in your meeting with the venture capitalist, you should show him a complete list of the backlog so he can see where the orders are coming from and who purchases the product.

2.24   Insurance

List the insurance carried by the company or intended to be carried by the company, including fire, casualty, product liability, flood insurance, fidelity bond, life insurance on key employees, and so on. However, list only the insurance that is important to the operation of the company, not health insurance, dental plan, or the like.

2.25   Taxes

Mention any special taxes that are levied against the company. If you are already in business, mention any outstanding taxes, such as payroll taxes or income taxes.

2.26   Corporate Structure

In this section you should mention whether it is a stock company, a partnership, or a Subchapter S, and whether it is 1244 stock. Tell where the company is incorporated, where it is licensed to do business, and what trade names it uses. You should mention if it is a parent company with a subsidiary. If it is a complex situation in which a parent owns part of or all subsidiaries, you should use block diagrams and show the separate legal entities and draw lines between them with percentages on them as shown in Figure 3-1.

2.27   Publications and Associations

As a point of information, the venture capitalist may be interested in trade associations for your industry. He may also want to know which trade magazines and trade newspapers are good ones, so that he may use back issues to learn more about your business.

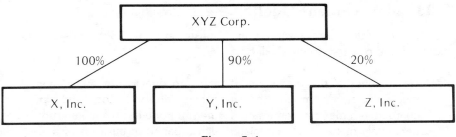

Figure 3-1

Part 3: The Management

In this section you should describe the management, the directors, and all others who are key to the operation of this business. Usually, there are no more than three key people in a very small firm and fewer than six in a larger one. Remember, the venture capitalist is looking for *key* people. You should refrain from using superlatives to describe the key people, but do not be shy about mentioning achievements.

3.01 Directors and Officers

List *all* the officers, directors, and key employees. You should include the full name of each individual, his or her position, and age. For example:

Name	Position	Age
Sam Smith	Chairman & director	38
Joseph Entrepreneur	President & director	36
Donna Dont	Vice-president & director	32

3.02 Key Employees

In this section you should identify the three or four individuals who are key employees and give a summary, in resume style, of their background and where they have worked. It is important to demonstrate that these key people are achievers.

There is a considerable body of psychological literature on achievers, but not much on entrepreneurs. Some people argue that achievers are born the way they are, whereas others believe the attributes of achievers can be learned. The point is simple in your case. You must present yourself as an achiever to the venture capitalist, or you probably will not be financed. Further, the more you have achieved in your industry, the more the venture capitalist will be motivated to finance your company.

3.03   Management Fidelity

It is difficult to demonstrate your honesty on paper. But a positive statement like the one that follows will be a big plus.

> No member of the management team, no director, or any major investor in the company, has ever been arrested, convicted, or charged in a material crime; and further, not one has been bankrupt personally or has been associated with a bankrupt business of any kind. Personal credit reports will verify that all individuals have excellent credit ratings and have no overdue debt outstanding.

Obviously, what you are trying to communicate to the venture capitalist is that you and your team are as clean as a whistle.

3.04   Remuneration

In this section you are to list all key employees, directors, or officers who will receive any payment whatsoever. You should list in tabular form the names of the individuals, the capacity in which they will be serving, and the salary or remuneration that they have received or propose to receive. Under the heading of remuneration, you should include all fees, director's fees, consulting fees, commissions, bonuses, salary, and so on—in other words, total remuneration by your company. An example is:

Name	Capacity	Remuneration
Joseph Entrepreneur	President	$75,000
Donna Dont	Vice-president	$45,000
Sam Smith	Chairman	$ 2,000

3.05   Stock Options

You should tabulate all stock options that are now outstanding. Beside each person's name you should indicate the number of shares that have been granted, the average exercise price, the number of shares that have been exercised since the options were granted, and the number of options still outstanding. Where options are outstanding to a corporation, you may wish to note why they are outstanding at this point. For example:

Name	Options Granted	Options Avg. Price	Options Exercised	Remaining Options
Joseph Entrepreneur	100,000	$.10	None	100,000
Donna Dont	50,000	$.10	None	50,000

3.06 Stock Option Plan

In this section describe the general stock option plan that exists at the company and how many options the plan has in it or will have in it at some date in the future.

3.07 Principal Shareholders

In this section list in tabular form the name of the individual, the amount of shares owned beneficially or directly, all shares under option, the percentage this ownership represents with regard to all the shares outstanding, and the percentage of ownership that will exist after the shares have been exercised. Also indicate the price paid for the ownership. For example:

Name	Number of Shares	Percentage of Ownership Before Financing	Percentage of Ownership After Financing	Price Paid for Ownership
J. Entrepreneur	400,000	50	40	$ 25,000
S. Smith	400,000	50	40	25,000
V. Capitalist	200,000	—	20	600,000

3.08 Employment Agreements

List in detail any employment agreements that the company has with any of the employees, and state specifically what the arrangement is with each employee. Employment agreements are not appreciated by venture capitalists. Most often they are used to insure that top management will not be fired and will continue to obtain a high salary. If you have a legitimate reason for employment contracts, state it in this section.

3.09 Conflict of Interest

This item is listed once again to make sure that any conflict of interest transactions that have transpired are revealed fully. In this section you should reveal transactions that management has had with the company. For example, a director may have contributed services to the company, and in return the director may have received stock or stock options in the company.

3.10 Consultants, Accountants, Lawyers, Bankers and Others

In this section you should mention the names of your consultants, if any, your accountants, lawyers, and bankers, along with their telephone numbers. If a special fee is being paid to any of them, or if any of them are on a monthly retainer fee by the company, mention it in this section.

Part 4:   Description of the Financing

In this section you will describe the type of financing you are trying to obtain, and some related items.

4.01   Proposed Financing

First, you should describe the loan, the options, the preferred stock, the common stock—whatever it is you are trying to sell to the venture capitalist. Be sure to provide enough details so that there will be no question about what you are selling.

If you are proposing a loan, explain the term of the loan. Is it five years or ten years? Will there be an interest-only period? What interest rate are you seeking? Will the interest rate be variable or fixed? Will the loan be convertible into common stock or preferred stock? All these items need to be covered. If you are open to suggestions on the structure, then state this important point in this section.

If you are selling preferred stock, what dividend will you pay? Will the dividend be cumulative (meaning that in case you do not pay it one year or one quarter, then you must make it up in some other year or quarter)? What redemption will there be of the preferred stock? For example, after five years will you have to begin redeeming the stock over a number of years to give the investor his money back? Is the preferred stock convertible into common stock? If so, what is the conversion price? What restrictions are there on these shares and does the preferred stock have voting rights? Does it control the board of directors? What preferential treatment will it have?

If you are selling common stock, will there be a dividend on the common stock? Will the dividend be cumulative in case you miss it? Will a redemption of the common stock be required after a period of time in order to give the investor his money back? What price will the investor pay for the common stock? Will there be restrictions on the shares? What voting rights will holders of common stock have? What registration rights will holders of common stock have? That is, can the venture capitalist make you register the stock and in so doing make you become a public company?

If you are offering stock options under any of the above conditions, you need to consider the price that the venture capitalist will pay for the option when he purchases the option from your company. You must also consider what price the venture capitalist will pay to exercise the option into common or preferred stock. How many shares will the options exercise into? What is the expiration period of the option? Five years? Ten years? You should spell out all these things about the stock options. If you are flexible as to the type of financing or the terms of the financing, state your willingness to negotiate in this section.

4.02   Capital Structure

Here you should describe the common stock, preferred stock, and long-term debt that is currently outstanding so that the venture capitalist will know the general capital structure of the company. For example:

	Before Financing	After Financing
Long-term debt	$100,000	—
Long-term venture capital debt	—	$500,000
Preferred stock	—	—
Common stock	$100,000	$100,000

In the case above, $100,000 of the debt from the venture capitalist is being used to pay off the bank debt. You only need this section if the financing is complex.

4.03   Collateral for the Financing

Obviously, if common stock is involved, there is no collateral. If the financing is to be subordinated debt, list the debts that will be senior to this debt. Explain what will be used to collateralize this debt.

4.04   Guarantees

Here indicate the personal or corporate guarantees that will be given to the venture capitalist for his investment. If there is to be a personal guarantee, you will be required to supply a personal financial statement on the guarantors. If a separate company is to guarantee the loan, you will need to provide a separate financial statement on the company guaranteeing the investment.

4.05   Conditions

Describe any conditions of the financing. For example, must the company provide a seat on the board of directors for the venture capital company's representative? Will the company have to live by any ratios? What milestones must the company achieve?

4.06   Reporting

Describe what reporting you intend to make to the investor with regard to this financing. For example, will you provide a monthly profit-and-loss statement, a balance sheet, and an annual audit?

4.07   Use of Proceeds

Specify where you intend to apply the funds. Do not use the amorphous name "working capital," but specify how the funds will be spent—for example, purchasing of inventory: $200,000; increase in accounts receivable: $100,000; and meeting payroll: $200,000. Be as specific as possible.

4.08   Ownership

In this section indicate the number of shares outstanding and the number that would be owned by the venture firm if this financing occurs. Indicate the price paid for the ownership, and the percentage of ownership the venture company will have of the company. Use a tabular format as shown.

	Before Financing	After Financing	Percentage	Price Paid
Existing shareholders	800,000	800,000	80	$ 50,000
Venture capitalist		200,000	20	600,000

4.09   Dilution

Here you want to describe the degree to which the new investor is diluted in terms of book value. Compare the cost per share that the venture capitalist will be paying with the price paid by others.

4.10   Fees Paid

In this section indicate whether you will pay any brokerage fees, and whether you will pay the legal fees of closing the investment. Specify what other fees you will pay or are obligated to pay. Be forewarned that most venture firms expect you to pay all fees.

4.11   Investor Involvement

The venture capitalist will want to have the right to attend board meetings and in many cases will want to become a member of the board of directors. He may want one or two, or even three board positions. You may wish to have the venture capitalist more actively involved. This is the section in which you describe the amount of investor involvement that you are seeking or would like to have from the venture capitalist.

There may be other opportunities for the venture capital firm to offer services to your small company. You may wish to set these out in this section. For example, you may want the venture capital firm to provide you with assistance in the area of finance and may offer to pay a fee for this assistance. You may require a particular type of financing, such as an industrial revenue bond. You may offer the venture capitalist a fee for placing the bond, for example, 2 percent of the amount being placed. Generally speaking, this section deals with the type of involvement you expect the venture capitalist to serve in the future.

Part 5: Risk Factors

In this section you want to describe the major risk that an investor will have by investing in your company. This section spells out all the drawbacks. Do not offer positive comments, except at the end of each paragraph. Some areas you may wish to cover are as follows:

5.01 Limited Operating History

If the company is new or has recently been organized, then the lack of operating history will be a significant item to discuss.

5.02 Limited Resources

The company may or may not have enough resources to continue operations for a prolonged period of time if everything does not work out as planned. Mention this as a potential risk.

5.03 Limited Management Experience

If management is young or new to this industry, you may need to discuss the experience level of management.

5.04 Market Uncertainties

You may wish to describe the market uncertainties that exist with regard to sales.

5.05 Production Uncertainties

Here you should describe any production uncertainties that may exist. Perhaps a prototype has never been built on a production assembly line, and therefore there are some uncertainties as to whether it can be built.

5.06 Liquidation

Here you should present a liquidation analysis of your company. That is, if the company were to get in trouble and had to be liquidated, what might it be worth on the auction block?

5.07   Dependence on Key Management

You need to explain either on paper or directly to the venture capitalist later, what changes you expect when any of the key managers die. Who will step into his place? Who could be designated to run the company if the top person died? If you do not cover the subject here, you can expect the venture capitalist to ask you the favorite question,"What happens if you are run over by a truck tomorrow?" Some entrepreneurs write a corporate "will." In it they describe what is to be done with the company when they die.

5.08   What Could Go Wrong??

Here the venture capitalist wants you to put on his hat and try to look at the business as an investment. He expects you to address the question, "What could go wrong?" The related question to answer here is, "How could the venture capitalist lose his money?" In other words, the venture capitalist wants you to use your objective, analytical skills to analyze your own business situation. He wants you to point out the major problems that can arise. As soon as you have pointed them out, you must indicate how you are going to solve them.

5.09   Other Items

You should mention such items as your estimated financial reserves, the lack of a public market for the shares, economic controls or other government regulations, control of the company by noninvestor stockholders, and the lack of dividends. You should mention these points if they are material, rather than wait for the venture capitalist to bring up these questions.

Part 6:   Return on Investment and Exit

In this section you need to discuss how the venture capital investor will eventually receive cash for his investment in the company. Remember, the venture capitalist wants to end up with all cash and no investment in your company. There are three generally accepted methods of giving the venture capitalist liquidity. You should cover all three, but should also indicate which one is the most likely exit for your investor.

6.01   Public Offering

The first possibility is a public offering; that is, the company could go public by offering its shares to the public. Part of the shares or all of the shares owned by the venture capitalist would be sold in the public offering. You may wish to discuss this with a brokerage firm before you discuss it with the venture capitalist.

6.02 Sale

Second, the company could be sold to a large company usually a conglomerate. In the case of this option, you should actually mention some conglomerates or large companies that you believe would have an interest in acquiring your company.

6.03 Buyback

Finally, you may offer the venture capitalist a "put" according to which your company will be required to buy the equity owned by the venture capitalist on the basis of a predetermined formula. Buyback formulas are covered in Chapter 6.

6.04 Return on Investment

Return on investment (ROI) will be important to the venture capitalist. You need to show what return he can expect if he invests the amount you are requesting. For example, you might say, "If an investor buys 30 percent of the company for $300,000 and after four years the company is a public company with pretax earnings of $3 million, then $3 million times a price earnings multiple of 8 for our particular industry is $24 million as a value for the company; take 30 percent of that and you have $7.2 million for your $300,000 investment. Assume that the 30 percent is sold after four years, then the undiscounted ROI is $7.2 million divided by $300,000, divided by four years, which is an ROI of 400 percent per year."

Part 7: Analysis of Operations and Projections

Here you will present your own analysis of the company's prior operating history as well as projections for the future.

7.01 General

In this section you need to start out with some general profit-and-loss information, which will be based on financial data from your company. For example, for the last three years and for the next three years in the future, take net revenues, cost of sales, operating expense, interest expense, and income. Project them forward and give historical information for them so that one can see at a glance where the company has been and where it is going. For example:

Stated in Thousands

	Prior Year Actual	Last Year Actual	This Year Projected	Next Year Projected	In Two Years Projected
Net revenues	100	400	1,000	4,000	10,000
Cost of sales	100	200	500	2,500	6,500
Operating expenses	100	100	200	400	800
Interest expenses	100	100	100	200	300
Net income	(200)	—	200	900	2,400
Current assets	20	40	400	1,400	4,300
Machinery, equipment	100	400	600	1,000	1,000
Land and building	—	—	—	—	—
Other assets	10	10	10	10	10
Current liabilities	20	240	100	400	1,000
Long-term debts	100	400	400	600	—
Equity	10	(190)	510	1,410	4,310

7.02   Ratio Analysis

In this section you should take the net revenue, cost of sale, operating expenses, interest expense, and net income and compute them as percentages. That is, use 100 percent for net sales, then calculate cost of sales as a percentage of sales, and so on. Place these percentages in columnar form so that one can see the percentage ratio. For example:

Percentage Ratios

	Prior Year Actual	Last Year Actual	This Year Projected	Next Year Projected	In Two Years Projected
Net revenues	100	100	100	100	100
Cost of sales	100	50	50	63	65
Operating expenses	—	25	20	10	8
Interest expenses	—	25	10	4	3
Net income	—	—	20	23	24

7.03   Results of Operation

In this section you should discuss the results of operation and projections. Why have the results increased or declined? Tell why they will go up in the future. Discuss why the percentages might change and mention any momentous events such as the year a new product was introduced or the year in the future when you will have large research and development expenditures, for example. In other words, you need to explain the numbers that you set out in the preceding section and should mention the attached financials and projections, which you are about to discuss in the next part of the proposal.

7.04   Financial Conditions

In this section you should discuss in detail the current balance sheet. Describe liquidity of the company. Tell why there are significant increases in certain items such as accounts receivable, accounts payable, and so on.

7.05   Contingent Liabilities

Describe the company's contingent liabilities such as an unfunded pension plan, or a lawsuit from a company contending that one of its former employees working for you has brought corporate secrets with him.

Part 8:   Financial Statements

This is not a section so much as it is a collection of supporting documents. It should consist of complete financial statements. If your financials are not certified by an independent public accountant, they should be reviewed by an independent public accountant. You should have consolidated balance sheets, consolidated statement of income, a consolidated statement of shareholders' equity, and a consolidated statement of changes in financial position. You should add appropriate notes of explanation to the financial statements. This exhibit should include the last several years of financial statements, as well as current financial statements that may or may not be audited by an accounting firm. These should all be attached as *Exhibit #1 — Financial Statements,* and your business proposal should mention these exhibits.

Whatever you do, don't submit a business proposal that does not include current financial statements. Too many business proposals arrive with old (six months or more) financial statements. If you are to demonstrate that you are operating a stable business, you should present its current financial statements. Some business proposals present financial statements that are a year old. How can anyone make a decision to invest in a company on the basis of financial statements that are history? Some entrepreneurs do not seem to be aware of the fact that financial statements are of prime importance in operating a business. Needless to say, this type of entrepreneur does not receive the backing of venture capital companies.

Part 9:   Financial Projections

This section, too, contains an exhibit. It should consist of the annual financial projections for the next five years, as well as a detailed monthly cash flow statement for the next twelve months. Anyone looking at the situation should be able to determine precisely the cash flow situation. The cash flow statement should show the inflow of this financing as cash inflow. These statements should be attached to the business proposal and should be marked *Exhibit #2 — Financial Projections* and *Exhibit #3 — Cash Flows*. Appendix 3 shows a typical format you may use for both projections and cash flows.

Part 10:   Product Literature, Brochures, Articles, and Pictures

You should include pictures of the product and literature about the company that will show off your product or service. Written descriptions in the business proposal are essential, but pictures will also help sell your proposal. A general article about the industry or about competitive products compared to your product is a useful addition. Newspaper articles or magazine pieces on the company are probably unnecessary and do not say much to a venture capitalist. It is advisable to leave them out. Sending along tapes, records, or other promotional audiovisual items is a waste of money and time; do not do it.

Do You Really Need All of This?

The business proposal discussed above represents a thorough approach. You do not need to include everything that is listed above. What you must put into your business proposal are the material and key elements about your business. If there are only two key employees, you do not need to list the top ten people. If you operate a service business, you don't need to discuss production problems. Your proposal does not have to describe all the minute details of the business. It does need to include those aspects of the business that any investor, including yourself, would want to know before investing in the business.

When you begin writing your business proposal, you should cover all of the above aspects in detail. That means you will have a very large draft proposal. Once you have finished that draft, you should weed out the parts that do not add materially to the proposal. The main goal of the business proposal is to present the major aspects of the business and to avoid or merely touch on the nonmaterial aspects of the business.

What Is the Venture Capitalist Really Looking For?

When all is said and done, what is a venture capitalist looking for when he reviews a business proposal? Many venture capitalists will tell you that they look for good management, that is, they immediately examine the management teams in depth. I think that most venture capitalists first look for what is special about this situation. In other words, they want to know why this company will make a lot of money. Basically, they are interested in the uniqueness of the idea or product or service and in management's ability to make it all happen. That means the venture capitalist will first look at the uniqueness of the product and what the team plans to do to capitalize on this uniqueness. Therefore it would be wise for anyone preparing a complete business proposal to address the question of uniqueness in several places in the proposal.

Uniqueness

Since uniqueness is the first thing the venture capitalist will look for in the business proposal, let's see where it can be mentioned. Uniqueness can first be covered in Part 2 of the business proposal, "Business and Its Future." The question can be taken up directly under "Product or Service." You can even have a section entitled "Uniqueness" as covered above. There may also be unique aspects of marketing and production. You should certainly comment on the unique qualifications or skills of the management team; it is not enough to say that they are good fellows.

Management

Most venture capitalists consider management to be the key to every successful venture capital investment. This is the second thing the venture capitalist will be looking for, but he will place more emphasis on this area. The old saw of the venturing business is: you can have a good idea and poor management and lose every time; conversely, you can have a poor idea and a good management team and win every time. Let us look at what is meant by "good" in this context. The first thing a management team must have is experience. Unfortunately for young people, venture capitalists believe entrepreneurs should be between the ages of thirty and forty-five. There seems to be a fifteen year open window of a person's lifetime which the venture capitalist believes is the best entrepreneurial age. Younger than age thirty usually means that the entrepreneur lacks management experience or the knowledge needed to conduct a strong growth-oriented company. Older than forty-five usually means he has the experience but lacks the drive and ambition. Certainly, there are exceptions to this pattern, but these are the general expectations of the venture capitalist.

Anyone preparing a business proposal should pay particular attention to the backgrounds of the management team. Explain in detail who they are, what makes them tick, and why these entrepreneurs among all the people in the world can take this unique product or service and make a great deal of money with it.

Projections

Money is the third key subject covered by a good business proposal. It is incumbent upon the entrepreneur to set out strong growth projections for his company. These financial projections must not only be reasonable in terms of the percentage of growth that occurs each year, but they must also be realistic when compared with the many projections presented to the venture capitalist by other companies. Every entrepreneur should spend a great deal of time making, evaluating, and understanding his financial projections. Some entrepreneurs have an accounting firm prepare the projections on the basis of assumptions made by the entrepreneur. This is probably a poor approach because the venture capitalist will undoubtedly interrogate the entrepreneur to see if the entrepreneur understands the projections and the underlying assumptions. If someone else makes the projections, the entrepreneur will not be able to explain them adequately or convincingly. The venture capitalist will continue to question whether it is possible to expect the amount of growth indicated. Many venture capitalists routinely cut the sales and earnings of a projection in half, and assume that these reduced figures are more realistic to expect. It will be incumbent upon the entrepreneur to persuade the venture capitalist that the projections are achievable.

Exit

How the venture capitalist will exit from this situation will be a critical factor influencing his decision to invest. He wants to know how he will get out before he gets in. The venture capitalist does not want to be a long-term owner in the company. He wants to invest his money, ride with the deal for a while, and then exit. There are three basic exits:

1. Public offering, whereby the venture capitalist sells his ownership to the public
2. Sale of the company, including the venture capitalist's ownership to someone else (usually a large company)
3. Sale of the venture capitalist's position back to the company, to you personally, or to a third party. You must cover this point in detail in your business proposal.

Remember, you need to cover: (1) uniqueness; (2) management; (3) projections; and (4) exit. To miss any of these points is to set yourself up for rejection by the venture capitalist.

How to Package Your Proposal

In the retail food business, the package is as important as what is inside the package. Retailers must emphasize whatever will attract the buyer because it is a buyer's market. Thousands of retail products are vying for the consumer's money. The same is true in the case of venture capital. Thousands of proposals are vying for the venture capitalist's money. The packaging can draw the venture capitalist to your proposal. You might write a great business proposal, but if its physical appearance is sloppy, it might not be picked up by the venture capitalist for weeks, and when it is picked up, what a sight! The venture capitalist's first impression of the proposal would be so colored by the poor packaging that he might turn down the business proposal without reviewing it in detail.

It cannot be emphasized enough that a venture capitalist receives hundreds of telephone calls and dozens of business proposals every week. If your business proposal is to compete with all the others sitting on his desk, you must have a distinctive proposal. So you need to know the basics of how to package a winning business proposal.

Copies

You should *not* send an original to the venture capitalist. You should have crisp, clean copies, preferably on white paper with margins wide enough for the venture capitalist to make notes. A margin of one inch on all sides is the standard. The copy paper you use should be of high quality; it should not be the old variety that has an oily touch and a foul smell. It should provide a crisp, clean imprint on every page. Colored paper is optional. It does not impress most venture capitalists, but it might appeal to a few. You can copy on the back and the front or just on the front of each page.

Style of Type

You should not use an unusual style of type such as script. A type that is easy to read is essential if people are to process your business proposal quickly. The type should be dark and sharp in the original and in the copies. Submitting handwritten items is forbidden unless it is absolutely necessary.

Graphs and Pictures

Generally speaking, graphs are fine if they are of high quality, but are usually not essential in a business proposal. Bar graphs of sales are not as effective as numbers. Pictures of the product or literature on the product should be attached to the business proposal in order to give the venture capitalist a better idea of the subject, but such material should be of good quality.

Copying Articles

You should copy articles carefully in order to make sure the copies are of good quality. A poor-quality copy of a newspaper article will not invite the venture capitalist to read it. Generally, articles are not recommended as part of your proposal.

Cover

If possible, the cover on your proposal should be an attractive color. Also, the cover sheet should be of heavy paper so that your proposal will stand out from all the others sitting on the venture capitalist's desk. Perhaps a bright yellow page with your logo in the middle and name at the bottom would invite the venture capitalist to pick it up and read it immediately. Once he opens it up, of course, the summary sheet should grab his attention and draw him into the proposal. You might wish to use a picture of the product on the first page in order to attract attention. Again, you are selling, so make sure your product's package catches the eye of the venture capitalist.

Binding

There are many ways of binding business proposals today. A staple probably will not hold your business proposal together. If an ordinary staple will hold it together, it is probably not long enough. Certain heavy-gauge staples are acceptable, of course. If such a staple is not available, you have three options: you can use a three-ring binder, have the proposal professionally bound, or put a large clip on it so that the venture capitalist can take the clip off and turn the pages. Of the three options, most venture capitalists prefer a professionally bound proposal. Otherwise, most would prefer to have a large clip. Most venture capitalists dislike three-ring binders only because they are almost impossible to store. While most venture capitalists prefer professional binding, they are perfectly willing to take any of the three options if they receive a professionally prepared proposal.

Professional binding is done in a number of ways. A device consisting of plastic "fingers" may be pushed through the pages after they have been cut with a special tool. This permits the book to be opened easily in the middle as well as at the front and back. In another type of binding, a thin plastic strip is applied to the left edge, and it forces the pages together with a plastic lock on the back. This type of binding does not permit the pages to open readily, but does create a clean-looking package. Gummed bindings that are available look highly professional, but are expensive. In addition, you can find plastic or paper folders at stationery stores that will create a professional look for the package. The most efficient ones bind pages that have been punched for a three-ring binder. As mentioned above, any of these will be fine for the venture capitalist, but you do need to make the package physically attractive.

How Many Venture Capitalists Should be Contacted?

Entrepreneurs normally make one of two mistakes in contacting venture capitalists. Either they contact too few venture capitalists, or they contact too many. The typical entrepreneur in the first situation contacts one venture capitalist, asks him to review the proposal, and then waits patiently for a response. This can consume a huge amount of time, especially if the venture capitalist happens to be occupied with something else. The venture capitalist may have a portfolio company or, heaven forbid, many portfolio companies in trouble. He may like your proposal but may not have the time to spend on it.

At the other end of the spectrum, some entrepreneurs prepare a summary sheet and mail it out to five hundred venture capitalists, assuming that this is the best approach. Although this is one way to contact many venture capitalists at once, it seldom moves them because the mail-out is not taken seriously. The best procedure to follow is to select the half dozen venture capital firms nearest your company, or those most likely to invest in your industry. Mail them the summary and the full business proposal with a concise but pleasant covering letter. After the proposal has been out for one week, call each of the venture capital companies and ask them if they have received the proposal and if they are interested. This telephone reminder will move them along a little faster.

The first venture capitalist who says he is interested in meeting with you should be approached with skepticism. You should discuss on the telephone what he has in mind. If his investment idea seems to be what you want, then by all means jump in an airplane or an automobile and see the venture capitalist face to face. If the fit does not seem quite right then hold out for a week or so while you wait for others to respond.

Some venture capitalists, having quickly read the proposal once, will tell the entrepreneur that they are interested in his deal. The entrepreneur, hearing the words, "Yes, I am interested," usually overreacts and assumes that the venture capitalist is ready to give him the money. The entrepreneur is ready to board an airplane to visit the venture capitalist. You can avoid wasting time on such trips by asking the venture capitalist to clarify his intentions on the telephone. For example, if the venture capitalist says, "Yes, I am interested, but we can't make any commitments for six months," you might not see the need to visit him via airplane. On the other hand, the venture capital firms might say they are interested in your proposal but after a few minutes of discussion, they might learn that the technology is more involved than they had perceived, and thus might decline. In short, a follow-up telephone conversation can help to clarify the venture capitalist's interest. Discuss by telephone what he has in mind. If there seems to be some common ground on which you can put together a deal, then you should visit the venture capitalist. Running off to visit each venture capitalist will consume a great deal of your own time, so be sure it's worth the trip.

Syndications

Often a venture capitalist will tell you he is interested in investing in your company, but that he can only invest part of the money that you need and will have to syndicate the rest. This means that he will look for other venture capital firms to join the investment in your company. The first question you should ask in this situation is, "Will you be the leading investor?" This means that the venture capital firm will act as the leading investor and will help persuade other venture firms to invest in your firm. Syndications are extremely common in the venture business and many venture firms routinely syndicate all their investments with other venture firms. It is important for you to determine who will have to persuade the other companies to join the syndication. In some cases, the venture firm, as the leading investor, will go with you to other venture firms or will meet with a group of them and will help sell your idea to them. In other cases, the venture firm will merely act as the first investor to commit funds, and all the others will have to do so on their own, in a separate action. This means you will have to be the syndicator and you will have to find the other venture firms to join the group. Of course, any firm that commits funds to you will have a list of other venture firms that they are interested in having in the investment with them.

Quite often, the leading investor is paid something for assisting in the syndication. Investment bankers, of course, are paid 5 to 10 percent for putting together a syndication of venture capital firms to invest in a small business. On the other hand, if the venture firms acts as a principal and syndicator, his fee is usually less. The typical fee to the venture firm will be 2 to 3 percent of the money he is raising through other venture firms. Sometimes he will share part of those fees with the other venture firms that are investing.

As mentioned, syndications are common in the venture capital business. However, in many instances they are difficult to organize because each venture firm will have its own way of analyzing your deal, its own way of making a commitment to you, and its own lawyer to close the loan. You will have to juggle all of these people in pulling together the investment into your firm. Although a syndication can be put together and this is done frequently, it is a complex and time-consuming endeavor.

Objective

Once you have created the proposal, it should sell you and your concept. If it does not accomplish this, you will not be given an opportunity to meet with the venture capitalist. Your objective is to create a business proposal that will lead to a meeting between you and the venture capitalist. That meeting is the subject of Chapter 5. Don't miss the opportunity to meet with the venture capitalist by giving him a number where you cannot be reached, especially one that rings and is not answered. A venture capitalist will try several times and then will stop trying. Remember, you are selling to him, so be available or have an answering service take your calls. Before you meet with the venture capitalist, you should prepare yourself for the many questions he will have. Chapter 4 deals with the questions most often asked by a venture capitalist and shows you how to answer some of them.

4

A Thousand Questions

Can You Answer a Thousand Questions?
Be Prepared by Answering All the Questions in This Chapter.

I t would be wonderful if the venture capitalist would read your business proposal and without another thought, write out a check for the amount you requested. Unfortunately, he never will. You will have to earn the money by proving your company is a good investment. The venture capitalist will have a thousand questions for you to answer before he will consider investing in your company. Before you submit your business proposal to a venture capitalist, you should have some friends read it, your accountant, if possible, and perhaps your banker. From these readings should come questions that will help you clarify your business proposal so that it can be easily comprehended by the venture capitalist. The questions will also prepare you for the venture capitalist's questions.

Questions are the subject of this chapter. Every venture capitalist will ask a thousand questions about your business, about you and your background, and about your plans for the future. You can answer some of these if you prepare a good business proposal. Other questions will be asked when the venture capitalist meets with you (more about this meeting in a later chapter). In order to prepare you for the many questions of the venture capitalist, this chapter presents a number of questions under the same headings used in Chapter 3 on the business proposal. Before moving on to these various headings and the corresponding questions, you should understand the four basic areas in which the venture capitalist will concentrate his questions. These critical questions will give you an overview of what the venture capitalist is seeking. Later, the specific areas of your business proposal will be discussed and the questions that might arise will be suggested.

What Are the Major Questions?

The venture capitalist will center his questions on four basic areas: management, uniqueness, projections, and exit. Let's look at them individually.

Management

The most important management characteristic that the venture capitalist will be looking for is honesty. The venture capitalist cannot determine your honesty from your business proposal. He will determine your honesty during his meetings with you. Basically, he will be looking at the management team and trying to determine how honest they are. No venture capitalist expects an entrepreneur to be honest to a fault, but *every* venture capitalist wants an honorable entrepreneur. If the venture capitalist thinks that the management team is dishonest, such a suspicion is the kiss of death. There will be no possibility of receiving financial support if the venture capitalist thinks the entrepreneur is dishonorable.

The venture capitalist's first questions about management will relate to their backgrounds. What is the business experience of the management team? What motivates the entrepreneur? Is the entrepreneur an achiever? Can the management team accomplish the job covered in the business proposal? These are the types of questions the venture capitalist will be asking about management in order to find out if the management team is competent.

After reviewing your business proposal and discussing it with you, the venture capitalist, you hope, will use terms such as *good people* and *impressive* to describe management. If a venture capitalist uses these key words, you can assume it means he has accepted the management team as the people he wants to back. Conversely, if the venture capitalist is hesitant about the management team, he will not finance the company.

Uniqueness

The venture capitalist receives many proposals from small businesses that are sound but that have no chance of strong growth because they lack uniqueness. Sure, the company may grow at 10 percent a year, it may be a good small business, but let's face it, *most* small businesses are very poor investments for the investor. They are poor because they never pay dividends and there is no place to sell the stock. You could own 49 percent of every small business in the United States and starve to death because the stock pays no dividends and there is no one to sell the stock to. So what makes your business different? Some of the questions that the venture capitalist will repeatedly ask are: "What makes this situation special?," and, "Why will it succeed?" And from another angle, "Among all the businesses of the world, why does this business have high growth potential?" Always be prepared for this type of interrogation and, conversely, never miss an opportunity, when asked a question that relates to uniqueness, to describe exactly why your company is special.

Projections and Return on Investment

A venture capitalist will try to determine how realistic your projections are. He will ask himself if the management team can make these projections happen. A related question the venture capitalist will ask is how much money his own company can make if he invests in your company. All these questions are concerned with the projections and the return on investment set out by you in your business proposal. You should be prepared to defend your sales and earnings projections. The projections should have a concrete foundation in reasonable assumptions. They should not be overly optimistic but must be aggressive enough to attract the venture capitalist. A projected sales growth of 50 to 100 percent in the very early years is common. Sales growth of 25 percent is minimum and may not be attractive enough to elicit funds from an investor.

Exit

Finally, the venture capitalist will ask himself, "How will I ever get out of the deal?" Venture capitalists ask themselves this question both about bad deals and good deals. Obviously they want to get their money out of bad deals, but they also want to get their money out of good deals. Owning 49 percent of a small business that is growing rapidly is wonderful if somewhere along the way there is an opportunity to sell part or all of that ownership position and realize cash for the investment. The goal of every venture capitalist is to exchange his investment in the small business that has appreciated in value for cash in the bank. It is a natural desire. You must be aware of this desire and the questions that will come from the venture capitalist on this subject. Your business proposal must tell the venture capitalist how he will exit from your situation.

Business Proposal Questions

We can conveniently consider the appropriate questions for each stage of the business proposal format, by following the headings presented in Chapter 3. Under each heading we will look at what the venture capitalist is seeking and the type of questions he will ask. In some cases, the information provided will coach you on the information the venture capitalist is seeking.

Part 1:   Summary

The summary will not evoke any questions unless it is inconsistent with the business proposal. Make sure the summary and the business proposal coincide. If you say something in the summary that raises a question and it is not answered in the business proposal, you will probably be questioned about it.

Part 2:   Business and Its Future

Generally the venture capitalist looks to this section for information about your industry and your business. Be aware that most entrepreneurs tend to describe the growth of their business in three phases. Why everyone selects three to mark their periods of growth is strange. You may wish to express your growth plan in something other than three phases.

2.01   General

The venture capitalist will have no questions here as long as you provide the name, address, telephone number of your business, and the individual who should be contacted. If possible, put in the Standard Industrial Classification. Remember, do not use a telephone number that is unattended. If you are not there, have an answering service or a friend answer the telephone for you.

2.02   Nature of the Business

Here you will try to describe in a pithy paragraph the nature of the business. It is important to be succinct and to give the venture capitalist a short phrase that he can use to identify your company. If you are in the computer terminal industry, that information should be in your opening sentence so that the venture capitalist can identify your company by an industry classification. If you are not succinct, then the venture capitalist will probably ask you to explain in two or three words what business you are in.

2.03   Business History

In this section the venture capitalist is seeking a synopsis. Even though the venture capitalist has read the business history section he will probably ask you to describe the history of the business. He is seeking the details of what has happened in the past. This section is not likely to spark any general questions, but there will be specific questions about events in the history of the business.

A typical question might take the form of, "Why have you done such and such?" Other likely questions are: "What are the major milestones your company has achieved? Why has your business been able to achieve the milestones?"

2.04   Business of the Future

Here, too, the venture capitalist is looking for general information about the milestones to be accomplished in the future. He will have particular questions about each stage of development that you intend to go through. His basic question will be, "How will you be able to achieve the milestones you have set out in the business proposal?"

2.05   Uniqueness

The basic question you must answer is,"What makes this business unique?" This question might be phrased in another way: "Given all the small businesses there are in the world, what will make this one succeed?" In the general area of business, big business usually overtakes small business. Given that axiom, why will your business succeed when it must compete with big business? In order to satisfy the venture capitalist, you must point to something out of the ordinary that makes your company a winner. If you will be just another "me, too" company, the venture capitalist will soon fall asleep.

2.06   Product or Service

Here the venture capitalist wants to find out what you sell and what need the product or service satisfies in the marketplace. He will be trying to determine if it is a commodity and if it has some originality. He is also interested in the maturity of the product, and the general life cycle of products like this. His questions will be: "Why is this product or service useful? What does it do for the user? Why does the user buy it? What is the expected life cycle of the product and when will another product have to be introduced? Is there a new product planned or on the market now that will help or hurt the company? What product liability is there? That is, if the user buys it and is hurt, what liability will the company have? What price can be charged for the product? How elastic is the price of the product? How durable is the product? How technologically sophisticated is the product? How mature is the product in the life cycle of such a product?"

2.07   Customers or Purchasers of the Product

The venture capitalist wants to know who buys the product or service and why. His questions concerning this topic will be: "Does this product meet a real need of the consumer or does it meet a perceived need that is not necessarily a real need? How does your consumer recognize your product among all the others? Does it have a brand name recognition? Is there only one type of buyer for the product? Are you selling to one large company or to the government?

Are there repeat users or does the customer need to buy the product only once? Is it a high-quality or low-quality product? Is it a high-styled or low-styled item? Is it a fad or a staple?" In addition, the venture capitalist will ask you to list each major purchaser of the product or perhaps the top ten or twenty purchasers of the product by dollar volume. He may also ask you to classify the purchasers by type and perhaps by demographic characteristics. He will want you to give him the name, address, and telephone numbers of the top ten users of your product. He will want to call the major purchasers and determine how satisfied they are with your product. You should prepare this list in advance because it is something the venture capitalist will ask for at some point in his investigations.

As for the purchases, the venture capitalist will want to know about the backlog. He will want to know how firm the backlog is and if the backlog can be modified. For example, you may have indicated that the United States government has purchased $1 million worth of your products subject to your shipping of them. This would be part of your backlog. As everyone who deals with the government knows, the federal government can cancel an order at any time. Thus, your backlog could drop by $1 million with one registered letter. It is important to be able to justify the various orders in a backlog and to show that the purchaser will be able to pay for the product once it is shipped.

2.08   Industry or Market

Here the venture capitalist will be trying to understand your industry. His questions will be: "What are the keys to success in your industry? How do your company and its products fit into the industry?" Some additional basic questions are: "How did you determine the total sales of the industry and its growth rate? What are the basic trends of the industry? What industry changes affect profits most in your company? What barriers to entry are there in this industry? That is, how easy or hard is it for someone to get started in the same business you will be in? Why is your product novel when compared with others in the industry? What seasonality is there to sales in the industry? Will you sell on a local, regional, national, or international basis?"

A word of warning: when you use the term *total sales* in talking about an industry, you must be careful not to include sales that are not addressed by your product. For example, one would *not* use total computer sales in the United States if one was planning to be a manufacturer of minicomputers. The minicomputer market is only one segment of the total computer market. The industry is the minicomputer market, not the total computer market. As a matter of fact, the minicomputer market itself is highly segmented now.

2.09   Competition

Here the venture capitalist will want to know who the competition is, how strong it is, what advantages it has, and what advantages you have. Typical questions will be: "What advantages do you have over your competitor? In terms of price, performance, services, and warranties, how do you compare with your competition? What advantages do your competitors have over you? Who, specifically, is your competition? Who are you similar to in your industry? Who do you compete with on a head-to-head basis? Are there substitutes for your product? If so, who makes the substitutes and how often are they substituted for your product? What is the price differential between your product and the product of your competitors? Are any competitors just entering the industry? If you plan to take a market share from the competition, how will you do it? How do you expect the competition to react to your company? Are any of your competitors public companies?"

2.10 Marketing

In this section the venture capitalist will focus on your marketing strategy. He wants to know how you are moving the product from the production facility into the hands of the ultimate user. Some of his basic questions will be: "Describe the channels of distribution for your product—that is, how does it get from your facility to the consumer? What are the critical elements of your marketing strategy? Is this primarily a retail or an industrial marketing strategy? How important is advertising in your marketing plan? What is your basic advertising program and how much does it cost? How sensitive are your sales to advertising expenditures? What market penetration have you had in the past? What degree of market penetration have you projected? What will be your marketing strategy when the product or industry matures? How difficult is the sale? Is direct selling necessary? That is, does the salesman call directly on the customer? Is the sale complex and long or is it relatively simple and straightforward? Is the purchase of the product a large cost item for the buyer or a small-budget item? Is it meaningful in terms of the consumer's budget when the consumer buys the product? What is the time lag between the time the buyer is contacted and the actual sale? Does the government regulate the marketing approach?"

2.11 Production

In this section the venture capitalist will try to understand how the product is produced. Some typical questions are: "What is the capacity of your facility? What are the key weaknesses of its capacity for manufacturing? That is, what component (such as quality control) is the main bottleneck in the operation? How important is quality control? What type of backlog exists now? Is this a standard product that goes through the production process or is it a job-shop operation in which each product is different? What type of health and safety problems are involved in this production process? Are there any revolutionary production processes on the horizon that would help or hurt the company?" If your service has a production cycle, you will also be asked to discuss how the service is rendered.

2.12   Production Characteristics

Here the venture capitalist will zero in on the critical factors in the production process. The questions will be: "Is it a sophisticated product that is difficult or easy to produce? Are there a large number of components? How much of the basic product is purchased from others in the form of subassembled parts? How much value does the company add to the production process? What components are crucial to the product? What liabilities are incurred by workers who must produce the product? Is the production process dangerous in any way?"

2.13   Labor Force and Employees

Here the venture capitalist wants to know the source and status of the labor force and the type of employees needed to produce and sell the product. His questions are: "Where does the labor supply come from? Is there an adequate supply of quality labor force or must they be trained? What is the relative cost of labor in this area versus other areas of the country for similar labor forces? What kind of union does the company have? What is the union's relationship with the management? Does the contract come up for renegotiation soon? Exactly how many employees are there, including full-time, part-time, white-collar, blue-collar, technical, nontechnical, degreed and nondegreed staff? What type of retirement plan is set up for the labor pool? Are there any liabilities in the form of unfunded pension or profit-sharing plans?"

2.14   Suppliers

Here the venture capitalist will try to determine the source of raw materials. His main questions will be: "Who are the suppliers of the raw materials used in the production process? Is there a single source for any components, especially key components? Are there shortages of some of the required components?"

You should prepare a list of suppliers that includes their names, addresses, telephone numbers, and names of individuals who may be contacted. You should list the largest dollar-volume suppliers first and the terms on which you purchase items from that supplier. You should also list any key suppliers and sole-source suppliers. You should prepare this list in advance for the venture capitalist.

2.15   Subcontractors

In this section you must describe any material relationship you have with any subcontractors. What role do they play in your business? How key is their operation? Can they be replaced? Give their names, addresses, telephone numbers, and the individual to contact at the subcontractors for reference purposes. This is another exhibit you should have available for the venture capitalist.

2.16   Equipment

In this section the venture capitalist will want to find out what type of equipment is available and what type is needed. His questions will be: "What type of equipment is absolutely necessary for the production of your product? Is special-purpose or general-purpose equipment essential? How long does it take to get parts for the equipment? Is it difficult to order a new piece of equipment? How long does it take to arrive? How old is your company's equipment? How much does it cost to repair each year? What is the dollar value of the capital requirements for equipment over the next five years? Is used equipment available? Will the equipment that you currently use be made obsolete by technological changes or by current items in the marketplace? What kind of equipment does the competition have? Do your competitors have an advantage because of their equipment? Do you have an advantage?"

2.17   Property and Facilities

Here you need to explain what facilities you are currently using and what you will need in the future. The venture capitalist will ask: "What are the terms of the lease? If you own the property, what did you pay for it and what is the balance owed on any mortgage due? What is the current value of the property? Are the facilities adequate for future production as envisioned under the projections? What is the total dollar volume that can be accomplished by using the facilities that you are in now?"

You should have available for the venture capitalist a copy of the lease on the property that you currently use if it is leased. If you own the property, it is appropriate to have on hand an appraisal of the property and a listing of the basic details such as acreage, square footage, and description of the building in terms of the type of construction.

2.18   Patents and Trademarks

The venture capitalist will want to know what patents or trademarks the company has. Typical questions are: "Is the patent issued? Is the patent in your name or the company's? If it is in the name of the entrepreneur, has it been fully assigned with all rights to the corporation? Have any licensing arrangements been entered into to give others the benefit of the patent? If so, what are the details of any licensing arrangements?"

2.19   Research and Development

The venture capitalist will want to know how much research and development has been completed in terms of dollars and time and how much will be needed in the future. Typical questions are: "What research and development are going on today? What dollars were expended in the past on research and development, and what sales have resulted from those expenditures? Has the research and development been written off or capitalized? What are the projected expenditures in the coming years and what do you expect to develop from the money spent on research and development?" Venture capitalists are not fond of funding research and development firms. They want companies to exploit new ideas.

2.20   Litigation

The venture capitalist wants to be informed of any legal actions that are in existence or that are being contemplated. Typical questions are: "What suits have been filed against the company? What suits has the company filed against others? Have suits been filed by trade creditors, customers, or users? Are patents being contested?" You should be ready to give full details of any legal situations. You should have your lawyer write a letter explaining each legal action in legal terms.

2.21   Government Regulations

Here the venture capitalist wants to know how the various layers of government might influence the growth of your company. His questions will be: "What are the state, local, and federal regulations affecting the operations of the company? Do any FTC, fair trade practice, OSHA, special IRS, SEC, or other government regulations affect the company? How can the company be helped or hindered by these government regulations?" For example, if you are in the drug business, you must have Federal Drug Administration (FDA) approval. Once your company receives FDA approval on a new drug, it has a monopoly on the use of the drug until another company can meet FDA approval.

2.22   Conflicts of Interest

The venture capitalist will be interested in any conflicts of interest. Examples of questions are: "Does the company buy from a supplier whose officer sits on your board of directors? Is there some relationship between a company in which you have a personal investment, and the company that is seeking financing?" You need to describe any conflicts of interest, or potential conflicts of interest between your company and boards of directors, management, key employees, large stockholders, and so on. If there is a potential conflict, describe how it is being solved.

2.23   Backlog

The venture capitalist needs to know what kind of backlog exists in terms of dollars, and in terms of units for each one of your products or services. The typical questions are: "Who are the orders from? How firm are the orders? Can the orders be cancelled? Do orders depend on a specific price? Do they depend on performance of prototypes? What is the nature of the backlog and how easily can it evaporate?"

2.24 Insurance

Here the venture capitalist wants to assure himself that you have adequate insurance to cover your company in a multitude of areas. He will pay attention to fidelity insurance, product liability insurance, the old standby of fire and casualty, and business interruption insurance. He may require life insurance on key employees. Basic questions will be: "What happens if you are hit by a truck? What happens if the building burns down?" A good answer to each question is, "The insurance company will pay our company millions."

2.25 Taxes

Here the venture capitalist will want to understand the type of taxes being paid by the company. Questions are: "Are any special taxes levied against the company? Can the company expect any special tax breaks? Are there any outstanding taxes today, such as payroll or income taxes? How can the company shelter some of its income from taxes?"

2.26 Corporate Structure

In this area the venture capitalist will want to understand the corporate structure. He will ask: "Is it a partnership or is it a corporation? Is the corporation a specialty such as a Subchapter S corporation?" Incidentally, if you are incorporated in one state, but are a resident in another, the venture capitalist will want to know why.

2.27 Publications and Associations

List the primary publications that cover your industry. The names of the industry magazine and the industry newspaper or newsletter are needed. Also give the venture capitalist the name of the person at your trade association who can be contacted to discuss the industry.

Part 3: Management

In this section the venture capitalist will want to evaluate the management team, their background, experience, and so on. Sometime during a relaxed period in the discussions you may be asked some "silly" questions. Be prepared for a wide variety of such questions: "What did you think of Physics 101 in college? What was your early childhood like? What has been your greatest accomplishment?" Most venture capitalists fancy themselves amateur psychologists. They hope to understand the individuals seeking funds and their motivations. You may receive some unusual questions in this section.

3.01   Directors and Officers

The venture capitalist may ask you questions about the individuals listed as directors or officers. He will want to know why certain people are directors if they have no obvious connection with the company. If the venture capitalist sees your lawyer on the board of directors, he will immediately ask why. When possible you should have working business people on your board because they will bring their business experience to the boardroom. Except for key directors, the venture capitalist will save most of his questions concerning key employees for the appropriate sections of your proposal, as indicated next.

3.02   Key Employees

Here the venture capitalist will want to know everything possible about the key employees because he will be betting his money on the management team. He will want to know the background, experience, age, education, work experience, and marital status of team members, and how many children they have. Most of the more personal questions will come over lunch, or in a friendly get-together somewhere along the way, such as the drive back to the airport in the car with you. Be prepared to provide anecdotes about where you have been and where you are today in terms of your personal life.

Formal questions about key employees will be: "What profit-and-loss responsibility have the key people had? What experience has the management team had in the industry? Do the key people have the technical knowledge necessary to operate this company in this industry? How dedicated are the key employees to this company? Can this management team make the projections happen? What functional responsibilities does each key employee have? How financially committed are the key employees to the company? That is, how much money has each of them invested? What other business affiliations do they have? What other businesses are they involved in? What ownership positions do they have in other businesses?"

3.03   Management Fidelity

Venture capitalists are regularly approached by swindlers. You should not take offense at the questions that cast doubt on your honesty. Because every venture capitalist has been swindled at least once, they feel they have to be on their guard. Most venture capitalists are slightly paranoid. Be kind and indulge their questions.

Most venture capitalists spend days trying to fathom the fidelity of management. You can help by letting the venture capitalist know your position on fidelity. You should forewarn him of any suits against individuals or any credit problems you have had with individuals. You may want to obtain a complimentary credit check from a local credit company to determine what your credit will look like to the venture capitalist when he runs a credit check. He will look for suits against the management team and their credit rating. The venture capitalist will want a list of references on the management. You should prepare an addendum to your resumes that provides a list of references, all of which should be business references. The venture capitalist will call these people in order to verify your fidelity and your business experience.

Some venture capitalists are studying the possibility of giving potential entrepreneurs tests that can be used to determine both their entrepreneurial ability and their honesty. I have not seen the merit in, or accuracy of, such tests but I could be convinced of their usefulness. It is rumored that one venture capital company employs a graphologist to examine the handwriting of entrepreneurs in order to determine their entrepreneurial ability and their fidelity. I have not been able to verify this rumor. Who knows, maybe the technique works!

One venture capitalist has his own method of evaluating entrepreneurs. After his M.B.A.'s have investigated the situation and have asked the entrepreneur every conceivable business question, the senior venture capitalist takes the entrepreneur into his office for a one-to-one discussion. For one or two hours the entrepreneur answers questions about everything conceivable except business. If at the end of that time the venture capitalist has a "good impression," then the entrepreneur has passed the final test. Most venture capitalists have a gut feeling about entrepreneurs. Unfortunately, even in this book it is impossible to define that feeling. It is a reaction that develops almost automatically as a result of interviewing, talking, and working with entrepreneurs over many years. This point will be discussed again in Chapter 5.

3.04 Remuneration

Here the venture capitalist is trying to determine how well you are paid now, and how much you intend to pay yourself in the future. You should let him know about all compensations to the key management team. His question will be, "Why are you paying such a high salary to your employees and to yourself?"

3.05 Stock Options

Here, too, the venture capitalist is trying to determine the management team's compensation. You should let him know precisely what you are thinking about in terms of stock options for current management, and any new people coming into the company. You should provide a copy of the stock option plan to the venture capitalist. If you do not have one, but intend to have one in the future, you should give him an outline of what you intend to do. The question is, "Why are you giving each person the number of options you have indicated?"

3.06   Stock Option Plan

The plan should be the standard plan or the venture capitalist will raise questions. If you have other deferred compensation plans, tell the venture capitalist about them.

3.07   Principal Shareholders

In this section the venture capitalist will want to know who owns stock, how much they paid for it, and why they received any low-priced stock. Anyone owning 5 percent or more of the company should be listed.

3.08   Employment Agreements

You should explain in detail any employment agreements and have copies available for the venture capitalist. He will ask: "Why do you have an employment agreement?" Be aware that venture capitalists disapprove of employment agreements unless they are one-way agreements, somewhat like the indentured servant's contract of old, that require you to work for the company but without a large salary.

3.09   Conflicts of Interest

Any conflict of interest between an employee and the company should be set out in detail. You might be asked which employees have any connection with other firms that the company does business with. For example, does an employee's father work for a company that sells products to your company? Is there any kind of financial relationship? For example, did his father's company lend your company $50,000? Does one of the employees own the computer that the company leases? These kinds of conflicts of interest should be revealed. The venture capitalist may uncover them so it is better for you to reveal them at the outset.

3.10   Consultants, Accountants, Lawyers, Bankers, and Others

You should prepare a list with the names, addresses, and telephone numbers of your lawyers, accountants, bankers, and consultants, along with the names of persons to contact.

Part 4:   Description of the Financing

In this section the venture capitalist will try to establish and negotiate with you the type of financing that is acceptable to both you and himself. The questions he will ask you in the meeting and the questions you should ask yourself beforehand are set out below under each heading.

4.01 Proposed Financing

If you are proposing a loan, what interest rate will it be? Why is the interest rate so low? Can the rate be increased? On what terms will the loan be made? Why do you need the money for such a long time? Why does there need to be an interest-only period? When can you begin repayment? Can repayment begin sooner? Will the interest rate be variable or fixed? Will the loan be convertible into common or preferred stock? Can the conversion rate be lower?

If it is preferred stock, what will the coupon value be, and can it be raised? Will it be cumulative in case you do not pay it for a calendar quarter? What redemption will there be and can it be sooner? Is it convertible into common stock? If so, what is the conversion price? Can the conversion price be reduced? What restrictions are there on the shares? Does the preferred stock have voting rights?

If you are selling common stock, will there be a dividend on the common stock? What is the price of the stock? Will the dividend be cumulative in case you miss it? Will you be required to redeem the common stock in case you miss it? Will you be required to redeem the common stock required in order to give the investor's money back? What price will the investor pay for the common stock? Will there be restrictions on the shares? What voting rights will holders of common stock have? What registration rights will they have? That is, can the venture capitalist make you register the stock so it will be a public company?

If you offer options with any of the above, you need to consider the price of the option, and why you selected a certain price. What is the exercise price that one must pay once the option is exercised into common stock? How many shares will it exercise into? What is the expiration period of the option?

4.02 Capital Structure

The venture capitalist will want to know if you listed all your debts under debt structure; this does not include accounts payable but all substantial debts, such as, long-term notes and any federal taxes due. These details will be of concern to him. He will ask you to list all the collateral for each of the term financings, and to give specific terms, conditions, and interest rates on each debt item.

4.03 Collateral for the Financing

What collateral can you offer the venture capitalist as security for his investment in your firm? What value does the collateral have, and why have you placed such a value on the collateral? Do you have an appraisal or something to show there is value?

4.04 Guarantees

What personal or corporate guarantees will be given on the investment? If you provide a personal guarantee accompanied by a personal financial statement, the venture capitalist will ask questions about the financial statement. He will want to know why you have put a high value on certain assets. If a separate company will guarantee the loan, its financial statement will also have to be examined by the venture capitalist, because he will want to know the financial strengths of the company.

4.05   Conditions

If the venture capitalist has invested in your company through a debt instrument, he may want your company to maintain certain ratios. If you select the ratios, he will want to know why you selected ratios that are easy to meet. When it comes to disbursing funds, the venture capitalist may make the disbursement conditional on certain milestones reached by the company. If you identify these milestones, the venture capitalist will want to know why these are significant, and why reaching them makes the company more valuable.

4.06   Reporting

Will you provide the venture capitalist a monthly financial statement? Will you give him updated projections at least once or twice a year? What special information will you give the venture capitalist? Will you give him a monthly summary-of-operations report?

4.07   Use of Proceeds

When you spell out the use of proceeds, the venture capitalist will want to know precisely why you want to spend so much money on certain items. By spending money on these items, what specifically do you accomplish for the company? You will need to be specific in the use of proceeds and the justification for each expenditure.

4.08   Ownership

The venture capitalist will want to know exactly how much of the company he will own if he invests. He will want to know how much others own, primarily key management. He will not accept the idea of a small ownership for key management because their incentive will be too low. Key management must have a substantial stake in the ownership of the company or they will not be motivated to make a lot of money and raise the value of the stock.

4.09   Dilution

This area will involve questions about the value of the company. Why, for example, should a venture capitalist pay a high price for his small ownership in a company when others have paid much less? You will need to justify why the venture capitalist is being asked to pay such a premium. One justification acceptable to the venture capitalist in a start-up is that you have put together the team and the idea and these have given the company value. If you have an existing company, then you should have reached some milestones that have increased the value.

4.10   Fees Paid

Is a broker's fee being paid for this financing? Why? What did the broker do to deserve the fee? If the broker performed a service, he deserves a fee. If the broker performed little service, he deserves a small fee.

4.11   Investor Involvement

Will you give the venture capitalist a seat on the board of directors? Will you give him veto power over certain transactions? Will you give him a consulting contract? Will he have control of the board for certain transactions such as the sale of additional shares? You need to offer a board seat as a minimum.

Part 5:   Risk Factors

The venture capitalist will ask you certain questions that will help him determine the amount of risk your business poses. These questions will tend to be negative. He will try to downgrade your company, and you will need to be positive and upbeat in conversations on this subject with the venture capitalist.

5.01   Limited Operating History

What makes you think you can start a new company? Have you ever started a new company before? What problems do you expect to run into starting a new company? How are you going to solve all the problems of a new company? What people on your management team will help you in this?

5.02   Limited Resources

If you do not have enough money to break even, what will you do for the next round of financing? Precisely, how much money is needed to carry this company to the point of cash flow break-even? What will you do if positive cash flow is not achieved?

5.03   Limited Management Experience

How many of your key managers are skilled in this industry? What have they been doing for the last ten years that makes their experience valuable in this industry? What outside help will enable them to overcome their lack of experience or ability?

5.04   Market Uncertainties

What could go wrong with the marketing plan? What is going on in the market that could destroy this company? What new inventions are around the corner that would make your product obsolete? What strategy might the competition use in the marketplace?

Often the best laid plans for marketing are destroyed by items that have never been thought of. Consider the venture capital company that financed the acquisition of a yacht club. The idea was to sell boat slips in somewhat the same way that condominiums are sold—that is, people would buy the boat slips and pay an annual fee to belong to the club. The proposal projected that 50 percent of the existing boat slip renters would convert to owners. Unknown to the entrepreneurs was the fact that the boat slip renters at this yacht club were extremely clannish. After it was announced that the slips would be sold, the renters banded together and boycotted the sale. They scared away many potential outside buyers by acting as a group. As a result, sales were not even close to projected sales and the conversion never took place. The entrepreneur and venture capitalist lost out. Venture capitalists may have a number of such war stories engraved in their minds. They may be able to come up with more market uncertainties than you will be able to explore in your business proposal. Be prepared for the questions that will be based on their bad experiences.

5.05   Production Uncertainties

If your product has never been produced before, why do you think you can produce it at the price you have projected? Have you ever run a production facility? Has anyone else on your staff done so? Has that person ever started a new production facility?

New production facilities are difficult to start. It seems that Murphy's law finds its true environment in a new production facility. There is the story of a venture capitalist who looked into financing a new yeast facility by asking several of the existing yeast facilities what problems a new yeast plant might have. He ran into a fellow who had actually started one only a few years before. Apparently when the yeast operations were moved from the old plant to the new plant, the yeast failed to grow. The fellow went back to the old plant to find out why the yeast would grow there without difficulty. He saw that the walls, the floor, and the roof were permeated with the yeast culture. This "cultured environment" was obviously conducive to growing a tremendous amount of yeast. The fellow reported that it took the new facility over a year to reach the same environmental state. The venture capitalist declined to invest in the venture for this and other reasons. Others invested and, sure enough, it took an extra year and an extra million dollars in working capital to break even. You can be sure that every seasoned venture capitalist has experienced starting a new production facility a number of times. He will be keenly aware of many of the problems that can occur in a new production environment.

5.06   Liquidation

Liquidation questions will be along the following lines. If the company had to be liquidated after the venture capitalist investment but some progress had been made, how much would an investor get back? Why do you say that you could liquidate it for those values? Have you ever liquidated a company before?

If you have had no experience in liquidating a company or do not know how it is done, the venture capitalist will be delighted to tell you about one of his liquidations. There was the venture capitalist who liquidated a knitting mill during the recession of 1975. Most of the collateralized lenders thought they had sufficient collateral to recover all their money on liquidation. The only problem was that many knitting mills had been liquidated during the year, and now all the usual buyers of used knitting equipment had their warehouses packed full. They were certainly not interested in buying additional knitting equipment. Before long, bidders on pieces of knitting equipment were asking whether they could just take off the parts they needed and leave the machine to be thrown away. In that environment, you know that you are going to lose. The venture capitalist and the bank lost a bundle.

5.07   Dependence on Key Management

If key management dies, how will the company survive? If key management dies, how can the company grow and prosper without the driving force of the key management? How would the venture capitalist be protected if a key manager died and could not be replaced? These are the types of questions that the venture capitalist will be pushing at you regarding the loss of key management personnel.

5.08   What Could Go Wrong?

The question that is uppermost in every venture capitalist's mind is "What factors could make the company a disaster situation?" The venture capitalist is almost certain to ask the entrepreneur, "What could go wrong?" In answering this question, you need to lay out several scenarios indicating the aspect of the business that could be fouled up and how you would react and solve such a problem. This is normally not a large section in the business proposal, but it will be a key point in the questions asked by the venture capitalist.

5.09   Other Items

Other questions may be quite random ones that are seeking general information. What financial reserves do you consider the company needs? Does a noninvestor employee control the company because he is key to the operation?

Part 6:   Return on Investment and Exit

In this section the venture capitalist will ask you how much money he can make, and when he will be able to make his exit. This is normally not a large section in the proposal, but it will be a key point in the questions asked by the venture capitalist.

6.01   Public Offering

Have you talked to a stockbrokerage firm about a public offering? When do you think you might be able to go public? What multiple do you think the stock would sell for in a public offering? How did you arrive at this estimate? What public company resembles your company most?

6.02   Sale

What other companies would be interested in buying your company if it made some of its projections? Is the technology or product desired by other companies? If so, name the companies that might want to buy them. Have you contacted any brokers about selling the business or parts of the business? If so, what interest level have they shown?

6.03   Buyback

If your company is to buy back the shares owned by the venture capitalist, what method could be used to value the shares? What basis has been used to place a value on companies that have been sold in your industry?

6.04   Return on Investment

If a public offering was made three years out and the venture capitalist was able to sell all of his holdings two years after that, what would be the return on investment to the venture capitalist? How much money would he make if you only made half of your projected sales?

Part 7:   Analysis of Operations and Projections

The venture capitalist will spend a great deal of time asking you about the numbers and assumptions in your projections. Some general questions are set out under the headings below, but you can also expect many specific questions about the assumptions and calculations behind the financial projections.

7.01   General

Many general questions will be asked about your assumptions, such as, "What makes you think the gross margin will be as set out in the projections?

What return on investment do other companies in your industry have? Why will you ROI be higher?

7.02 Ratio Analysis

If the ratios you presented for each year seem to be different, the venture capitalist will want you to explain why they are not the same each year. For example, if your gross margin changes every year, going up and down, or steadily upward, the venture capitalist will want you to explain this inconsistency. If payroll or other items go up drastically, the venture capitalist will want to know why the salary levels, as a percentage, increased so rapidly.

7.03 Results of Operation

The venture capitalist will be particularly interested in any past performance. Questions about the numbers will center around profits and projected profits. Normally the venture capitalist will not be upset by losses in the early years as long as the company shows some progress toward losing less money on a monthly basis. If you have increased losses, the venture capitalist will look at the situation as a turnaround.

7.04 Financial Conditions

The balance sheet will not be of primary importance to the venture capitalist unless he is lending money, and then he will look through the balance sheet seeking some collateral for the loan. Balance sheets showing that large amounts of research and development have been capitalized or a balance sheet that has a large slug of goodwill, will require special explanations to the venture capitalist. In his review of the balance sheet the venture capitalist will subtract all goodwill and capitalized research and development in order to arrive at a book value closer to liquidation value of the company.

7.05 Contingent Liabilities

Most venture capitalists are greatly concerned about contingent liabilities. They will ask many questions as they look for contingent liabilities. Have you guaranteed loans or other debts for some other business? Have you agreed to purchase a specific quantity of goods from some supplier? Have you signed a lease that escalates quickly?

Part 8:   Financial Statements

The venture capitalist will spend a lot of time analyzing your financial statements. He will ask you questions about profitability. He will ask you about the auditor. He will ask you about any subsidiaries and how they are consolidated.

Above all, he will want to know why certain things appear on your financial statements.

Part 9: Financial Projections

In this section the venture capitalist will want to know how your projections have been constructed. That is, why do your projections go up so drastically? What are the basic assumptions in your projections? What are the sensitive items in your cash flow projections? The venture capitalist will perform a type of sensitivity analysis on your financial projections. He will adjust certain items in the projections in order to see what other items change drastically. He will want to see to what extent increased sales will demand an increased amount of working capital. The venture capitalist will spend a great deal of time asking you questions about the financial projections, and you should know your projections very well in order to answer these questions easily.

Part 10: Product Literature, Brochures, Articles, and Pictures

The venture capitalist will look at the pictures and try to determine how your product fits into his way of looking at the world. Be ready for any offhand questions about the product. For example, why did you use plastic in the handle of the product? What colors does it come in?

Other Information the Venture Capitalist Will Need

You should have answers for the questions set out above regarding your business proposal. You should also have ready answers for the questions that are not directly concerned with the business proposal but that we have covered so that you will be prepared on all fronts. If you can answer the questions in this chapter, you will be prepared for the questions from the venture capitalist. Many of the questions asked above require you to give the venture capitalist additional items besides the business proposal. Listed below are the other papers you should have ready for the venture capitalist when he visits your location.

References on the Business

Give the name, address, and telephone number of people who are familiar with your business and can give you a good reference. (Chapter 6 covers the questions the venture capitalist may ask your references.)

References on Key Employees

In this instance, you need the name, address, and telephone number of the person who is familiar with the key employees of the business, and who can vouch for the reliability of each of the key employees. It is usually better to have each of the key employees draw up his own reference list.

Bankers, Lawyers, Accountants, and Consultants

Make a list of all the people who are key to your business such as your bankers, lawyers, accountants, and consultants. List their names, addresses, telephone numbers, and the person to contact within the company.

Largest Suppliers

Here, enumerate your ten largest suppliers and give names, addresses, telephone numbers, and persons to contact at each supplier. List the dollar volume that you have purchased from each supplier or that you expect to purchase in the coming years.

Largest Purchasers

In this list give the names, addresses, telephone numbers, and the key persons to contact for the largest purchasers of your product. Give the dollar volume that has been purchased in the past, and the amount you expect to be purchased in the future.

Backlog

The venture capitalist will ask you many questions about your backlog. He will want to know how firm the orders really are. He will call a number of the purchasers and confirm their backlog. He will want to know the history of backlog orders. How many of them were actually fulfilled? For example, if you have converted your backlogs into actual sales 99 percent of the time, the venture capitalist will be pleased. If the conversion is only 50 percent, then your backlog should be cut in half. Prepare a list of the customers in the backlog, listing the person that the venture capitalist can talk to in order to verify the order. Give the person's name, address, and telephone number, plus a description of the order.

Aging of Accounts Receivable

Here you should provide all your accounts receivable and arrange them in columns by age. The first column should contain the amounts of those accounts under thirty days, the second column over thirty days, the third column over sixty days, and the fourth column over ninety days. The venture capitalist will be trying to determine the quality of your accounts receivable. In one venture capital situation the entrepreneur indicated that he had $2 million worth of accounts receivable to pledge as collateral. The company had only $100,000 in sales. Needless to say, this looked unusual. Further investigation revealed that the entrepreneur had agreed to sell his product, a specialty type of copier, if the buyer would sign a note to pay for it over the next twelve months. These notes were conditioned upon delivery of the product. The entrepreneur tried to suggest these notes were accounts receivable. He wanted to use them as collateral for loans from banks and for investment capital from venture capitalists. Needless to say, he never received any financing.

Aging of Accounts Payable

In this tabulation give the age of the accounts payable just as you did for receivables above.

Debts and Terms Summarized

Here, enter each major debt that you have. Give the terms of the debt, such as interest rate, repayment terms, and final due date. List the collateral for the loan and personal guarantees of the loan. Be prepared to give the venture capitalist a copy of the actual loan documents.

Leases

Summarize information about each lease that you have, and have a copy of the lease on hand in case the venture capitalist asks for it.

Tax Returns

Be prepared to give the venture capitalist a copy of the tax returns for the last three years.

Other Government Data

Be prepared to give the venture capitalist a copy of any OSHA reports, EPA reports, SEC reports, and so on.

Union Contract

Summarize on one page the union contract, and be sure to have a copy of the contract for the venture capitalist if he asks for it.

Personal Financial Statements

Prepare a personal financial statement for each key employee, listing his assets, liabilities, net worth, any contingent liabilities, and his annual income. You may want to use a standard bank form for the personal financial statement.

The personal financial statement is usually supplied only if the venture capitalist requires a personal guarantee of the loan by key employees.

Long Resume

Have each of the key employees complete a two- to three-page detailed resume on himself showing where he has worked during the last ten years (minimum) and the dates, the specific job titles, and names of people who can be contacted at these various places. This information should be arranged chronologically so the key person's progress can be seen. Any other materials, such as published articles or other achievements, should be included in this long resume. It is important to bring out all achievements.

Will the Venture Capitalist Ask All These Questions?

The venture capitalist will *not* ask anywhere near the number of questions listed in this chapter. He will be doing well if he asks one-third of the questions listed here. The point is that you must be ready for all of the questions because you don't know which third he will ask. Many of the questions do not have a "right" answer. In some situations the answer could be completely different than it is in others. It is important that you practice answering these questions and that you have a reasonable answer for the venture capitalist. One thing is for sure; some of the questions the venture capitalist will ask are listed in this chapter.

Objective

Your objective in this chapter has been to understand your own business proposal, and to be ready for *every* conceivable question that the venture capitalist can throw at you. Your motto must be, "Be prepared!" Now let us turn to Chapter 5, which tells you what to expect in your first meeting with the venture capitalist.

5

Meetings and Negotiations

Can You Have It Your Way?
What You Need To Know To Get The Best Deal.

After reading the summary and business proposal, the venture capitalist will normally telephone you to ask some basic questions about your business. He will determine what kind of deal you are seeking. If all signs are "go," the venture capitalist will probably request a meeting in his office. Some venture capitalists will make a trip to your office to discuss your company. Most venture capitalists like to have the initial meeting at their place because it saves time. It reduces their travel, which is heavy in the venture capital business. Also, from the standpoint of negotiations, they are in slightly better negotiating position on their own turf.

The Office of the Venture Capitalist

The location and surroundings of a venture capitalist range from modest to opulent. The venture capitalist who interviews you in opulent surroundings should be no more believable than one in modest surroundings. After all, jerks can rent expensive furniture too. The surroundings you visit probably are not related to the personality of the person you are meeting. It may be fairly difficult for you to gauge how you should act by the surroundings of the venture capitalist. For example, you might think that ultramodern surroundings reflect an interest in ultramodern investments. However, it could just mean that the venture capitalist's spouse or decorator likes unusual furniture.

The meeting place may indicate the venture capitalist's approach to your deal. Some like to conduct business in their offices, others in a conference room. From my experience, venture capitalists who receive people and conduct their business in a conference room are by and large less creative, less imaginative, and most often follow a set procedure in any venture capital situation. Venture capitalists who receive you in the office, and who conduct discussions and negotiations there, are generally receptive and open to your approach to life, and to making a creative decision. These observations, it should be remembered, are based on my own limited survey.

What Do Venture Capitalists Look Like?

Venture capitalists look like everybody else. They are part of the great American middle class. Most venture capitalists act and dress like investment bankers on Wall Street. Some of them dress and act like bankers in any major metropolitan bank. In some of the smaller venture firms in small towns, they act and dress much as you would expect any small town banker to act and dress. Most are fairly conservative in their dress and wear white shirts and dark suits. There are some notable exceptions. A number of venture capitalists have full beards. In a room full of venture capitalists these fellows stand out. Many venture capitalists from California dress in traditional banker suits, others are more casual in their attire. Despite some regional differences, all in all, you will find the group fairly similar in their appearance and in their approach to investing in companies.

How Long Will the Meeting Last?

The initial meeting in the venture capitalist's office will usually last from one to five hours, depending on the depth of the discussions. On the average, you should expect to be in the meeting approximately two hours. During the meeting the venture capitalist will attempt to "read" your personality. He will want to obtain a good impression of you as an individual. He will be analyzing your character and judging your ability as an entrepreneur. Most venture capitalists believe that first impressions are meaningful. If it is a poor one, most likely the deal will never go further. Needless to say, the initial meeting is a critical one for you.

In this meeting you should dress appropriately in your dark suit and white shirt and conservative tie. You should probably act reserved but at the same time show entrepreneurial energy. I have noticed in many initial meetings that small businessmen have great difficulty talking to the venture capitalist and have to clear their throats many times. I have never determined whether this behavior indicates nervousness or uneasiness about not telling the truth. In your meeting with the venture capitalist you should be straightforward. Present yourself as the person who can get the job done.

What Is the Object of the Meeting?

The venture capitalist holds a meeting with you to accomplish three basic objectives:

1. He wants to obtain more information about the business and how it will make money.
2. The meeting provides an opportunity to evaluate you, the management, in a face-to-face situation.
3. The venture capitalist wants to "cut the deal," meaning structure the investment, which is the ultimate goal of the meeting.

The deal may not be completely structured in this initial meeting. If, however, you leave an initial meeting without having discussed even a preliminary structure of the investment to be made by the venture capitalist, you've probably lost the investment. He is not interested unless he "cuts the deal," at least on a preliminary basis.

The preliminary deal is contingent upon the venture capitalist's final review of you, your business, and your industry. If his original perception changes for any reason, he will want to change his preliminary deal, or even worse, not go through with it. As the venture capitalist compares your business proposal with his findings, his original impression should be confirmed. If there is a difference, then the deal you have struck during your meeting will be void.

What Happens in a Typical Meeting With a Venture Capitalist?

In a typical session, the entrepreneur enters the office and a few pleasantries are exchanged. The venture capitalist usually begins the conversation with, "What can I do for you?" or some other open-ended question. It is surprising how many directions a conversation can take from that question. What most venture capitalists want to hear from the entrepreneur is a verbal presentation of what the business is all about, how much money they need, and what they plan to do with the money. You need not be detailed and long-winded unless asked specific questions. Your presentation should be energizing not dull.

It is important to appear energetic. Starting and running a small business and developing it into a medium-sized business takes a tremendous amount of energy. If you seem to be slow and methodical, you will probably not get his backing. After all, it is your energy, your creativeness, your organization, and your leadership that will make it all happen. Also, you need to appear cheerful. If you come across as an unhappy soul, it is very unlikely that anyone will want to put money behind you. So, besides looking for innate intelligence and knowledge of the business, the venture capitalist will be looking for an energetic and cheerful entrepreneur. Personally, I also look for a good sense of humor. Two people whom I backed and who failed both lacked a sense of humor and that experience may account for my interest in this quality in an entrepreneur. I have worked with other venture capitalists who say they have backed humorless, boring people who made a lot of money. The basic qualities venture capitalists look for seem to be energy and a will to succeed. Remember, throughout your meeting you are selling your business proposal and you are also selling yourself as the one person the venture capitalist should back. Show them you are a fireball!

What Type of Presentation Should be Made?

In most of your meetings with the venture capitalist you will both be working from the business proposal that you have previously sent to the venture capitalist. Many entrepreneurs think they should show slides or large flip charts. Neither of these props is necessary. Most venture capitalists do not want to see a professional presentation. Slides are seldom as good as a set of pictures that you can pass across the table to the venture capitalist. Pictures will show him what your product looks like. You do not need to leave the pictures with the venture capitalist although a plain paper copy of several of the pictures could be included in case the venture capitalist wants to keep pictures. If you have a model or sample of the product you are manufacturing, bring it along. An individual once gave a demonstration of a new surgical technique in my office using a cushion to represent a person's stomach. It was very effective in illustrating the proprietary method used for holding a patient's stomach open during surgery.

Another effective mechanism is a book of pictures. This method, akin to a scrapbook, shows prototypes as well as operating units and can effectively illustrate how a new technology operates. You do not need to leave the book with the venture capitalist. Once he has an understanding of the process, the pictures will not be necessary for presentation purposes.

What Type of Entrepreneurs are Venture Capitalists Seeking?

The general consensus among venture capitalists is that entrepreneurs are achievers. They have a positive and optimistic approach to life. In your meeting with the venture capitalist, you want to project yourself as an achiever—a person who has achieved things already, which you should stress, and a person who will achieve in the future. In essence, you should adopt a positive mental attitude when making your presentation to the venture capitalist. Various analyses that have been completed indicate that certain attributes correlate positively or negatively with the achieving personality. For example, a high positive correlation has been found in individuals who have been Eagle Scouts. The lowest correlation has been found among pipe smokers. Venture capitalists do not take to heart such generalizations. In the meeting, you should be yourself; do not try to act like someone's stereotype of an entrepreneur. Display a positive attitude and an intelligent, inquiring mind and have answers for the questions being asked. Be pleasantly aggressive in the meeting and sell, sell, sell. You should convey your concept with as much positive verbiage as possible. Unfortunately, a few venture capitalists do make investments on a phyletic basis. Others are sexist in their decision making. If you happen to encounter one of those poor souls, go on to the next venture capitalist. Do not waste your time trying to change emotional prejudices.

What Are the Characteristics of the Entrepreneur?

The venture capitalist will be looking for seven basic characteristics. This doesn't mean he is looking for an ideal human being, but merely that he would like to see a number of these qualities. Thus, your lack of strength in one area or another may be acceptable. Different venture capitalists will emphasize different items in the list, and some industries will require more strength in some areas than will other industries. You should keep in mind that this is a laundry list of the qualities of the ideal entrepreneur. No one is expected to have them all. People will differ in their strong qualities, but we can examine these seven according to the way they are ranked by venture capitalists, most of who put honesty at the top of the list.

Honesty

Every venture capitalist wants an honest entrepreneur. Some venture capitalists believe that a dishonest entrepreneur can still make money for them. That may be true as long as the dishonest entrepreneur cheats only other people and not the venture capitalist. Most venture capitalists will only work with an honest entrepreneur because they realize a dishonest one might someday turn on them. Honesty is made up of a number of components:

1. *Integrity,* in that the entrepreneur tells the truth and is honest to the venture capitalist.
2. *Fidelity,* meaning that the entrepreneur is trustworthy in his dealings with the venture capitalist and with others.
3. *Loyalty,* meaning that the entrepreneur stands by his commitments.
4. *Equitability,* meaning that the entrepreneur believes in fair play.

In your relationship with the venture capitalist, remember honesty and its components. Build your credibility with the venture capitalist by demonstrating whenever possible that you are an honest entrepreneur.

Achiever

Venture capitalists want to believe that you have a strong desire to win, that you want to accomplish your goals. They need to know that you use money as a measure of performance in your activities. Building the best computer in the world may be a tremendous achievement, but it means nothing to the venture capitalist unless it can be sold at a profit. You must translate your feelings and your drive into goals that are measured in terms of money. You must demonstrate that you have a desire to make money, not so much because of greed, but because money is the ruler by which you measure your performance. The venture capitalist must understand that you are an achiever or he will not back your venture.

Energy

This quality comes in many forms. First you must have physical and mental energy to accomplish the tasks that have been set out. You must have the strength to complete the years of effort that will be needed to bring about your financial plan. You must demonstrate to the venture capitalist your capacity for hard work. You must demonstrate that you have drive, enthusiasm, and initiative. The venture capitalist must know that you are tenacious in your desire to achieve goals, and that you have a long-term commitment to achieve them. He does not want to back a stubborn person, but one who has the commitment and the energy to make it all happen. Being an entrepreneur will consume large amounts of energy. Without physical and mental energy, most business proposals cannot be accomplished.

Intelligence

The venture capitalist will want to know that you are an intelligent individual. There are many components to intelligence. It is certainly demonstrated by advanced degrees from recognized universities. But many intelligent people have not attended college. By intelligence, the venture capitalist means a rational human being, one who is logical in his thinking, one who has the ability to understand complex situations, and the reasoning power to analyze those complex situations. He will want to know that you have good judgment and that after analyzing a problem you have the ability to select the right solution. You must be able to take the appropriate amount of risk for the reward at hand. There is no way that the venture capitalist or anyone else can measure the type of intelligence that is needed in entrepreneurial activity. Your intelligence will be judged by your response to the questions and the solutions you have provided in your business proposal. Your entrepreneurial ability will be judged on the basis of the venture capitalist's experience in dealing with other entrepreneurs.

Knowledge

Knowledge also comes in many forms. Certainly an education at a good university indicates a knowledge of basic subjects. But the venture capitalist is more interested in your experience. What lessons did you learn from past failures? How much experience do you have in the industry you are about to enter? Do you have within your brain the information about the industry that is necessary for success? Have you analyzed the industry and determined the keys to success in your business? Can you accept criticism and profit from it? The venture capitalist will want to determine what knowledge you have about this particular situation that makes you able to make money at it.

Leadership

Leadership has been studied almost to excess in business schools, yet it has seldom been studied from the perspective of entrepreneurship. The venture capitalist must understand that you have the leadership qualities necessary to be the center of attraction in a small growth oriented company. You must have the courage to take personal responsibility for an entire corporation. You must have the courage to take risks and to tolerate these risks during adversity as you go in the direction others have not tread. With respect to personality, leadership involves self-confidence, a positive attitude, and some degree of self-centeredness. The venture capitalist will be trying to determine if you have those leadership qualities. Can you set the standards for yourself and for others, and carry them out? Do you have the leadership capability to see the problems at hand, and to change the strategic plan if necessary in order to ensure profitability? You must not be so self-confident or egocentric that you refuse to do a menial task or solve a problem that is "beneath you." Leadership in many ways means getting the job done either by doing it yourself, or, most often, by doing it through other people.

Creativity

Although it is important for an entrepreneur to be creative, too often the creative side of entrepreneurship has been emphasized to the exclusion of many other necessary traits. The venture capitalist will want to know that you are resourceful, and that you are a problem solver. He wants to see that you have a new or unique approach in this situation, that you have brought originality to a situation that makes it exceptional.

All seven of these characteristics are important. You should review them in detail and try to see where your own personality fits into these categories. If you are weak in an area such as knowledge, you may want to bring along a person in your organization who has extensive knowledge of the industry. He can answer the questions about the industry that you will not be entirely familiar with. If you are not the creative genius in the group, you may wish to bring along the person who has created the idea. Again, you personally do not have to embody all of these qualities, but you must show achievement and honesty. Your team should have all of them well covered.

Know Your Stuff

During this meeting with the venture capitalist, you will be asked a thousand questions about your business. Many of these questions were covered in Chapter 4. Often two venture capitalists will be in the room, both firing questions at you from every direction. There will be marketing questions, production questions, financial questions, and a number of questions about your projections. You need to know every part of your business proposal in detail. You must know your business inside and out or the venture capitalist will think that you are not knowledgeable about your business, your industry, or the people.

If you are a heavyweight in marketing but a lightweight in finance, you may wish to bring along a strong financial partner. If you do not have a controller who can stand up to the questioning, your accountant may be willing to play this role. If you are not a heavyweight in the production side or some other segment of your business, you may wish to bring along the person in your business who is strong in this area. It is not unusual for the entrepreneur and one or two others on his management team to be at the meeting and participate in the discussions. If these people are not part owners in the business and you do not want them to know what kind of deal you are negotiating, you may wish to tell the venture capitalist ahead of time. Tell him that you would like to discuss your management team, the financial details, and projections, and after those discussions, you would like to dismiss the other people before you negotiate a deal. He will be receptive to this type of situation and will be sympathetic to confidential discussions.

Things You Do Not Say to the Venture Capitalist

Your conversation may run for hours. During this period of time you may relax and become quite talkative. You may say some things you should not be saying at this point in your relationship with the venture capitalist.

Big Plans

During the discussion you should concentrate on your business proposal. You should avoid certain topics. Leave out all the grandiose plans you have for the future. The idea that your company might someday have thirteen divisions in forty-seven states and might approach $1 billion in sales is not relevant to the venture capitalist's analysis of your business proposal. In fact, such grandiose plans will probably scare him away and make him see you as a dreamer. If somewhere in the back of your mind you have an idea for another product, or for additional bells and whistles on your existing product, or the hope of acquiring another business, or other things that are not part of the business proposal, do not bring them up during the meeting. To do so will only sidetrack the venture capitalist from the written business proposal and reduce your chances of obtaining financing. If you bring up additional plans during the meeting, the venture capitalist might think that you are trying to run before you can crawl. It will make him question your business judgment. He will think you are spreading yourself too thin.

Make Money

One of the things venture capitalists like to ask an entrepreneur after the in-depth discussion of his business proposal usually goes something like this:

Venture Capitalist: After discussing this business proposal in detail with you, I think it is going to take a tremendous effort on your part. It is going to take a great deal of work and may involve many long hours. It will mean a sacrifice. It's going to be a grind for the next four to five years. Why in the world would someone like you want to do something like this?

Entrepreneur #1 (Wrong Answer): I have always wanted to own my own business. I just don't like working for someone else. Where I am now, I have to report to people who just don't understand how to get something done. There is just too much bureaucracy and there just isn't enough opportunity for me to express myself. My boss doesn't understand me. I want to be my own boss so that I don't have to answer to anyone.

Entrepreneur #2 (Right Answer): I have always wanted to own my own business but that is only part of this whole plan. What I really want to do is make a lot of money. I see this as a unique opportunity for you and me.

We'll put together my ideas and your money and have a winner. It's a golden opportunity for us both.

As you can see, the two answers above are quite different. The first entrepreneur seems to think that by owning his own business he will not have to answer to anyone. Nothing could be further from the truth. An entrepreneur must answer to his investors, his banker, his accounts payable when he has not paid them promptly, the Internal Revenue Service when he has not paid his taxes, and the state sales tax collection agency and payroll taxes. The list is far greater than most entrepreneurs ever imagine. I remember asking a friend of mine who had finally obtained his own business how it felt to be president. He responded, "I think about it every night when I sweep out the place." Being an entrepreneur with your own business does not mean riding around in a big car while making decisions. It means hard work that involves scrimping and saving, and it is a tough life. When something goes wrong, you have to fix it.

The second entrepreneur said the right things as far as the venture capitalist is concerned. That is, he focused on making money. Keep in mind that the venture capitalist is not interested in your psychological or sociological need to be independent. He has no interest in solving your personal problems. He is interested in making money.

Honesty

As we discussed previously, honesty is the most important characteristic of an entrepreneur. Honesty is probably the most difficult characteristic to evaluate. Most venture capitalists recognize that there are two levels of dishonesty. First there are con men. They tell you how much they will make money by cheating others, and at the same time tell you how they will share it all with you. They describe the method by which they are going to cheat the government, how much money they are going to cut out of suppliers through negotiations, how they will lie to lending institutions to gain credit, and in short, do anything to make money. Then they look straight across the table and tell the venture capitalist how much his share will be. They are seeking to gain his confidence. Once confidence is gained, the con man will take the money and be gone. This type of dishonesty is not too difficult to spot even if it does not come out in the meeting. It usually sticks out like a sore thumb when checking the background of the individual.

The second kind of dishonesty is known in business school parlance as "constructive deception," or is more commonly known as telling white lies. An example of a constructive deception is the statement, "My board of directors will never agree to that proposal." Since the board usually follows the lead of the management, the statement is a disguise for the real response, "I don't like your proposal." The statement is a way for management to hide behind the board of directors in order to give the answer, no.

Another form of constructive deception used by venture capitalists can be illustrated by the comment, "Your type of investment just doesn't fit into our investment strategy." What the venture capitalist may mean by this response is that the deal is not to his liking. He is using a neutral excuse to turn down the proposal, rather than give a direct rejection. I have used both of the above constructive deceptions in order to negotiate or turn down a deal. That type of constructive deception is acceptable in business.

Constructive deception is not the same as evading answers, nor does it mean not doing what one says one will do. For example, constructive deception cannot be equated with not answering a question when directly asked about it. When someone tries to avoid an issue or a question, that behavior is like a con man's. Similar to the con artist is the entrepreneur who does not take the action he agreed to take. This type of behavior, too, casts doubt on a person's honesty. In other words, it is all right to tell a white lie to a venture capitalist but not to tell big lies. Such behavior will kill the deal. A venture capitalist looking at you for the first time will be trying to determine the degree of your honesty. If you tell him a lie and he catches you, you can wave goodbye to your financing. Be sensitive to the fact that venture capitalists will not back dishonest people.

Things Not To Do in the Meeting

Because the venture capitalist has to see people all day long and talk to them about their business plans, he develops certain pet peeves. Here are a few of them.

Do Not Avoid Answering Questions and Do Not Give Vague Answers

The venture capitalist does not have the time to tolerate coyness so avoid answering questions in a circuitous way that forces him to repeat his questions. If you are handing out vague answers, the venture capitalist will in turn give you a fairly vague answer when you ask if he wants to invest in your company. Play it simple and play it straight. Give a direct answer to a direct question. If you do not understand the question, do not give a vague or meandering answers. Ask specifically what the venture capitalist is looking for and then answer directly. Most venture capitalists spend their days asking questions. They have become highly skilled in interrogating people. If they find you leading them around in a circle, you can bet you will not be getting any money from them.

Do Not Hide Significant Problems

If your company has had significant problems such as lawsuits, or large thefts in the past, especially in the immediate past, do not hide them from the venture capitalist. Assume that he will eventually find out about them and that when he does he will be quite upset that you have not revealed them. If the venture capitalist asks the rather vague question, "Are there any other significant problems that I haven't asked about?," go ahead and give him the significant problems you see. Many times a venture capitalist asks, "What can go wrong and how can this entire situation fail?" In this instance you should give him a solid answer. The answer should not be, "Nothing can go wrong." Obviously things can go wrong and there are probabilities that things can go wrong. You should answer in that vein, perhaps by saying, "It is possible that a new competitor will enter the marketplace." Then you should respond to that probability by indicating how your company would react. Do not hide significant problems from the venture capitalist. To do so can only buy you trouble.

Do Not Bring Your Lawyer to the Negotiations

Lawyers are by nature combative. They spend three years in law school arguing with one another. Then they join a profession that is argumentative. Many lawyers spend the entire day writing legal documents that try to cover every conceivable possibility. They are constantly thinking about what can go wrong, and how their clients can be hurt. This is what they should be doing. As a result, however, when lawyers come to negotiating sessions they tend to be long-winded and eloquent. They tend to be combative on minor issues and argumentative about probabilities. If you want to make a deal with the venture capitalist, leave your lawyer at his office. It will be cheaper for you and you will negotiate a business deal that the lawyer can put in legal language later.

Do Not Press for an Immediate Decision

Asking the venture capitalist for an immediate decision will only make him nervous. The best approach is to ask the venture capitalist, "If we assume that what I have presented in the business proposal is correct, can you please outline in general terms what you might be thinking of?" If he is unwilling to outline the terms, you may wish to coax him along by suggesting certain terms and can observe his reaction. The idea is not to get the venture capitalist to shake your hand and say, "We have a deal." After all, he has just read the business proposal and met you for the first time. Do not expect him to conclude the transaction at that meeting. However, you should expect him to give you an indication of whether he is interested in the deal and if so, to give you the general parameters of the type of deal he believes would best fit the situation.

Do Not Be Rigid in Pricing

If you have structured your deal to sell only common stock at a certain price per share for a certain percentage of the company, and if you are unwilling to move from that position, you probably will not receive financing from any venture capital firm. It would be a rare coincidence if the terms you set for an investment fit precisely those offered by a venture capitalist. Do not enter into negotiations with the idea that you can obtain only one deal. Negotiate with the venture capitalist. To negotiate means to give and take. After the negotiations are over and you have reached some conclusions, you can still change your mind. A discussion does not mean you have to live with the conclusions. At the end of the day you can say, "I understand what the deal is. I want several days to think about it before I firmly agree to what we have discussed." This is a perfectly acceptable position to take. You should always negotiate with the venture capitalist because in the negotiations you may arrive at a position that is more advantageous than your original position.

How to Negotiate in the Meeting

Negotiating is the subject of numerous books, each author professing to have the right technique. The method you use will be a reflection of your approach to business. In addition, negotiating techniques depend primarily upon the situation, the personalities, and the relative strengths of both parties. In negotiations between individuals of high education, calm personalities, and similar strengths, the technique that usually works best is logical persuasion. That is, each party has a point to sell and each one attempts to sell it to the best advantage. There is give and take. Both parties have needs and each is seeking a solution.

Another technique is touted in many seminars and highly publicized books. It focuses on the overbearing personality with little education, dissimilar positions and strengths, and communication in the form of grunts and demands. A number of other books concentrate on "hard" negotiating techniques, and describe how you can browbeat anyone into submission. There is a good lesson to be learned from these outrageous negotiating techniques. If, after the negotiations are completed, each party goes its separate way, then this technique can be used successfully. However, if the two parties must "live" with one another after the negotiations are completed, as must be done after a venture capital investment, then any technique that injures the other party cannot be employed. It will impair the relationship for the duration of the investment.

There is a saying in the investment business that "the Golden Rule prevails." The Golden Rule is, "He who has the gold makes the rule." However, if a venture capitalist uses this axiom exclusively he will have problems with his investments. After the investment is made, the entrepreneur will have the gold and he will make the rules. In reality, each party has something to give. You have your company, the proposal that you have put together, and an idea of what you can do in the future. The venture capital investor has his money, his experience in the business world, and his financial contacts. Each has a position to protect and each must give good value to the other party or the relationship will not work. Remember this in your dealings with venture capitalists, and if you find yourself negotiating with a hard, uncompromising venture capitalist, walk out of the office.

In negotiating with the venture capitalist, you should keep in mind that if you both can agree on the terms, you will be living with each other for a considerable amount of time. Therefore, during the negotiations it is appropriate for you to conduct yourself in a manner that is conducive to a long-term relationship rather than a short-term one. If it takes a struggle to obtain the commitment, you will only be hampered in your long-term relationship. In the negotiations you should listen to the needs of the venture capitalist but you should not forget your own needs. Do not be afraid to ask for anything you think is meaningful and try to negotiate a deal that you both can live with.

How to Cut the Deal

Once the venture capitalist has heard the entrepreneur's presentation and has asked questions about the business, the next logical step is to negotiate the terms of the investment. If the venture capitalist gives a weak answer to an entrepreneur such as, "Well, we'll have to study your proposal some more and get back to you in a few days," you have failed to generate enough interest for the venture capitalist to negotiate a deal with you. As a rule, if you leave the venture capitalist's office without having negotiated at least a preliminary deal, chances are you will never obtain a deal.

Many new people in the venture capital field live and die for deal making. Experienced venture capitalists, on the other hand, like reviewing proposals and hearing from entrepreneurs. Cutting the deal is relatively unimportant to their personal satisfaction. By the time they have come to the point of negotiating the investment terms, the experienced venture capitalist usually knows what it will take before he will invest his money. If he cannot move the entrepreneur close to his position, then the deal dies. An experienced venture capitalist will never reach for deals nor will he try to browbeat the entrepreneur into a position the entrepreneur does not want. If an entrepreneur must accept terms that he feels are unreasonable, he will be out to retaliate throughout the investment period. As everyone in the venture capital business knows, if an entrepreneur wants to do in the venture capitalist, the entrepreneur has ample opportunity to do so while running his business. Fortunately, most venture capitalists do not have to reach for an investment because a great many excellent investments are available. Perhaps when good investments become scarcer, venture capitalists will have to be more aggressive in seeking deals. In the interim, most are content to sit in their chairs and try to create deals that fit their needs and the needs of the entrepreneur.

Ownership by the Venture Capitalist

The opening gambit in determining how much equity the venture capitalist will own in a company is usually a question to the entrepreneur: "How much equity are you willing to give up?" Some entrepeneurs are willing to give up more than the venture capitalist needs to make the deal. Of course this makes "negotiating" quite easy. Some entrepreneurs are stingy when it comes to the ownership they are willing to give up, and this approach usually kills the process for most venture capitalists. Trying to persuade entrepreneurs to give up more than a very small percentage of their company is a waste of good time. When the entrepreneur is unwilling to give up a reasonable portion of the company, no persuasive argument will work.

Entrepreneurs will think of hundreds of persuasive arguments to suggest why a venture capitalist should own a small percentage of the company. Some entrepreneurs start by discussing the return on investment that the venture capitalist will have if he invests. The discussion usually proceeds as follows:

Entrepreneur: If you invest $300,000 and you get 10 percent of the company you will make a fortune.

Venture Capitalist: But if I get only 10 percent of the company for $300,000, this means that 100 percent of the company is currently worth $2.7 million. I don't see how a company at this stage of development is worth $2.7 million because of an idea.

Entrepreneur: Wait. Let me finish. When we hit the projections that we are shooting for in three years, the company will be earning about $3 million after taxes. Using a price-earnings ratio of twenty to one on pretax dollars, the company will be worth $30 million. Your 10 percent will be worth $3 million. You will have received a ten to one return on your investment in only three years. That seems to be super.

Venture Capitalist: And if your company fails, I lose $300,000 and you lose very little. And if the company goes as you say it is going to go, you will have made $27 million and invested a small amount, while I invest $300,000 and received $3 million. This is just not an equitable distribution of the potential return if you consider the risk you are asking me to take on my $300,000.

The discussion above has occurred so many times with venture capitalists that they literally cringe when they see or hear the "return on investment" argument. The fallacy of the entire argument is that the entrepreneur is basing his valuation on future earnings, as though the company was a public company with assured future earnings, when in reality the company is not even in existence or is merely in the formative stages. In addition, the entrepreneur is using earnings that are three years away, when most analyses use the present year's earnings.

It is not an appropriate methodology, and using it with the venture capitalist will only set you on the wrong trail.

How Do Venture Capitalists Price Investments?

Venture capitalists think about a company on the basis of pricing. That is, if they are buying a percentage of the comany, what does that make the entire company worth? The variables that the venture capitalist uses to determine price are the entrepreneur's investment, upside potential, downside risk, additional funds, and exit vehicle. Each of these is now discussed in turn.

Entrepreneur's Investment

How much money is the entrepreneur investing, relative to the total amount of money that is being invested by all investors? If the entrepreneur is investing very lit'le, then he should expect to receive less equity in the entire deal.

If you do r . intend to invest any money, the deal will have to be extremely attractive before any venture capitalist will wish to invest in your company. If you are like most of us in the middle-class segment of society, you don't have much money to put into a business. But taking out a second mortgage on your house or borrowing on your personal signature at a bank to raise some money to invest in the company will be a sign of your commitment to the venture capitalist. The venture capitalist realizes that you are putting your sweat and blood into the company. He realizes that if it fails you will have a black mark on your record and you will be set back for many years of your life. Nevertheless, he still wants to know that you cannot walk away from the deal without suffering some economic loss. In the above example, where the entrepreneur was seeking $300,000 with only a small personal investment, the venture capitalist will want 80 percent ownership in the company. With an investment of $30,000 (10 percent of the deal), the entrepreneur is probably in a position to negotiate 50 percent of the equity for himself. If you invest one-third, then you can probably obtain two-thirds of the equity.

Another way to insure that you have a large piece of the equity is to give collateral to the venture capital company. A venture capital company does not often obtain good collateral for its loans and investments in small business. However, if collateral is available—such as machinery and equipment, perhaps a second mortgage on real estate, or other hard assets—you will be in a much better position to negotiate with the venture capitalist. The downside risk for the venture capitalist will have been curbed to some extent. The more collateral you can provide, the greater the opportunity you will have to own more of your comany.

There is no scientific method of setting the equity ownership. It will be up to discussions and negotiations between you and the venture capitalist. If he believes in you, and if he believes the downside risk is relatively small, then you will come away from the negotiating table with a larger share of equity ownership in your company. By having a strong, straightforward business proposal, by presenting yourself as an aggressive, eager, energetic, intelligent entrepreneur, you can obtain a substantial position in your own company after receiving a substantial amount of venture capital.

Upside Potential

What is the upside potential of the investment? How much money can the venture capitalist make? What kind of profits can the company generate? What is the probability the projections will be achieved on schedule? Any negative factors in this area will mean that the venture capitalist will have to receive more equity ownership and the entrepreneur less.

In your negotiations with the venture capital firm on the amount of equity that it ought to own, it will generally be looking for return on investment. Most venture capital firms think of return on investment in technical terms known as internal rate of return. Internal rate of return answers the question, "How much interest would I have to receive on my money in order to equal the return on investment I will get from investing in this project?" The venture capitalist is basically saying to himself, "One can invest the money today in a money market fund and have a certain interest as a return on investment. If one invests in your company and at the end of some period of time receives a great deal of money back, then what interest rate would one have had to have received (on a compound, annual rate of return) in order to equal what one would get from investing in your company?"

Most venture capital companies are thinking in terms of a five-year horizon. You might think that if you could double the venture capitalist's money every five years he would be quite satisfied. Actually, this only computes to an internal rate of return of 15 percent per annum—not very much for taking the amount of risk he is expected to take. A triple in five years yields 25 percent per annum, which is no slouch in terms of investment. If all the venture capitalist's investments returned 25 percent, then he would be considered a success. However, some investments fail and therefore the venture capitalist must receive a higher return on investment than 25 percent in order to pay for his mistakes. Five times his money in five years is 38 percent per annum. Now you have the venture capitalist's attention, and now you see what you are going to have to do. You must give him a return equal to five times his initial investment in order to attract him. Below is a table that carries the computations of internal rate of return for various periods.

When Profit is Returned	Compounded Annual Return on Investment (%)
2 times the investment in 5 years	15
3 times the investment in 5 years	25
5 times the investment in 5 years	38
7 times the investment in 5 years	48
10 times the investment in 5 years	58

The table above suggests that you have to give the venture capitalist about one times his money per year while he is invested. This works out fairly well in the initial years. The problem, of course, is that the longer the money stays out, the lower the internal rate of return is because of the time value of money. The time value of money means it is better to have a dollar in one year than to receive the dollar in ten years. Below is a chart that sets out the internal rate of return on investment for periods equal to the number of years.

When Profit is Returned	Compounded Annual Return on Investment (%)
3 times the investment in 3 years	44
4 times the investment in 4 years	41
5 times the investment in 5 years	38
7 times the investment in 7 years	32
10 times the investment in 10 years	26

Every venture capitalist has a profit target for his investments. It may be as low as 20 percent for investments that are not particularly venturesome, to as high as 100 percent for those that consistently make a high return on investment. Actually the profit target is determined by the type of investment. If there is a lot of collateral, the venture capitalist will take a lower return on his investment. The rate of return will depend on the stage or type of company that the venture capitalist is investing in. Obviously, start-ups and turnarounds demand a higher return on investment than would a leverage buyout or a third-round financing. Set out below is a chart that some venture capitalists adhere to.

Type of Investment	Range for Compounded Annual Rates of Return (%)
Start-up	50 +
First stage	40–60
Second stage	30–40
Third stage	20–30
Turnarounds	50+
Buyouts	30–50

These figures are only general guidelines. For each investment the venture capitalist makes, the expected return is based on the risk taken. If there is sufficient collateral and a good cash flow, the venture capitalist will take a lower return on investment. The lower the venture capitalist perceives the risk to be, the lower return he will take. You should not expect any venture capitalist to accept less than 20 percent return on investment. After all, this 20 percent is calculated before his overhead. You should also remember that many venture firms are leveraged. That is, they borrow their money from other institutions. These leveraged funds will calculate their internal rate of return before interest cost but will be looking for more immediate return on investment.

Most venture capitalists invest with the idea of hitting a "big winner," but they also try to avoid any losses. If they think the probability of loss is fifty-fifty, your return on investment figures will have to be spectacular in order to attract them. A 20 percent chance of loss is more in line with the venture capitalist's perception of risk and reward. As that figure goes from 80 percent to 90 percent, and perhaps even close to 97 or 98 percent, the venture capitalist will lower his return on investment expectations.

You might ask yourself why the venture capitalist needs such high returns on investment if there is only a 90 or 95 percent chance that he will lose his money. Actually, the venture capitalist will not invest in situations in which there is a reasonable chance of losing his principal. No one actually thinks the risk is great when he invests. As all venture capitalists say, "No one invests in a bad deal." All investments look promising when they are first made.

Most venture capital investments turn out to be mediocre investments. That is, the venture capitalist does not lose his money, but neither does he make a great deal of money. Probably seven out of every ten are mediocre investments for venture capitalists and it is the other three that bring in a sufficient return on investment to overshadow the mediocre seven investments. You should understand the venture capitalist's aversion to losing his principal. He is much like a gambler standing at a casino table. He can continue to play the game and stand a chance of making a great deal of money as long as he doesn't lose all of his chips. If each time he places a few bets down and he can at least get his bet (his principal) back, he can continue to play the game. Once he begins losing the principal chips, he has less and less opportunity to win. In your negotiations with the venture capitalist you should keep in mind his risk-and-reward analysis and be sensitive to it. It is his guiding light.

Downside Risk

The third principle that venture capitalists follow in pricing investments is the downside risk. They ask, "What is the downside risk?" In other words, how much of the investment made by the venture capitalist would be lost in a liquidation? What is the probability that a liquidation could occur? The higher the downside risk and the lower the liquidation value of the company, the more the venture capitalist will have to receive in equity ownership to compensate for the risk; conversely, the less the equity that will be available for the entrepreneur.

Downside risk is very difficult to evaluate. As an entrepreneur you are probably optimistic about the business and cannot see the downside risk. You do not understand that if the business fails, nothing will be left for the investors. You can reduce the downside risk to the venture capital firm in two basic ways: by means of collateral and structure of the deal.

Offering the venture capital company collateral can give him more hope of not losing his money. Obviously, if you have land and a building or machinery and equipment, these can be used to collateralize his investment. Having an appraisal prepared on the machinery and equipment or land and the building to show their true worth will help. Providing the venture capital firm with a second mortgage or a third mortgage on valuable land and the building, or providing a security interest in the machinery and equipment, will help mitigate the venture capitalist's fear of losing his money. This means that you will have to give up less equity ownership to the venture capitalist.

Other items can be used as collateral. You may have valuable patents for your new product. These patents may be worth a great deal. You may have already received an offer from a large company to purchase the patents. Such an offer would establish the worth of the patents. By giving the patents as collateral, the venture capital company will need less ownership in the company. You may also have a valuable lease on a retail location for your business. This, too, could be used as collateral through an assignment of the lease to the venture capital firm. If you have some personal net worth or have the ability to earn money as an expert in your business, you may wish to give your personal guarantee to the venture capital firm. Your personal guarantee, of course, could mean that you would have to pay off the investment made by the venture capital firm if the business failed.

There is another way of solving the downside risk problem. You can structure the venture capitalist's investment in order to give him confidence that the business will not fail. For example, you could purchase common stock in the business with your funds and the venture capitalist could purchase preferred stock. This would give him a preferred position if the company was liquidated. Furthermore, you could give the venture capitalist a debt position in the company; that is, as a debtor of the company he would have certain rights that stockholders, either preferred or common, would not have. Finally, you could give a secured position on your assets to the venture capital firm. By moving the venture capitalist from an unsecured to a secured creditor position, you will make him feel that the downside risk is less for him, and therefore he will need less equity. You should always remember that there is a direct correlation between the amount of risk the venture capitalist believes he is taking and the amount of return on investment he is seeking.

Additional Funds

How much additional money will be needed in the years ahead to keep the business growing? Obviously a venture capital investment will not produce a large conglomerate. It takes successive rounds of financing either in the public market or private placements to bring a company from its early stages to maturity. Each successive requirement for capital will cause dilution of ownership by existing stockholders, unless the venture capitalist is willing to put up his pro rata share each time. Since it is unlikely the venture capitalist will invest every time funds are needed, there will be some dilution in his ownership position. The more the dilution, the more equity ownership the venture capitalist will want on his initial investment so he can be diluted to an acceptable ownership position rather than being diluted to nearly nothing.

There are two methods of approaching the problem of additional funding. The first is obvious; you could raise enough money to take you from your current position to the stage of public offering and positive cash flow. This may sound ludicrous but it is happening more and more in the venture capital field. In the past, an entrepreneur came to the venture capitalist with an idea. The venture capitalist put out a small amount of money to see if the idea would work. Once it was determined that the idea worked, the venture capitalist invested additional funds. More people would be hired and the prototype would go into production. During the production process more money would be invested, perhaps for a complete marketing of the product. Each successive round of financing would cause further dilution in the venture capitalist's position if he did not participate.

In recent years a more organized approach has appeared. A group of entrepreneurs working as a team have shown up on the doorsteps of venture capitalists. They have raised enormous amounts of money for the venture, enough to take it from its initial starting point through sales and break-even. This new approach to venture financing has consumed large quantities of cash and has increased the size of the loss by the venture capital firm. On the other hand, when the full management team is in place and there are supposedly enough funds to take the venture to cash flow break-even, the venture capitalist is in a position to quantify many of the risks not quantifiable under the old scenario described above. At any rate, the venture capitalist will be looking at your cash flow statement to determine how many rounds of financing are going to be needed, and therefore how much dilution might occur if he doesn't participate. You should be aware of this approach and make sure the venture capitalist understands needs for additional funds so that he can evaluate his risk and dilution.

Public Offering or Exit

As a final measure for pricing an investment, the venture capitalist will ask, "What is the probability that the company can go public so that a price-earnings ratio can be used on the earnings to determine value rather than a private valuation?" This is important both for bringing liquidity to the venture capitalist and for providing a marketplace valuation on the company. The less likelihood there is for the company to go public, the less likely the entrepreneur will own a large share of the stock. If there is little chance of a public offering, what other exit is available?

When you are negotiating with the venture capitalist, keep in mind that he always wants to sell his position. Even if he ends up with an equity position greater than 51 percent, he still wants to sell it to you or to someone else. The entrepreneur should not be concerned about the long-term ownership by the venture capitalist's company and his desire to own a majority of the company. In order to avoid having the company sold to someone, you should insist on having the right of first refusal on the sale of the company's stock owned by the venture capitalist. This will give you the opportunity to buy the stock owned by the venture capitalist if it is being sold at an unreasonably low price.

Also the entrepreneur should not be worried about the fact that a venture capitalist could own more than 50 percent and control the company. Telling the entrepreneur what to do is not the method of operation for most venture capitalists. Most venture capital companies are not active operators in their investment companies unless the small company gets in trouble. Then they will have something to say about the management of the company. The entrepreneur should not be concerned that the venture capitalist might own more than 50 percent and somehow tell the entrepreneur how to run his business. The venture capitalist physically does not have time to run the companies in which he has an investment. Most professional venture capitalists would not dream of telling an entrepreneur how to run his business on a day-to-day basis because the venture capitalists do not know enough about the business.

After the Negotiations

When the negotiations are complete, you must feel satisfied with the deal you have negotiated. If you feel you have ruined the negotiations and that the venture capitalist will now own too much of your company for what he is putting in, you are advised not to go forward with the deal. Going forward with a deal that you don't feel satisfied with, will only end in a great deal of misery for you and for the venture capitalist. It will only contribute to your failure. However, before you throw away the deal by turning down the venture capitalist's offer, you should discuss the offer with as many people as possible: your stockbroker, your lawyer, your banker, and other people you think will have the ability to evaluate what is happening. You may be pleasantly surprised that the offer and deal you have structured are the best that you can expect in the current marketplace.

Objective

After the negotiations are over, each party will have an idea of what they believe they have agreed to. It has been my experience and the experience of many others that these perceptions of the agreement rarely coincide. It is surprising how people can sit in the same room for hours and come away with a different notion of what was agreed to. These misunderstandings are the basic reason behind the simplified commitment letter that is discussed in the next chapter.

Your objective now is to obtain a commitment letter from the venture capital firm evidencing the agreement that resulted from the meeting. Any good venture capital firm should take no longer than twenty days to send a commitment letter. Many venture capital firms have to go to their board of directors for approval, but they can issue a commitment letter subject to board approval. Any commitment letter at this stage will be subject to the "due diligence" of the venture capitalist, as described in Chapter 7. The quicker you can reduce the amount of discussion and obtain a commitment letter, the further you will progress toward obtaining money. If you have not received such a letter within fifteen days after your meeting, you should call the venture capitalist and discuss when you might be able to obtain such a letter. In the next chapter we will discuss the contents of the commitment letter.

6

Commitment Letter

Can It All Be Put Into Words?
Your Agreements Must Always Be Put In Writing.

Every venture capital company has a different way of making a commitment to you. It may seem hard to believe, but many venture capital companies will not issue a commitment letter. They will tell you about the proposed deal. They may write it down on paper, but they will not sign a letter that is a formal commitment. Once you have reached an oral agreement with them, they will begin to draw up the legal documents and attempt to close on the investment on the basis of the oral understanding you have reached.

Personally, I like a commitment letter. It seems to me there should be an intermediate step between oral understanding and legal documents. This step involves writing down in a commitment letter the bargain struck by each side so that both can agree to it in a semibinding manner. Obviously, if neither can agree on the terms and conditions of a letter, no legal documents can be drawn. There are, in essence, two types of commitment letters: the one-page commitment letter issued by banks and some venture capital companies, and the long detailed ones issued by venture capital companies.

A short letter may contain a paragraph that sets out in simple terms everything the bank is willing to put in writing. Below is a typical short commitment letter:

Mr. Joe Entrepreneur, President
The Entrepreneur Company
123 Main Street
McLean, Virginia 22102

Dear Mr. Entrepreneur:

The First National Bank does hereby commit to lend your company $500,000 for five years at 3 percent over prime on our standard terms and conditions. Our loan will be secured by a first deed of trust and a first secured interest in all the assets of your company and will be personally guaranteed by you and your wife.

Sincere best wishes,

Mr. B. Banker
Assistant Vice-president

You might wonder why some venture capital companies will not issue commitment letters or why commitment letters from banks lack detail. Primarily, it is because banks operate in a competitive community. If they give you a commitment letter and if you take it to another financial institution, then there is a high probability that after seeing a competitor's commitment letter, the other bank will be more interested in your company. The competitor might offer you better terms and conditions. Needless to say, entrepreneurs who use commitment letters as a bargaining tool are frowned upon in both the banking and the venture capital community. Any potential lender hearing of such behavior may rescind the commitment letter as soon as possible. The preferred method of operating is to stay with one venture capital company until you agree or disagree. If you cannot agree, then you should move to the next venture capital company. If the agreement is in the form of a commitment letter, you should stay with the agreement.

Commitment Letters

The normal method for preventing an entrepreneur from using a commitment letter to bargain with other financial institutions is to require the borrower to make a commitment deposit in order to hold the commitment outstanding. This procedure seems only fair since the venture capital company at this point will have reserved some of its funds for your company. Also, the venture capitalist will have to make a commitment of time and expenses to analyze you, your company, and your industry. There should be some commitment on the part of the entrepreneur. Be advised that the points or percentages of the investment are normally required as commitment deposits, especially by those venture capital companies that are leveraged. For example, if 2 percent is required as a deposit on a $500,000 commitment, then you will have to put up $8,000 to hold the commitment. The current norm is 1 to 2 percent as a commitment deposit. Usually the fee is paid before the venture capitalist visits your company. If for some reason the venture capital company does not go through with the commitment, the fee is refunded. If you do not go forward, normally you lose the fee. You are legally free to shop for the best deal you can find from the venture community. You should remember that the venture community is small and friendly. It is more like a fraternity. You may damage your relationship if a venture capitalist hears that you are using his commitment as a bargaining tool. Even worse, the venture capitalist may cancel his commitment.

Some venture firms do not issue commitment letters because they believe such letters would bind them to make the investment. They do not want a suit if they back out. Even the firms that do issue commitment letters make certain the letters contain loopholes that let the firms off if they do not wish to go forward. Some venture capitalists do not like commitment letters because they reveal their full intentions to tie the entrepreneur in knots with conditions the entrepreneur must meet. Nonetheless you should insist on a commitment letter, or at least a letter outlining the basic terms of the agreement.

A detailed commitment letter is the subject of this chapter. It is the first step toward obtaining your funds. In the example below, the structure is a loan with options to own stock. This structure is typical for Small Business Investment Companies.

What Is In the Commitment Letter?

The commitment letter contains five basic segments. The first segment states the terms on which the loan is being made to your company and the terms of the equity option. The second section states the collateral for the loan. The third part talks about the conditions of the loan, both negative and positive. The fourth outlines the representations you have made that have induced the venture capital company to make a commitment. The fifth part deals with the conditions on which the commitment was made. Each part is discussed below.

Section 1: Terms of the Investment

In this section the venture capital company will try to state in clear terms precisely what it intends to do.

1.01 The venture capital company will make a loan of $500,000 for ten years at an interest rate of 12 percent per annum paid monthly on the first of each month.

In this sentence, which is self-explanatory, the venture company agrees to lend you $500,000 at 12 percent interest.

1.02   The loan shall be interest only for the first thirty-six months, and beginning with the thirty-seventh month you will pay principal and interest sufficient to fully amortize the loan over the remaining sixty months. All principal and interest outstanding at the end of eight years shall be due and payable in full.

The venture capital company will receive interest only during the first thirty-six months. After three years it will be paid interest plus principal in an amount sufficient to fully amortize the loan over sixty months or five years.

1.03   The loan may be prepaid in whole or in part, at any time with no prepayment penalty.

This part indicates that you may prepay the loan in whole or in part at any time. Thus, if you had a large public offering and had surplus cash, you might want to pay off the note in order to free any collateral that the loan had encumbered. Of course, it is difficult to obtain a loan at 12 percent interest so you may never pay it off. At any rate, this gives you the flexibility to pay it off. Always avoid prepayment penalties in this section.

1.04   Disbursement and takedown of the loan shall be 100 percent of the loan at closing.

This is a very important section. Sometimes the venture capital firm will agree to invest money in your company but will not let you draw it down unless certain conditions are met. Here, no conditions are stated. Disbursement by the venture capital firm and the takedown of all the funds by you will be 100 percent at closing. This means you will get all the money on the day the loan closes. If possible, you should attempt to have all the money disbursed at closing with no conditions. This gives you control over the funds.

1.05   In connection with this financing, the venture capital firm shall receive at the closing separate stock options to purchase stock in the company. The cost of the options to the venture capital firm will be $100. These options when exercised will provide stock ownership in the company of 20 percent at the time of exercise. The exercise price will be $20,000. The options will expire ten years from closing. The venture capital firm will share pro rata in any redemption of stock by the company in order to expand its pro rata ownership.

This paragraph explains the equity option granted to the venture capital firm. A piece of paper signed by you will give the venture capitalist the right to own stock in your company. This piece of paper will cost the venture capital firm $100. However, when the firm exercises the piece of paper and receives the stock, it will have to pay $20,000 for it. It will have this option for up to ten years. That is, the option will hang over the company for the next ten years unless a different agreement is negotiated in that period of time. The venture capital firm will also share in any redemptions of stock. If there are various stock-holders and the company agrees to buy out one who owns 10 percent of the stock, the venture capital company would receive an option to acquire 2 percent more of the company and thus have an option to buy 22 percent of the company for $20,000. Sometimes the actual number of shares and price per share are stated in this section. If so, there will also be an antidilution clause stating that if you sell stock below the price to be paid by the venture capitalist, then you will issue additional shares to him.

> 1.06   There shall be an "unlocking" provision whereby if there is a bona fide offer to purchase the company and the venture capitalist wishes to accept the offer whereas the company does not, then the company is required to acquire the venture capitalist's interest on the same terms and conditions as the bona fide offer. If you do not buy out the venture capitalist, then you must sell the company according to the terms of the bona fide offer.

This "unlocking" provision gives the venture capitalist an opportunity to exit from your company if there is a bona fide offer to purchase the company. In essence, it says that if someone offers to buy your company and the venture capitalist thinks you should sell the company but you do not agree then you must buy the venture capitalist's percentage portion of the offer on the same terms and conditions as those made by the bona fide offerer.

> 1.07   There shall be a "put" provision whereby anytime after five years the venture capital firm may require the company to purchase its stock options or the resulting stock from the options at the higher of the following:

1. $50,000 cash.
2. 120 percent of book value times 20 percent ownership.
3. Five times net pretax earning for the year just ended times 20 percent ownership.
4. 10 percent of sales for the year just ended times 20 percent ownership.
5. Ten times cash flow times 20 percent ownership.
6. Appraised value times 20 percent ownership.

A very important provision in the option agreement will be the "put" provision. Here it is agreed that the venture capitalist can require the company to buy his option according to six possible formulas. The minimum amount is obviously the first alternative, the cash price of $50,000. This means that any time the venture capital company wants, it can require you to purchase its stock option for $50,000. The other formulas are related to the equity ownership of the venture capital firm. For example, the third formula uses the company's pretax earnings for the year just ended times five, and then multiplies that number by 20 percent. If pretax earnings had been $100,000, then the venture capitalist could require you to buy his equity position for $100,000 cash ($100,000 earnings times five, times 20 percent, equals $100,000).

> 1.08   There shall be a "call" provision for a period of three years whereby after five years from closing and after the venture capitalist's loan has been paid in full, then the company can purchase the stock options or resulting stock from the options on the same terms and conditions as 1.07 above.

This section enables you to buy back the stock option held by the venture capital company after five years at a price based on the higher of the formulas set out in 1.07. In this situation you have a limited time to buy back the option. It is three years, and the clock begins running five years after closing. Most venture capital companies will not give you a call because it puts a cap on the amount of profit they can make. So don't be disappointed if you can't obtain a call. The call does not obligate you; it is a benefit.

> 1.09   Anytime after five years from closing the venture capitalist may require a registration and public offering of the shares owned by the venture capitalist at the company's expense.

This section gives the venture capitalist the right to make you register and publicly offer the shares owned by him. This could be quite expensive in that you would have to go to the Securities and Exchange Commission, register the shares, and give the venture capitalist the right to sell the shares in the public market. In theory, this seems to be an onerous task. In practice it is not. Most venture capitalists would not dream of requesting a public offering of the company's shares without having a stockbrokerage firm as an underwriter. An underwriter will not register and sell the shares of a floundering company or one that cannot meet strong projections. Therefore, if your company is not doing well, a stockbroker will not be willing to take your company public. It is is doing well, the venture capitalist does have a means of pushing you into a public offering. It might be at a time when you do not want to have it, but nonetheless, he would have the right to push you in that direction. If you can avoid this paragraph in your commitment, do it.

> 1.10   The venture capitalist shall have full "piggyback" rights to register his shares whenever the company or its management is registering shares for sale, and such registration of the venture capitalist's shares shall be paid for by the company.

This paragraph enables the venture capitalist to ride your coattails if you register shares for public distribution and sale. This means that if you have lined up a stockbrokerage firm and it is willing to sell shares in a public offering; then the venture capitalist will have the right to ride piggyback on that registration and sell its shares also. Generally, a brokerage house will not permit the venture capitalist to sell more than 10 to 20 percent of his holdings in the initial public offering. The fact that the venture capitalist has the right to sell all of his shares in the public offering could provide for an impasse between the brokerage house and the venture firm. This is seldom more than a momentary impasse since most venture firms recognize that having 20 percent sold is better than none and they will probably go along with the offer to sell some shares. The "piggyback" paragraph is a standard one.

Section 2:   Collateral and Security

This section of the commitment letter sets out the collateralization of the loan with certain assets of the corporation, and in some cases your own personal assets.

> 2.01   A second deed of trust on land and building of the business subordinated as to collateral to a first mortgage of $200,000 from a bank on terms acceptable to the venture capitalist.

According to this paragraph, the venture capitalist will have a second deed of trust mortgage on the land and building owned by the company subordinated only to a $200,000 first mortgage by a bank. There may be no equity in the land and building at this time, but the venture capitalist is hoping that if the business gets in trouble after a year or two, perhaps inflation will have increased the value of the land and building and there will be some collateral for him. If you agree to give a mortgage, then this paragraph is standard.

> 2.02   A second secured interest in all the tangible and intangible assets of the company, including but not limited to inventory, machinery, equipment, furniture, fixtures, and accounts receivable subordinated as to collateral to a first secured bank loan of $100,000 on terms acceptable to the venture capitalist.

In this instance the venture capitalist has a second secured interest in all the tangible and intangible assets of the company. They are subordinated to the first secured interest of a $100,000 term loan from the bank. Many venture capitalists seek to secure their loans in order to remove themselves as general creditors of the company. This gives them protection in case the company falters or goes into bankruptcy. It's better to be in a second mortgage position and a second secured interest in the company than to be just another general creditor. Sometimes there is something for secured creditors when there is nothing for general creditors.

> 2.03   Pledge and assignment of all the stock of the company and assignment of any and all leases of the company.

Here, you will pledge the stock that you own in the company as collateral for the loan. If the loan was in default, the venture firm could take the stock and become the owner of your company. That is unlikely. If the company actually was in trouble and the venture capitalist became an owner, he could be held responsible for some of the liabilities, such as payroll taxes. Often a venture capitalist will take a valuable lease assigned to him as collateral, especially in a retail situation. Under a default scenario, the venture capital firm can take over the leases and sell them to a third party.

2.04   Personal signature and guarantees of you and your spouse.

Many venture capitalists will require the individuals involved in the business to guarantee their investment. Frequently the guarantee is required in order to satisfy the venture capitalist that the entrepreneur will not run away from the business. This requirement is particularly common in cases where the entrepreneur puts in few equity dollars.

2.05   Assignment of a life insurance policy on your life for the amount of the loan outstanding with the venture capitalist listed as the loss payee to the extent of his loan.

Venture capital firms almost always require a life insurance policy on the life of the key entrepreneur. If the key entrepreneur dies, the policy will pay back the venture capitalist the money it has invested. This is not an unreasonable request since the venture capitalist is betting on you to make him some money.

2.06   Adequate hazard and business insurance, which shall include flood insurance if your business is located in a designated federal flood area. All such insurance shall be assigned to the venture capital firm, which shall be listed as the loss payee to the extent of its interest. In this regard, you will supply the venture capital firm with a list of all business insurance, and such insurance and coverage shall be acceptable to the venture capital firm.

Business insurance is also a requirement before a venture capitalist will invest in a company. Much like any other creditor, the venture capital firm will want the insurance policy assigned to it so that if the business is destroyed, at least it will be repaid for the amount of money it is owed.

Section 3:   Conditions of the Loan

This section enumerates the conditions under which the loan will exist. Wherever possible you should try to remove many conditions.

3.01   The company will provide the venture capitalist with internally prepared, monthly year-to-date financial statements, in accordance with generally accepted accounting standards (including a profit-and-loss and balance sheet) within thirty days of the end of each month.

As a condition of the loan, you will be required to prepare monthly financial statements and give them to the venture capital firm within thirty days of the end of each month. So, by the end of June each year, you will have supplied the venture capitalist with the May financial statements. This is a standard requirement.

> 3.02   The company will provide the venture capitalist with a monthly one- or two-page summary of operations with the financial reports furnished in 3.01 above.

Venture capitalists also like to have in writing a monthly summary of the operations and an indication of important events. If you are in this situation, you must include this summary with the financial statements.

> 3.03   Within 90 days after the year end the company will provide the venture capitalist with an annual certified audit from an independent certified public accounting firm acceptable to the venture capital company.

A certified audit from an independent certified public accountant is mandatory in any company financed by a venture capitalist. Some venture firms will permit an accounting firm to review the finances of a small business, but most often they require an audit. Although an audit is expensive, it is useful in the early years because it will permit you to have a public offering at a much earlier date. Normally you need to have the last three years audited in order to have a public offering.

> 3.04   Within thirty days of the year end, provide the venture capitalist with projections for the next fiscal year in the same format as the financial statements.

Venture capitalists want to have updated financial projections. In this instance, you will have to provide the venture capitalist with projections for the next fiscal year within thirty days of the year end. You can expect the venture capitalist to discuss these new projections with you in detail.

> 3.05   Within thirty days after they are filed, provide the venture capitalist with a copy of all material documents filed with government agencies such as the Internal Revenue Service, Environmental Protection Agency, and Securities and Exchange Commission.

In an effort to obtain additional information on the company, the venture capital firm will want a copy of filings before government agencies. These documents will enable the venture capital firm to continue to monitor your company.

> 3.06   The president of the company will provide the venture capital company with a certificate each quarter stating that no default has occurred in the terms and conditions of this loan.

In this instance, you will certify that to the best of your knowledge nothing has come to your attention that would indicate the company is in default on any of the default provisions in the loan agreement. Falsifying this kind of statement could lead to charges of fraud. You should take every precaution to make sure that what you are signing is correct.

3.07   On a quarterly basis and within thirty days of the end of the quarter, provide the venture capital firm with a list of inventory, accounts receivable, and other collateral to be compared with certain ratios.

The venture capital firm often follows certain ratios and levels of assets and sales. You may be required to provide the venture capitalist with this information, including the calculation of certain ratios.

3.08   In accordance with generally accepted accounting principles, the company will maintain:

1. A current ratio of one to one.
2. Accounts receivable to loan balance of one to one.
3. Inventory to loan balance of percent.
4. Sales of $1 million per year.
5. Net worth of $300,000.

In your quarterly statement set out in 3.07 above, you will have to mention the ratios that you agreed to in section 3.08. When you agree to one of these ratios or absolute numbers, you should look at your projections to make sure the ratios will be maintained throughout your projected future. Ratios are less popular among venture capitalists, and you will be able to remove all or most of them.

3.09   There will be no change in control or ownership of the company without the venture capital firm's expressed written approval.

Under the terms of section 3.09, the venture capitalist does not permit a change in control of the company. If you or the others who own the company sold it to somebody else, the venture capitalist would then be in bed with a different partner. No venture capitalist wants to wake up the next morning to find himself with a different management team and different owners.

3.10   Management will not sell, assign, or transfer any shares it owns in the company without written approval of the venture capital firm.

Here the venture capitalist makes sure you will not sell, assign, or transfer your shares in the company without his approval. After all, if you sold all of your shares, even though they did not amount to control of the company, the venture capitalist, again, would not have the same manager he had before. Your incentive would no longer be to make the stock of the company worth a great deal since you no longer would be an owner of the stock. The venture capitalist bets on a racehorse, and wants to make sure the same racehorse finishes the race. He does not want to change horses midstream unless you are not doing a good job.

3.11   The company will have board meetings at least once each quarter at the company's business offices. Although the venture capital firm's representative will not serve on the board, its representative will have the right to attend each meeting at the company's expense and the venture capital firm shall be notified of each meeting at least two weeks before it is to occur.

By agreeing to this paragraph, you and he agreed to have a meeting at least once each quarter and the venture capitalist will come to the meeting. Venture capitalists will often become board members and, therefore, they will not attend the meeting as a representative, but as a member of the board of directors.

3.12   The company will pay no cash dividends and the company will not sell any assets of the business that are not part of the regular course of business without the venture capital firm's approval.

The company will be prohibited from dividend payments. In all likelihood, the company is in its strong growth mode and does not intend to pay any dividends. Nor will the company sell any assets of the business that are not in the regular course of the business. This clause will prohibit the company from selling its machinery or equipment if it wants to shut down a certain part of the business because that would not be in the regular course of business. The only assets that could be sold are assets that are regularly sold. For example, if you are manufacturing a certain type of product (a small machine), you may sell these assets of the company, but not the assets of the company used to produce the product (a small machine). This is a standard paragraph.

3.13   The company will not expend funds in excess of $30,000 per year for capital improvements without written approval of the venture capital firm.

In this instance the company is prohibited from making capital improvements. In total, this will cost more than $30,000. Obviously the venture capitalist does not wish to have the company buying a great deal of capital equipment without his permission. If your company needs additional machinery, equipment, or other assets, you will need to negotiate the $30,000 figure up.

3.14   The management team, including you, will live in the metropolitan area where the business is located. The business will not be relocated without the express written permission of the venture capital firm.

Many venture capitalists require entrepreneurs to live in the city in which the business is located. It is a universal rule among venture capital firms that a business cannot be run on an absentee basis. This is possible in a few situations, but most often you will be required to live where your business is located. If you intended to move away and retire after the financing, you would not be allowed to do so.

3.15   The company will not pay any employee nor will it loan nor advance to any employee money that in total exceeds $50,000 per year without the written approval of the venture capital firm. If the company is in default for nonpayment on its loan to the venture capital firm or in default on any senior lien, or if the company is not profitable for any calendar quarter, then the company will not pay any employee nor will it loan nor advance to any employee money that in total exceeds $30,000 without written permission of the venture capital firm.

The venture capitalist will want a ceiling on the salary the entrepreneur can take from the company. He will do this for one basic reason. If the entrepreneur is taking out hundreds of thousands of dollars in salary, then there will be no incentive for the entrepreneur to take the company public or to go forward with any action that will give the venture capitalist an opportunity to cash in on his investment. It is my experience that most venture capital firms do not mind entrepreneurs making a large salary but they would prefer this to come in the form of bonuses at year end rather than a monthly payment. The board can agree to the bonus subject to approval of the venture capitalist. Then permission can be obtained from the venture capitalist.

3.16   The company will not pay any brokerage fees, legal fees, or consulting fees in excess of $20,000 per year without written approval of the venture capitalist.

Venture capitalists do not like to have a consultant or broker on the payroll unless it is one of their own. For this reason, they limit the amount of money that can be paid out in legal fees, consulting fees, and brokerage fees.

3.17   You will pay all closing costs and recording fees, which include all attorney's fees, even those of the venture capitalist's attorney. You may use any attorney to draw up the legal documents; however, they must be reviewed and approved by the venture capitalist's counsel. A simple review by the venture capital company's counsel will not incur a legal fee; however, if the work done by the venture capitalist's counsel is beyond a simple review, a fee will be charged and the fee will be paid by you.

Invariably, you will pay all closing costs, recording fees, and attorney's fees, including the fees of the attorney for the venture capital firm. Probably the best decision you can make is to have the venture capitalist's attorney draw up all the legal documents and have your attorney review and change them. In this way, you know the legal documents will be acceptable to the venture capital firm. Whenever I have seen attorneys for small firms try to draw up these documents, the venture firm's counsel has usually been dissatisifed. To avoid the resulting delays, you are better off letting the venture firm's counsel draw up the documents. You do not have to agree to each term and condition set out in the legal documents. You can negotiate anything.

Section 4:   Representations

The approval was based on the following representations made by you and were inducements to the venture capital firm making this commitment. If any of these representations are not true, this commitment letter may be declared void by the venture capital firm. Do not sign a representation you cannot fulfill.

4.01   The company is a corporation in good standing in _____ (your state). You will provide the venture capital firm with a certificate of good standing, and a copy of the charter, the bylaws, and the organizing minutes of the company.

This is a standard certification that your company is in good standing and incorporated in a certain state. Your attorney can make sure that these representations are correct.

4.02   The company is primarily engaged in the business of _____ (type of business).

The venture capitalist seeks to define in legal terms what business you are in. It is a representation to him that you are not in some other business.

4.03   There are no lawsuits against the company, its directors, or its officers, nor do you know of any that may be contemplated. If there are any suits outstanding or contemplated, your attorney will provide the venture capital firm with a letter stating the nature of such suits and a copy of such suits at least thirty days prior to closing. You will provide the venture capital firm with a copy of all lawsuits you have filed against others.

You will have to certify to the venture capitalist that there are no lawsuits against your company. This is a moment of truth. If you do not inform the venture firm of any lawsuits that are outstanding, you are in effect certifying that there are none.

4.04   The company is current on all taxes owed; in this regard you will provide the venture capital firm with a copy of the last three years' tax returns plus a copy of the receipts for payment of the last four quarters for payroll taxes.

Here you are certifying that you have paid all payroll taxes or other taxes owed, including real estate taxes. If you owe any taxes, again, this is the time to let the venture capital firm know. Indicate in the commitment letter whether you owe taxes. In the instance above, you are certifying that there are no taxes outstanding.

4.05   You have presented financial information, business information, and a business proposal that you represent to be true and correct.

In this paragraph the venture firm is seeking to incorporate all the information that you have supplied to it under a representation that you believe this information to be correct. If you state in your resume that you received an M.B.A. from a renowned business school and you did not, then the commitment letter could be automatically voided by this misrepresentation. Is everything you stated to the venture capitalist true? Be sure it is before you sign this statement.

4.06   Your personal financial statement showed that you have a net worth of $500,000.

According to this paragraph, you presented information to the venture firm that your net worth was $500,000. If this representation is incorrect, then the commitment letter will be voided.

4.07   You will invest an additional $50,000 of cash in the company as equity on or before the closing on this loan on terms acceptable to the venture capital firm. You will provide the venture capital firm with written information on the terms of this investment.

Somewhere along the way you indicated to the venture capital firm that you intended to invest additional equity in the business, in this case, $50,000. The venture capital firm is documenting your representation.

4.08   A group of investors will invest $150,000 in the business as equity on terms acceptable to the venture capital firm. You will provide the venture capital firm with written information on these investments.

You have also represented to the venture capital firm that a group of investors would invest another $150,000 in equity in the business and the venture capital firm is documenting this representation.

4.09   The money borrowed will be used as follows:

1. Pay accounts payable, $100,000.
2. Pay bank debt, $300,000.
3. Provide working capital, $100,000.

You have represented to the venture capital firm how you intend to use the money. Later, if you do not pay $300,000 on the bank debt but pay off only $100,000, you will be in violation of a material representation and your loan may be defaulted. Be sure the representations you make with regard to use of proceeds are correct. Then follow through when you receive the money.

4.10   Upon closing of the investor's loan, you will have approximately the following assets:

1. Cash, $300,000.
2. Inventory, $700,000.
3. Accounts receivable, $1,000,000.
4. Machinery and equipment, $500,000.
5. Land and building, $300,000.
6. OTher assets, $20,000.

Here the venture capital firm is representing part of the after-financing balance sheet, that is, the assets your company will have after the financing occurs. Look at this representation to make sure it is accurate, because if it is not, your loan agreement could be in default.

4.11   With regard to all material leases, you will provide the venture capital firm with a copy of each lease.

In this section you are agreeing to provide the venture firm with a copy of all material leases pertaining to the company. If you have forgotten to tell the venture firm that you are leasing a large warehouse and you do not provide it with a copy of this material lease, the loan agreement could be in default.

4.12   You will pay no brokerage fees, legal fees, or other fees in connection with this loan without the venture capital firm's written approval; and, in addition, you will indemnify the venture capital firm against all such fees.

Many financial brokers who have not been involved in financing a venture later claim that they were the brokers in the financial transaction. In this paragraph you are representing to the venture firm that there are no brokers and you are indemnifying the venture capital firm against such fees.

4.13   During the past ten years none of the directors, officers, or management has been arrested or convicted of a material crime or a material matter.

You are representing to the venture firm that none of your officers are criminals.

> 4.14   The company has a commitment from a bank or other finan-
> cial institution to borrow $200,000 on terms acceptable to the ven-
> ture capital firm. With regard to this commitment, you will provide
> the venture capital firm with a copy of your commitment and closing
> documents.

You are representing that a bank is willing to lend the company $200,000. If the bank has said only that it was interested in making the loan, you may have difficulty living up to this representation, as you do not have a commitment letter. You should obtain a commitment letter from the bank for $200,000 before you sign this representation.

Section 5:   Conditions of Commitment

If the following conditions are not obtained, the venture capital firm's commitment will be void:

> 5.01   In connection with this financing, the venture capital firm will
> receive a 2 percent ($10,000) fee. Upon acceptance of this commit-
> ment letter, you will pay the venture capital firm $5,000 of the fee
> and the remainder at closing. Should closing not take place through
> the fault of the venture capital firm, then the fee in total would be
> returned. Otherwise the paid portion of the fee would be forfeited
> and the unpaid portion of the fee would be due and payable immedi-
> ately. Acceptance by you of this commitment letter and the return of
> one copy of this letter to the venture capital firm fully executed by
> you with the fee must be received before _____ (date).

It is customary in the venture business for the venture firm to receive a commitment fee. After all, the venture firm is committing to invest the money in your company. In the instance above, it is to receive a 2 percent fee. You may be able to negotiate a smaller fee. Note that the commitment above is open until a certain date. If you miss that date, then the commitment letter is void. Once you pay the fee and sign the letter, then the commitment is open until the date set out in 5.02, below.

> 5.02   Closing on the investment before _____ (date).

Closing on the investment means the day the legal papers are signed and the money is transferred from the venture capitalist to you. If you do not close by the date listed in this section, then the venture capital firm can keep your commitment fee and does not have to go through with the deal.

> 5.03   All legal documents must be acceptable to the venture capital
> firm.

The venture firm does not have to close unless all the legal documents are acceptable. Obviously, if your lawyer inserts provisions in the legal documents, whether or not they seem reasonable to you and your lawyer, they must be acceptable to the venture capital firm. If they are not, the venture capital firm will not have to go to closing.

> 5.04   A favorable credit check of you and your business and a favorable "due diligence" review of you, your business, and your industry must take place with no adverse occurrences before closing.

Venture firms will run a credit check on you and the business. If they do not like something in your credit file, such as an unpaid bill, they can renege on their commitment. Also, an adverse occurrence before the closing, such as a 15 percent drop in sales would allow the venture firm not to close on this loan. The due diligence report is prepared by the venture capitalist. Almost anything could make it unfavorable. All venture firms include these types of loopholes in their commitment letters.

> 5.05   A favorable visit to your business operation by the venture capitalist must take place.

This short sentence is probably the open-ended item in this section in that no one knows what a favorable visit to your business really is. If the venture capitalist wanted to get out of his commitment, he could make a visit and say that it was unfavorable for almost any reason. This would void his commitment to you. It will be hard to remove this due diligence visit clause. Every venture capitalist wants to see where he is investing his money.

> 5.06   The entire funds set forth in this commitment letter must be raised.

This section merely states that unless all the funds that are sought have been raised, then this commitment is void. If you are not willing to put in the $50,000 in equity, if the investors are unwilling to put in their $150,000, and if the bank is unwilling to lend you the $200,000, then any of these occurrences can void the commitment letter.

Comments on the Commitment Letter

The reason behind each of the above items seems self-evident. To the extent that you can remove some of these items from the commitment letter or keep them from being added to the legal documents, you will simplify the relationship between you and the venture capitalist. However, the venture capitalist's lawyer will make sure that whatever is in the commitment letter is in the legal documents, so remove troublesome items before you sign the letter. The above letter contains most of the reasonable items a venture firm should ask for. Most letters will contain only some part of the ones listed above. You should negotiate every point in the letter but do not quibble over details.

What Is An Investment Memorandum?

For some strange reason when a venture capital firm purchases stock in your new enterprise it does not call the commitment letter a commitment letter. The firm calls this letter an investment memorandum or a term sheet, even though it is in the form of a letter. An investment memorandum usually states all the terms and conditions of the stock purchase. Set out below are the five categories as they appear in an investment memorandum, for the purchase of stock. This is usually the approach of large venture capital companies and not Small Business Investment Companies.

Section 1: Term of the Investment

In this section the venture capital company will state exactly what it intends to do in purchasing the shares.

1.01   The venture capital firm will purchase 300,000 shares of common stock in the company at $3 per share.

1.02   All shares will be purchased at closing.

1.03   If any stock of the company is sold by the company for less than $3 per share at any time within five years from this sale, there shall be antidilution for the ownership of these 300,000 shares.

1.04   If the company has not had a public offering of its stock within five years from the closing date, then the venture capital firm will have a "put" provision whereby the venture capital firm can require the company to redeem the shares resulting from this purchase at the higher of the following:

1. Book value per share.

2. Earnings per share times 10.

3. $6 per share, fixed price.

1.05   Anytime after five years from closing the venture capital firm may require a registration and public offering of the shares owned by the venture capital firm at the company's expense.

1.06   The venture capital firm will have full "piggyback" rights to register shares any time the company or its management is registering shares for sale, and such registration of the venture capital firm's shares shall be paid for by your company.

Section 2: Collateral and Security

In this section of the investment memorandum the venture capital firm will set out what security or what preferences are given to its shares.

2.01   Should the company be liquidated, it is agreed that the shares being issued to the venture capital firm shall have priority in liquidation to the shares owned by anyone else. This means that any funds remaining after all creditors have been paid will be first paid to the venture capital firm to the extent of its investment of $900,000 and the remainder shall go to other stockholders who are assumed to be management until the cost of the shares is repaid. If any funds remain, they shall be divided pro rate.

2.02   You will have a life insurance policy on your life for the amount of $900,000 with the venture capital firm listed as the loss payee.

2.03   The company will have adequate hazard and business insurance. In this regard, you will supply the venture capital firm with a list of all business insurance, and such insurance and coverage shall be acceptable to the venture capital firm.

Section 3:   Conditions of the Investment

In this section the venture capital firm will set out the conditions under which it has made the investment and you must live up to these conditions even after the closing date.

As long as the venture capital firm owns any of the shares resulting from the purchase of shares at the closing, and as long as those shares are equal to 5 percent of the stock outstanding, then your company will comply with the following items:

3.01   Provide the venture capital firm with monthly, year-to-date, financial statements, in accordance with generally accepted accounting standards, within thirty days of the end of each calendar month.

3.02   Within ninety days after the year end, the company will provide the venture capital company with an annual certified audit from an independent certified public accounting firm acceptable to the venture capital firm.

3.03   Within ninety days of the year end, provide the venture capital firm with projections for the next fiscal year in the same format as the financial statements.

3.04   Within thirty days after they have been filed, provide the venture capital firm with a copy of all documents filed with government agencies, such as the Internal Revenue Service, Environmental Protection Agency, and Securities and Exchange Commission.

3.05   There will be no change in control of the company nor will there be any change in ownership of the company without the venture capital company's express written approval; and further, management will not sell, assign, or transfer any shares it owns in the company without the written approval of the venture capital firm.

3.06   The company will have a board of directors that does not exceed five persons. The venture capital firm will have the right to elect two members to the board of directors and you and your associates will vote all your shares to effect such election of two members to the board of directors.

3.07   The board of directors will meet at least once each month at the firm's business office. The venture capital firm's board members will be notified at least two weeks before each meeting and your company will pay the transportation expenses of the venture capital board members as well as customary fees.

3.08   The company will pay no cash dividends and the company will not sell or assign any assets of the business that are not part of the regular course of business without the venture capital firm's approval.

3.09   The management team, including you, will live in the metropolitan area where the business is located. The business will not be relocated without the express written permission of the venture capital firm.

3.10   The company will not pay any employee nor will it loan nor advance to any employee money that in total exceeds $50,000 per year without the written approval of the venture capital company.

3.11   You will pay all closing costs, and recording fees related to this financing, which include attorney fees of the venture capital firm.

Section 4:   Representations

The approval and commitment made by the venture capital firm was based on representations that were made by your company as listed below.

4.01   The company is a corporation in good standing in the State of _____ (state). You will provide the venture capital firm with a certificate of good standing and a copy of the charter and bylaws and organizational minutes of the company.

4.02   The company is primarily engaged in the business of _____ (type of business).

4.03   There are no lawsuits against the company, its directors, or its officers, nor do you know of any that may be contemplated.

4.04   The company is current on all taxes owed and in this regard you will provide the venture capital firm with a copy of the last three years' tax returns and the past four quarterly tax receipts for payroll taxes.

4.05   You have presented financial information, business information, and a business proposal, all of which you believe to be correct and true.

4.06   The money will be used as follows:

1. Research and development, $900,000.
2. Accounts payable, $100,000.

4.07   You will pay no brokerage fees, legal fees, or other fees in connection with this investment without the venture capital firm's prior written approval; and in addition you will indemnify the venture capital firm against all such fees.

4.08   During the past ten years none of the directors, officers, or managers has been arrested or convicted of material crimes of any manner whatsoever.

4.09   You have a commitment from a bank to borrow $100,000 on terms as presented in the bank commitment letter attached to Exhibit 4.09.

4.10   There are 300,000 shares of stock outstanding and no stock options.

Section 5:   Conditions of the Commitment

This investment commitment is conditioned on the following, which, if not obtained by you, will make the venture capital firm's commitment void.

5.01   In connection with this venture capital investment, the venture capital firm will receive a 1 percent, $9,000 fee. Upon acceptance of this investment memorandum, you will pay the venture capital company the $9,000 fee. Should closing not take place through the fault of the venture capital firm, then the fee in total will be returned. Otherwise, the fee will be forfeited. Acceptance by you of this investment memorandum and return of one copy of this investment memorandum fully executed by you with the fee must be received before _____ (date).

5.02   Closing on this investment must take place by _____ (date).

5.03   All legal documents must be acceptable to the investor.

5.04   A favorable credit check of you and your business and your management team with no material adverse occurrences before the closing date.

5.05   A favorable visit by the venture capital company to your business operation.

Consulting Agreement

As you can see the above investment memorandum is similar to the commitment letter; however, it is less cumbersome because it refers to stock, not debt. The investment memorandum may contain one other condition that is not listed above; that is, a consulting arrangement with the venture capitalist. The consulting arrangement usually reads something like this:

1.11   The company will enter into a consulting arrangement with the venture capital firm whereby the venture capital firm will provide consulting services to the business for $2,000 per month. This consulting agreement will be in effect for the first twelve months subsequent to closing on the investment.

Sometimes the venture capital company uses the consulting contract as a mechanism for becoming part of the mangement team and for improving its understanding of the business. Sometimes it wants to make sure that the invested funds will not be squandered by the management team. Often it is just another method for the venture capital company to take money out of the small business. It has been my own practice to avoid such consulting arrangements unless the venture capital firm has someone to provide actual services to the company.

Voting Trust

Another item that often appears in the commitment letter is the voting trust arrangement. That is, all the shares owned by the entrepreneurs (which, in essence, represent control of the company) are placed in a voting trust. The voting trust is controlled by the venture capital firm. Should things get out of hand, the venture capital firm can exercise its rights under the voting trust, vote the shares of the company, and elect a new board of directors favorably disposed to the venture capital firm. Then they can make any needed changes, including firing the management team. Many of the conditions set forth in a voting trust could trigger the venture capital company into wanting to operate your business. Some of the basic causes for concern are: (a) failure to meet all projections agreed upon; (b) losses greater than anticipated; and (c) key employees leaving the company. A typical voting trust clause is set out below:

> 1.12   All shares of the company will be placed in a voting trust. The trustee shall be an officer of a bank acceptable to both you and the venture capital firm. If the company's sales are less than $50,000 in any month, then the venture capital firm may name two additional trustees to the trust. A majority vote of the three trustees may vote the shares placed in the voting trust.

Voting trusts used to be common in the venture capital business but are now less common. Nonetheless, as an entrepreneur trying to raise venture capital, you should be prepared to deal with the voting trust arrangement should it arise.

Nonlegal Commitment Letter

You should remember that the commitment letter is not intended to be a legal document. Its main purpose is to convey in writing the business understanding between the venture capital firm and your company. If you ask a lawyer to go through the commitment letter and bring it up to snuff as a legal document, you will probably pay a great deal and not achieve the objective you are seeking. Good business judgment on your part is probably worth more than a lawyer's review of the commitment letter. Remember, you still have one more pass at this with your lawyer when the legal documents are drawn up. If one of the legal documents contains a paragraph that is supposed to expand and clarify a portion of the commitment letter, and you do not understand the clarification, you have the opportunity to walk away from the deal.

It is important that the commitment letter spell out the business deal, not the legal deal, between the two of you. If it does not clearly state the business deal, then you should revise it and make sure it states the business deal. Once a commitment letter is signed, it is usually given to the lawyers to use in drawing up the legal documents.

Arguing Over Minor Points

The commitment letter contains some definitive statements. It states some factual information and it has all the elements of the venture capitalist's deal with your company. If any of these major items are not what you have agreed to, then you should not sign the commitment letter. You need to renegotiate the business deal.

You should not spend a great deal of time arguing over minor points, word changes that are insignificant, commas, misspellings, and so on. The letter is not a legally binding letter that you will be able to use in court because it has too many loopholes for the venture capitalist to jump out of. The commitment letter is nothing more than a letter of understanding. It represents two business-men trying to put on paper what they believe they have agreed to in a meeting. Commitment letters can go through several iterations but only on major points. You should not revise the commitment letter for any minor points. Don't waste your time and your venture capital partner's time. Minor points can be ironed out in the legal documents.

Items You Should Not Sign in the Commitment Letter

If the commitment letter contains any items that you believe are not true or you do not wish to enter into with the venture capital firm, then don't sign the letter. The commitment letter is not written in a foreign language. It is written in English, and if it does not say what you expected it to say, then you should not sign it.

You should also review the commitment letter for what it doesn't say. If you and the venture capitalist reached an agreement on certain points and they are not covered in the commitment letter, then you should ask to have them inserted. Once you sign the commitment letter, that is the business deal. If you receive legal documents that don't contain items that you thought should be in it, and that weren't in the commitment letter, you shouldn't be surprised. I remember signing a commitment letter with an entrepreneur who was part of a large syndication. The letter specifically said in one of its paragraphs that we would invest a certain amount of money. The company actually needed three times as much as we were willing to invest. The commitment letter nowhere specified who would raise the additional funds. It did indicate that all the funds had to be raised before our commitment would be valid. For some strange reason, the entrepreneur assumed that we would be raising the money for him, even though there was no agreement on the part of our company to do so.

Objective

As can be seen from the investment memorandum and the commitment letter, the venture capital company can void its commitment to you in a number of ways. Some of the basic items listed are due diligence, credit check, and favorable visit. This means that the venture firm has not completed all of its investigations of you, your business, and your industry. Five items could cost you your commitment: (1) a visit to your business to meet the people and to understand the business; (2) detailed checks of the background of you and your management team; (3) credit analysis of the business; (4) a study of the industry; and (5) change of heart by the venture capital firm.

Needless to say, the commitment is not a commitment at all. The venture capitalist can simply say he does not believe the business will make it, renege on his commitment, and return your commitment fee. This option is always open and you should be aware that you do not have a commitment until you have the money in hand. Most venture capital firms are reputable and will honor their commitments. If they want to get out of a commitment, it is very easy for them to do it. Your objective is to get the commitment letter. Afterwards, you should continue to push for closing. When you have the money in your hand, you know the venture capitalist has made a real commitment.

7

Due Diligence

What Does the Venture Capitalist Want When He Visits?
What To Expect from Investigations of Your Proposal.

When you and the venture capitalist have reached an understanding on the terms and conditions of the investment, the venture capitalist must begin what is known in his world as "due diligence." He may carry out some of his due diligence before reaching an agreement with you on the terms of his investment. Some venture capitalists will not issue a commitment letter until all of their due diligence is completed. Due diligence simply means that the investor must conduct background checks on the management team, complete an industry study, and verify the representations in your business proposal. In essence, his review of you, your management, your company, and the industry is a more detailed study of your business proposal. The venture capitalist will try to find misrepresentations in your proposal or other reasons not to invest in your business. He will attempt to determine the potential of your company to make money. Even though some venture capitalists will conduct their due diligence before they make a formal written commitment, you should know the kind of deal to expect from them before they perform their investigations and analysis of your business.

What to Expect From a Visit to Your Business

One important step in the due diligence process is a visit to your business. Most venture capitalists will fly into your city and will need transportation from the airport to your plant or business. Although not necessary, it is a friendly gesture to pick up the venture capitalist at the airport or to have someone from your company pick him up. Furthermore, the drive to your office will give you some extra time to become familiar with each other on a personal basis. During the drive you will have an opportunity to exchange some pleasantries and take the edge off a new relationship. It is a good time for the venture capitalist to ask some of his personal questions: "How many children do you have? What do you do for relaxation? What recreational activities do you like?" He may ask some political questions. These give him a better understanding of the person he is dealing with. The trip will also give you a little time to better understand the venture capitalist and make him feel at home. Remember, you are still trying to sell him the idea that this is a great deal for his venture capital company.

How to Give a Good Cook's Tour

The starting point in a visit is normally a Cook's tour. This means a tour of the entire operation with introductions along the way to key people in the company. During such a tour, the venture capitalist tries to see as much of the business and as many people as possible. He may stop along the way and ask questions of people who are working. Once, while walking through a plant with several venture capitalists, a friend of mine tarried behind the group. He asked a lady who was running a drill press what she was making. Her answer was, "Oh, I'm not making anything. They just hired me for the day and told me to look busy." It seems the entrepreneur wanted the plant to look busy so he hired a few extra people for one day and told them to pretend they were busy employees. Needless to say, the venture capitalist did not make that investment. Such deception is unacceptable.

A tour of the business will usually take twenty minutes for a small operation and one hour or more for a larger company. During the walk-through the venture capitalist will try to understand the daily operations of the business. He will try to understand the type of people needed to make the business successful. He will absorb as much visual information about the business as possible. During the tour, the venture capitalist may ask some seemingly stupid questions that have nothing to do with the real world of your business. They will reflect his ignorance of your business. Please forgive him; it is the only way he can learn.

During the tour, you should be the tour leader and explain the various aspects of the operation as you walk through the plant and offices. Introduce the people along the way and describe the role they play in the organization. Leave time for the venture capitalist to ask questions of each person. As you both walk through, explain the layout of the business. Help the venture capitalist visualize sections such as accounting, purchasing, and manufacturing of the first and second product. Show the venture capitalist the manufacturing process. Begin with the raw materials entering the factory; follow them as they progress through the manufacturing process and end up in shipping. It is your responsibility as the tour director to make sure the venture capitalist understands how your business operates. You may want to practice the tour once before the venture capitalist arrives.

You might think a venture capitalist who has seen many plants would not need a tour of another facility. As it turns out, every plant is different. Often a tour will reveal some interesting details about the entrepreneur. Venture capitalists have one generalization about plants. A clean operation indicates the desire to have a well-run company. The way the physical operation is run, the way the facilities are laid out, and the cleanliness of the place are a direct reflection of how the entrepreneur operates the business.

Another reason for the visit is to see the entrepreneur in his environment. It is interesting to observe how he works with his people, and to see what type of surroundings he feels comfortable in. Most venture capitalists become disturbed if they discover plush surroundings and a go-go environment. After all, why is the company using so much capital for the physical comforts of the entrepreneur? Why does it need more money? Perhaps to complete an indoor swimming pool and sauna for the management?

If your proposal is for a start-up venture, obviously the plant or retail operation does not exist. There is no opportunity for a tour. Usually the entrepreneur has rented office space with some of his team around him. Some venture capitalists will nonetheless make a trip to see this initial operation in order to observe the people on their turf. Such a visit helps the venture capitalist understand the team and how they interact. If the proposed plant site or retail location is nearby, the venture capitalist will want to drive by the site. Pictures of the site can sometimes substitute for a visit, especially in start-up situations for a retail location.

Additional Questions About the Proposal

After the tour of the operations, usually two to four hours of discussion takes place. This may include lunch or it may be one long session. Typically, the venture capitalist will have begun his due diligence and as a result will have further questions about the industry, about the product, or other critical areas of the business. The venture capitalist may delve into every aspect of your business in order to test you. Again, you must know your industry and your product in detail and be able to answer questions without hesitation. If you do not know the answer, write down the question and deliver an answer to the venture capitalist as soon as possible. Also, your financial projections will raise numerous questions; be prepared to answer them.

Sometimes a venture capitalist will be confused about one item in the business proposal. It may take him an inordinate amount of time to understand the concept. Be patient. He is trying to understand something taken for granted by people in the industry. The venture capitalist is also likely to ask the same question twice. This may be due to his own ignorance, or it may be that he did not like the way you answered the question the first time. He wants to hear how you answer it the second time. Then, again, the venture capitalist may ask the same questions twice as a test of consistency. That is, he may want to see if the entrepreneur will answer it the same way twice. If the entrepreneur fails, the venture capitalist may think he does not know what he is talking about or worse, that he is lying and cannot remember his lies.

Additional Questions About the Business

The venture capitalist will ask you all the questions you have not answered in your business proposal. You should expect the type of questions that were set out in Chapter 4. After the operations tour some venture capitalists sit down with the entrepreneur and methodically run through a list of questions that they use in every investigation. These may be questions that were not asked during the meeting in the venture capitalist's office. During the visit to the entrepreneur, the venture capitalist will want to spend time with the person in charge of marketing and will ask him about the industry, the competition, and the marketplace. The venture capitalist will also want to meet the person who is in charge of production and will ask him questions about production, inventory control, labor, and management. The venture capitalist will spend even more time with the person who is in charge of finance, and will ask him about the banks and other places he has obtained financing. The venture capitalist will ask him about financial ratios for the business and will compare them with others in the industry. The cash flow of the business will be of keen interest.

Finally, if the deal has not been completely negotiated, the venture capitalist will set aside some time to discuss the final aspects of the deal. He may take out the commitment letter and go through it point by point to make sure all parties have the same understanding. If the venture capitalist thinks the risks are higher than he perceived before he conducted his due diligence, or if the potential return is viewed as lower, the venture capitalist will open the negotiations by saying he needs additional equity, a higher interest rate, additional collateral, or some portion of the three. You should listen to the venture capitalist's concerns and attempt to reduce the risk he perceives. If you cannot reduce the risk, you will have to negotiate your deal again. Negotiations may take a short time or may be left unresolved. If possible it is better to settle the negotiations at this sitting; this will make it more difficult for the venture capitalist to open the negotiations again.

Additional Questions About Management

During your first meeting with the venture capitalist in his office and later during this visit to your business, the venture capitalist will be trying to answer the question, "What makes you tick?" He wants to know what motivates you— in other words, what is the driving force in your life. He wants to know why you, of all people, think you can make a venture successful. You should remember that during any meetings between you and the venture capitalist, the venture capitalist will be looking for the seven items discussed in Chapter 5. They are honesty, achievement, energy, intelligence, knowledge, leadership, and creativity. Before every meeting with the venture capitalist, you should review these seven items again so that you can present yourself in the best light.

The venture capitalist will ask you some personal questions. They will usually not be as direct as his business questions. They will usually come during a more relaxed part of the meeting. He may ask you where you grew up, what your background is, what sports activities you have been involved in, what hobbies you like, when you were married, how many children you have, and the ages of your children. Basically, the venture capitalist is trying to understand your personal environment. He wants to determine if your private life is strong enough to withstand the time and energy you will have to put into this new business. Being an entrepreneur will put a great deal of pressure on you at work and at home. If you have a spouse and family, your business will take up much of your time and leave only a little for your family. The venture capitalist will want to know if your personal life can withstand the pressures of your entrepreneurial activities.

Also, when he looks at your personal life, the venture capitalist will be looking for stability and maturity. He will be trying to determine if you are a person who has reached the point in your life that allows you to cope with the difficulties of running a growing small business. An unsettled personal life will detract from your ability to operate the small business that is being financed by the venture capitalist. Personal problems will not allow you to give the business all your time and attention. Your energies and emotions will be reduced by your personal situation.

One situation I am familiar with concerned an entrepreneur with tremendous personal problems. For five years the entrepreneur had diligently worked to build his company and neglected his home life. One cold January day the entrepreneur's wife left him and his two small children. She boarded an airplane with her boyfriend and left the entrepreneur forever. The separation destroyed the entrepreneur. Suddenly he was faced with taking care of two small children as well as trying to run his business. He needed to overcome his emotional reaction to his wife's departure but could not. After six months, a crisis developed in his business. The number two man in the business was not strong enough to step into the number one position. The business was on a disaster course. The venture capitalist moved in and tried to save the business. The only alternative was to sell the company. Now you can understand why the venture capitalist is concerned about the personal life of the entrepreneur. A stable personal life is a crucial element in the equation.

Investigating the Individuals

Before or after the visit, the venture capitalist will investigate the backgrounds of the individuals. This will be a never-ending process for the venture capitalist. He will continue to follow leads that might give him additional information about his entrepreneurial team.

The venture capitalist often feels like an FBI agent when he looks into people's backgrounds. In checking out the background of an entrepreneur, he first requests a personal credit check on the entrepreneur and on each member of the management team. Credit checks often give the potential investor leads to follow. The venture capitalist looks for bills unpaid, which can indicate an entrepreneur who is a deadbeat or who is living beyond his means. Also, unpaid debts indicate how the entrepreneur is likely to treat the venture capitalist after the investment in his business takes effect. If he does not pay his personal bills, why should one believe he will pay the venture capitalist?

The second method of checking the background of an individual is to call business and personal references. Of course, entrepreneurs always give references that will say favorable things about them. The venture capitalist usually asks business references if they know someone else who knows the entrepreneur. This question enables the venture capitalist to develop secondary references. Then he can call the secondary references and ask additional questions.

Venture Capitalists Are Paranoid

While the venture capitalist looks for achievements and a record of hard work in the entrepreneur's background, he is developing a picture of the entrepreneur's reputation. Venture capitalists are suspicious by nature. They start each relationship believing the entrepreneur is trying to cheat them. As a result, their constant concern is to determine whether the entrepreneur is honest. You should appreciate the predicament of a venture capitalist. Anyone who has money to invest is bombarded with proposals from crooks. Normally it is difficult to fool the venture capitalist and swindle him of his money, but it happens from time to time.

There is the story of a group of venture capitalists who invested a million dollars in a new business started by an entrepreneur with impeccable credentials. In their background check the venture capitalists found that the entrepreneur was born and raised in a small midwestern town, had attended a distinguished midwestern university, and had worked for several conglomerates on the west coast. In both his university and business environment he had served with distinction. No sooner had the venture capitalists invested their money than the entrepreneur disappeared, leaving a trail indicating he was in a South American country. After contacting the FBI about the possible fraud, the venture capitalists found that the entrepreneur was a crook. He had previously testified for the U.S. government in the criminal prosecution of underworld figures. He had been given a new identity under the witness protection program. Needless to say, the venture capitalists were extremely upset with the U.S. government.

In revealing information to a venture capitalist, you must tell him of any problems in your background. If you do not, and the problems are uncovered during the background check, your deal will most likely be killed. The venture capitalist will perceive your omission as an attempt to deceive him. Your reputation will be shattered. Venture capitalists do not like to run into surprises when they check your background. They like continuity.

Another story tells of the venture capitalist who was investigating a promising entrepreneur. The venture capitalist was sure he wanted to invest in the business. The venture capitalist could not find anything derogatory in the entrepreneur's credit record and many of his references praised his business acumen. A secondary source happened to mention that he thought the entrepreneur had encountered severe difficulties ten or fifteen years ago, and had actually served time in prison. When the venture capitalist asked the credit-checking service to go back further in time and search specific criminal records the agency found that the entrepreneur had spent three years in prison. The fact that this important item in his past was never revealed to the venture capitalist killed the deal, even though the entrepreneur may have been a good investment risk since he had paid his debt to society.

The venture capitalist's analysis usually starts with an individual's early life and follows in detail, both where he has lived and where he has worked since college, or at least for the last ten years. Most investigations follow a chronological order. This kind of continuity check gives the venture capitalist an idea of what type of person he is dealing with. Does the entrepreneur hop around from job to job, moving frequently, or is he a solid citizen with an outstanding record in his business?

The venture capitalist usually takes the entrepreneur's resume and verifies where the entrepreneur was and what he was doing each year. The venture capitalist will often check on a military record. Was the individual honorably discharged? Was he really a second lieutenant, or a corporal? Invariably, the venture capitalist will call the school mentioned in a resume to verify that the entrepreneur received the degrees that he claims to have received. More than one venture capitalist has found an entrepreneur lying about his detail. All of these checks are necessary in order to confirm that what you see as a talented entrepreneur is what you'll get.

Other Aspects of the Background Check

There is a saying in the venture capital business: "You can predict an individual's future by what he has done in the past." This is particularly true of successful entrepreneurs. Success seems to breed success, and conversely, failure breeds failure. It is hard for an entrepreneur to come out of a slump once he is in it.

What the venture capitalist is looking for in an individual's past is his achievement level. What has he achieved in the past? Most venture capitalists believe there is a high correlation between achieving personalities and success in entrepreneurial endeavors. So if the venture capitalists finds many achievements in your background, he will be happy.

Of course, every venture capitalist is looking for an honest individual. He will ask references point blank if the entrepreneur is honest, if he is trustworthy, if he is hard working, if he has bad habits, would cheat under pressure, and in a general way, is a person somebody should trust. Although many people will not answer these questions, most will give some indication of how they feel about the individual. After a venture capitalist has talked to half a dozen people about an entrepreneur, he will begin to get an idea of the entrepreneur's honesty and the personality traits that make up his basic character.

Do They Have a Test for Entrepreneurs?

Most venture capitalists do not use personality tests on entrepreneurs. Most believe they can learn as much as they need to about the entrepreneur's personality by using conventional question-and-answer methods. Giving an entrepreneur a psychological test seems to be an invasion of his privacy. Further, most venture capitalists do not believe that any reliable tests for entrepreneurship exist today. The reason there are no such tests is simple. Entrepreneurship spans all industries. At the same time, various industries may require different personality types. For example, in a white-collar, highly technical environment, management by objective (MBO) may work best. MBO works well among highly motivated people who need to achieve goals.

In an industry where the entrepreneur must deal with some rough-and-tumble employees, management by intimidation (MBI) might work best. Unless the entrepreneur has an aggressive personality and is willing to scream and yell, he may not get his point across. Giving a businessman a test to determine if he is an entrepreneur would not indicate if he could succeed in both businesses. The management style required is different and no one test on entrepreneurship would be applicable to these two different businesses.

A few large credit companies use handwriting analysis (graphology) to determine whether an individual is credit worthy. Perhaps a graphology test could be used by venture capitalists to determine if an individual is a good credit risk and if he has an achieving personality. Most venture capitalists are skeptical about such a possibility. There is a rumor among venture capitalists that one firm is using a graphology test. It seems hard to believe, but given the difficulty of the problem it is not surprising to see any technique tried at least once. Palm reading and physiognomy tests are probably used by someone, somewhere, in the business community, but I do not know of any. A pretty hand or face are not part of the investment criteria used by venture capitalists.

A battery of tests on the market today are used to determine an individual's honesty. Many employers give these tests to employee applicants. These tests are prevalent in the retail business. Venture capitalists do not use these tests yet. It is doubtful that they would work on intelligent entrepreneurs because such tests are easy to foil. Perhaps the test would help the venture capitalist weed out some of the stupid individuals seeking money.

Experience Is the Watchword

When a venture capitalist looks at an individual's background, he tries to determine how much experience the entrepreneur has had in the chosen industry. People who profess a general management ability in operating any business have yet to prove themselves to the venture capitalist as operators of small business. Being a general manager in the small business environment seems to be a contradiction of terms. It may be true that the president of one large company can be just as effective as the new president of another large company. Managing a bureaucracy in one large company is probably similar to managing a bureaucracy in another company. However, the rubber meets the road in small business entrepreneurship, where it is difficult for a general manager to survive at all. An entrepreneur must have in-depth knowledge of the business in order to play the game according to the rules of each industry. An entrepreneur entering the construction business, for example, would probably be eaten alive by subcontractors unless he had experience with them. Similarly, an entrepreneur with experience in the construction business who entered a manufacturing environment, would probably be slain by his white-collar workers and his accounts receivable.

It is true that a smart individual can become adept at handling practically any industry, but it will usually take a year or two. It takes time to become proficient in operating a small business because there is no layer of middle managers between the president and daily problems. The president is on the firing line every day. If a business can survive during the time it takes the new entrepreneur to learn, the business may become a profitable enterprise for the entrepreneur. However, the venture capital investor must realize that he will have to wait an additional year or two for his investment to gain momentum. The venture capitalist must wait while the entrepreneur learns the ins and outs of the industry and the business itself.

When it comes to due diligence by the venture capital company, the entrepreneur should know that most venture capitalists will be quite thorough in investigating his background. To lie about your experience or to distort it in a manner that would fool the venture capitalist on paper will only be your undoing when the venture capitalist begins his background check. The venture capitalist will use a lot of energy to determine how strong your credentials are for operating the intended small business. So if you worked in the marketing department of a company but did not run the place, do not say in your resume that you ran the company's marketing department.

Investigating the Entrepreneur and His Team

When investigating the experience of the entrepreneur and his management team, the venture capitalist generally starts with the references. The questions most venture capitalists ask references are the standard ones about achievements, competence, character, commitment, honesty, and so on. You may be surprised to hear that some other questions are asked of your references. One will be, "Does he have a problem with drugs?" This has become an important question for new entrepreneurs as drugs can diminish one's ability. A long-standing question asked by venture capitalists continues to remain on the list: "Does the entrepreneur have a drinking problem?" Many venture capitalists reviewing the poor performance of a small business have looked behind those problems and found an alcoholic. A company that has gone up and down over the years will often place so much strain on an individual that he will resort to drugs or alcohol as a temporary treatment for the problem. People with an alcohol problem are not successful entrepreneurs.

Other questions asked by venture capitalists are: "Does the entrepreneur like a high style of living? Does he run around like a playboy?" This is often a problem in sales-oriented companies where the entrepreneur-salesman is on the road a great deal. If you act like a "big shot," you may impress your friends but not the venture capitalist. In order to determine whether the entrepreneur is living "high on the hog," the venture capitalist will often drive by his house, note what kind of car he is driving, and ask for a copy of his personal tax return. Some entrepreneurs think this kind of investigation is an invasion of privacy, but if the venture capitalist intends to risk his money on an individual, he wants to know who the individual is, what his lifestyle is, and what problems he has.

Questions for Other People in the Organization

The venture capitalist may go one step below the management team and talk with other people in the organization. A specific individual the venture capitalist wants to talk to, if he is not part of the management team, is the marketing manager, to understand how he perceives the marketplace. The venture capitalist also wants to find out how the production man views producing the product and what problems he thinks he will have. Of course, the venture capitalist always spends a great deal of time with the finance man in order to understand the numbers that have been presented. As part of his procedure, one venture capitalist spends at least several days with the management team and lower people in the organization. After hearing the bright picture painted by the management team, he is often quite surprised to hear the controller's remarks about the financial status of the company. He may be rudely awakened when the production boss says the item in question cannot be produced easily. More than once marketing people have told him the products in question are difficult to sell. Lower echelon people should be as convinced as the entrepreneur that the company is a great opportunity. If they have not been convinced, it probably will be difficult to convince an investor like the venture capitalist.

In addition to these inside people, the venture capitalist tries to talk to each director of the company to find out what their involvement may be in the company. He will want to know how they came to be on the board of directors. Also, the venture capitalist wants their views of the company. The venture capitalist will talk to principal stockholders. Now and then a stockholder of 10 or 20 percent of the company is not a director or part of management. The venture capitalist will want to know why he owns such a large percentage of the company, what he paid for it, why he thinks it's a good investment, how he got involved, and so on.

Every venture capital firm is hungry for information about the people who will make the company grow. The more information you can give the venture capitalist about your team, the happier he will be.

Investigating the Business, the Product, and the Industry

While the venture capitalist is investigating the entrepreneur and the team, he will also be investigating the product, the business, and the industry. To do so, he will call many users or potential users of the product. He will ask them many of the questions that a marketing survey would include: "Why do you like the product? Is it too expensive? Is it a major purchase for you? How could the product be improved? Are you satisfied with it?" One other question he will usually ask a user is, "Do you intend to purchase additional products or services from the business?" If the answer is yes, he tries to determine the dollar volume of their purchase. This helps him understand the backlog. He will normally call many of the people listed on the backlog in order to verify that they do have an order for the amount specified in the backlog report. He will usually ask those people on the backlog list why they ordered a product from the company and what they like about it.

On the other end of the scale, the venture capitalist almost always calls suppliers in order to determine how promptly they have been paid, what they like about the company, and how they are treated as suppliers. Suppliers can be a tremendous source of capital for a small business since they can extend credit. For this reason alone, you should have good relations with suppliers. The venture capitalist will conduct his discussions with suppliers in order to determine what kind of business you operate. If you do not pay the supplier on time, the venture capitalist will assume you will not pay him on time.

Industry Study

A study of the industry is often difficult to undertake, especially if it is a new and dynamic industry. Credit reports of companies in the industry may not give a clear picture of what to expect. Industry studies by "think tanks" or large sophisticated research firms may not yield a great deal of information, either. If the industry is new, the estimates may be based on hunches or on inadequate data. If the industry is further along in its development, some companies in the industry will be public, and the reported information on public companies will help the venture capitalist understand the industry. Sometimes a competitor's financial statements can be obtained through normal credit reference services. They can give an added dimension to the industry. All of these sources give the venture capitalist insight into the potential for your business. You may have covered some of this same ground when you studied the industry. You can help the venture capitalist in his survey by providing him with details you have already uncovered.

After becoming acquainted with the industry, the venture capitalist usually tries to relate the industry study to the projections made by the entrepreneur. How do the projections compare with the growth of other public companies in the industry? How do the ratios in the projections compare with published ratios for companies in the same industry or those in similar industries? These are important questions. The entrepreneur should not merely pick some ratios out of the air that he thinks are attainable. A common mistake of entrepreneurs is to assume gross profit ratios or other ratios will hold up, when in fact, the industry does not function in that manner at all.

Uniqueness of the Product

The venture capitalist will investigate the uniqueness you describe in your business proposal. He will attack the problem from various perspectives. Often an idea may seem unique to the venture capitalist but it will be old hat to people in the industry. It does not take long, however, for a venture capitalist to determine whether the entrepreneur has a unique approach to a problem or if it is just a variation on a theme. When the venture capitalist talks to people in trade associations and experts in the field, he will soon uncover the uniqueness of a product or service. The Standard Industrial Classification of investments made by venture capitalists can be consulted for the names of venture capital firms that have direct experience in the industry. These firms can give your venture capitalist a sophisticated appraisal of the uniqueness and the projections presented in your business proposal. If necessary, the venture firm will hire an expert to review your patents or other out-of-the-ordinary ideas. Many firms have an advisory council to which they refer all unusual technological ideas.

Trying to give the venture firm a "snow job" on your product will waste everyone's time, especially yours. It will also tarnish your image in the close-knit venture capital community. I remember an entrepreneur who made his product sound unique. After a few hours of investigation, we determined that most of the components, and indeed, the product itself could be purchased from a local retail electronics store. The store had been selling the product for the last three years. Needless to say, I no longer trusted this entrepreneur. He had spent no time researching the product. He thought he had "invented" it and so concluded that it was unique.

Another entrepreneur had a product that seemed unusual by every measure that one might use. However, when the venture capitalist began to talk to users of the product, they did not mention specifically the product's special traits touted by the entrepreneur. When the venture capitalist asked about the extraordinary aspects of the product, customers informed him that those particular aspects had no bearing on their choice. They liked the product simply because "it worked" and because "it was delivered on time." The unique aspect did not influence their purchase of the product. The users informed the venture capitalist that many products on the market could do the job without the special feature of this product. In essence, the entrepreneur was touting a uniqueness that did not make any difference to his customers. Venture capitalists find it disconcerting to uncover this type of information on their own, especially when the entrepreneur has told them how important the unusual feature of his product is to each sale.

Many entrepreneurs think that a patent on a product "proves" its uniqueness. A patent may prove uniqueness, but the worth of the product and the extraordinary features must be demonstrated conclusively. Having a patent does not make a product worth something. There are millions of worthless patents.

A patent is not conclusive evidence of uniqueness. Patents have been overturned and patents can be granted on grounds that can be disproved in later years. A patent may preclude a competitor from manufacturing an identical product, but a competitor can change minor details and bypass the patent protection. If a patent exists, the venture capitalist will usually talk to the patent counsel to determine how strong the patent is and how wide it reaches, and to hear the patent attorney's justification of the uniqueness of the product.

Questions for Business References

The venture capitalist will want to speak with many business references, not only users and suppliers, but banks, accountants, lawyers, and various other people who know the business and the reputation of the management team. The venture capitalist will call a number of the outsiders that you have mentioned during your discussions with him and those on the list you have provided. He will ask each of these outsiders a number of questions, and you should be aware of what he is seeking from these various sources. You may wish to forewarn some of them that the following questions will be asked.

Suppliers

You will probably have given the venture capitalist a list of suppliers. He will call many of these suppliers, especially the largest and most critical ones, to ask them some simple questions such as, "Does the company pay on time? Have you had any problems with payments? Will you continue to supply him? What credit limit do you have for the company? Have you ever shipped supplies COD?" Any company that is being shipped supplies COD is a company that the supplier does not trust. If the supplier is short of goods, he will cut off the COD orders and ship only to his best customers. If the supplier's product is a critical item, the venture capitalist will want to know that the supplier has financial strength and a capacity large enough to provide the items needed. At one time the toy business did not have enough computer chips to satisfy the demand for electronic games. Therefore, slow-paying manufacturers of electronic games usually had to wait an inordinate amount of time in order to receive the chips they needed for their games.

Customers

If you have industrial customers or are selling to retail outlets, the venture capitalist will call the largest of these, and perhaps a number of the smaller customers, to determine your reputation. He will want to know if the customers have been shipped poor products and what happened when the customer received faulty items. He will want to know if the customers will continue to buy the product. Is the customer satisfied with the price? How many units can the customer use or sell? What is the current outstanding order that the customer has with the business? This last question will be used to check on the backlog that you have reported to the venture capital firm. The venture capital company may call many of the customers listed on the backlog to verify that the backlog is correct. The venture capitalist will also ask the customer who else he buys from; that is, who the competition is. The venture capitalist will try to understand who these competitors are and how they are regarded by the customer.

Competition

Many venture capitalists investigate the competition's product and even talk to salesmen representing the competition. They may pretend to be a customer looking at various products. The venture capitalist might indicate that he is buying your company's product as opposed to the competition's product in order to hear how the salesman sells his product against yours. Sometimes the venture capitalist may know someone who works for the competition. He will be able to obtain additional information about the competition and how they view your product.

Stock Market Analysts

Stock market analysts often follow a particular industry. Many of the companies they follow will be the competition for your business. The venture capitalist will contact several of these analysts to discuss the industry and the competition in order to determine what the market is like. The stock market analyst may also be the person who will help the venture capitalist and you with a public offering of shares somewhere down the road.

Associations

Every industry has an association, and lists of these associations are compiled by several publishers. Every public library has a business section containing an updated publication on associations. The venture capitalist will locate your association and discuss the industry, the competition, and the market with the association executives. The association may not be knowledgeable about the market and may suggest another individual that it uses for market analysis; the venture firm will probably contact him. Most associations will have data on the market, its size, and its growth rate. The venture capitalist will obtain this information in order to back up statements you have made in your business proposal.

Government Sources

The U.S. government publishes billions of words about business. It has conducted study after study of various segments of our society. Some of these studies are filled with useful information. Venture capitalists generally know where to uncover such sources of industry information in the government. You should be aware that they will contact the Commerce Department and the Bureau of Business and Labor Statistics seeking information on your industry.

Accountants

Many venture capital companies will not contact your accountant. Those who do contact your accountant will ask only minor questions about accounting principles. Other venture capitalists have learned the importance of verifying the accuracy of the audit they received. I was once involved in a case in which the entrepreneur had used the letterhead of an accounting firm to construct his own audit, complete with the accountant's unqualified opinion. The original audit had shown him losing $450,000, but after the entrepreneur redid the audit, it showed him making $250,000 in profit. Only a telephone call to the accountant to verify the numbers unraveled the scheme. The entrepreneur was sent to jail for this fraud.

Accounting firms often issue management letters, which the venture capital firm will want to read because they are critical of your operation. Some venture capital firms will hire an accounting firm to complete a "businessman's audit" of your company. This means the accountants will come into your operation and go through the books and records in order to determine if they are being accurately kept. Some venture firms ask accountants to review projections in order to determine if they are reasonable.

Lawyers

The venture firm will contact your lawyer, primarily to find out whether any lawsuits are outstanding and to ask if any suits are pending. The venture firm will ask if the entrepreneur has discussed any suits with the lawyer. All venture capitalists are lawsuit shy and will not invest in any company that has a long history of litigation or that shows signs of many possible suits in the future.

A venture capitalist will contact your patent counsel if you represent that your unique product has a patent. The basic questions for the patent attorney are, "On what basis was the patent applied for or granted? What makes this product so unusual?"

Bankers

The venture capitalist will discuss your general business with your banker. He will verify that you have a credit line, and he will want to know if you have made payments on your prior bank loans on time. If you have switched banks in recent years, he may call your prior banker to ask if any problems arose in the prior relationship.

Consultants

Some venture firms will hire experts or consultants to review specific parts of your business. You should welcome these free experts since they will be studying a situation that you intend to build a business upon. Sometimes you may hire a consultant to do a study, in order to prove or disprove that a product will work, or that a market exists. You should expect the venture capitalist to contact your consultant and discuss the report he has rendered.

Insurance Agent

If your company deals with a hazardous product, your venture partner will want to know if the product liability insurance covers all the aspects of the business. The venture capitalist will also want to know if the company carries liability insurance for directors. This will be important to him if he intends to be on the board of directors.

Union

If the work force is unionized, the venture capitalist will want to see a copy of the union contract and he may wish to contact the union leader. He will question the union leader as to the relationship between the union and the company, and more particularly, the relationship between you and the union leadership. If the venture capitalist finds an intransigent union that will surely make enormous demands the next time the contract comes up, he may not invest.

Appraiser of the Property and Equipment

If you give the venture capitalist an appraisal of property and equipment he will talk with the appraiser to determine how competent the appraiser is and to ask questions about the appraisal. Sometimes the venture capitalist will hire his own appraiser for property and equipment, especially where he is to be collateralized by these assets.

Manufacturers of Machinery

A manufacturer of machinery is in some respects a supplier, but a very special one. Often the machinery is used for a special purpose and is built to the customer's design. The venture capitalist will want to know if the machinery will work, and he will try to determine this by speaking directly to the manufacturers of the machinery.

Other References on the Business

Any references you give the venture capitalist will probably be contacted. Any other names that he may come up with that relate to a special part of your business will be approached to determine how critical they are to the success of the business.

When the Venture Firm Finds Something Wrong

You can be sure that the venture capital firm will find something wrong with your proposal or will uncover something during its due diligence work that will be worrisome. There is no such thing as a perfect proposal. You should not be overly alarmed by this prospect. In the venture capital business it is an accepted axiom that no deal is perfect, and that every deal has something wrong with it. You should try to minimize the effect of this negative item. Make sure the venture capital firm understands that the problem is not critical, and that the business can go forward and make money. Some negative features are the result of a lack of knowledge about a certain subject. To satisfy the venture firm, you may conduct an intensive research effort in order to obtain additional information that will remove the item from the critical list for the venture firm. You can be sure that the venture firm will find something wrong. Do your best to minimize it for them as well as for yourself. After all, if the venture capitalist is concerned, you should be concerned, too.

You may have already listed the primary risk in your business proposal. The venture capitalist will be concerned about the risk. He will ask you to explain why you are willing to take such a risk. If the risks listed in your business plan are the only concerns of the venture capitalist, you are 90 percent of the way to a deal with the venture capitalist.

Questions for the Venture Capitalist

While the venture capital company is conducting its due diligence on you and your industry, you must conduct your due diligence on the venture capital company. Chapter 1 covered the first five questions you should ask a venture capital firm, but it is worth mentioning them again at this point.

Question One on Money to Invest

Do you have money to invest? Obviously, this question must be answered in the affirmative or you should not be spending any time with this venture firm. If the venture capital company does not have funds, you should ask for the name of a venture capital company that does have money.

Question Two on Review of Proposal

Do you have time to complete a review of my proposal? If the venture capitalist is so busy that he does not have time to complete a review of your proposal for two months, then you may wish to work with another venture capital firm. If the venture capitalist gives you a date in the future, you will have to gauge in your own mind the likelihood that he will keep his promise.

Question Three on Available Time

If the venture firm is interested in investing, how long does it take to disburse the funds? Again, if it takes the venture firm a long time to go through the process, you may wish to seek money from another firm. Investing in a company in two weeks is very quick. The average time from inception to investment is approximately six to eight weeks. A waiting period of over eight weeks is considered long. Keep in mind that complex companies and syndications of venture investors will take longer than a simple investment.

Question Four on Interest in the Industry

"Are you interested in investing in my industry?" A no here means you are bucking a mental block. You should go elsewhere. If the venture capitalist does not like your industry, do not try to persuade him that he can earn money on it. You are wasting your time.

Another way of approaching the situation is to ask, "Have you ever invested in this industry or do you have specific knowledge of this industry?" If the venture capitalist is interested in your industry or is already investing in the industry, you will find it easier to convince him that your deal is a good one, since he already understands the economics of the industry. It is helpful if you can find a venture capital firm that has experience in your industry, but it is not essential.

Question Five on Other Venture Firms To Contact

"Do you mind if I contact other venture capital firms at the same time I am working with you?" Obviously, this is a touchy question. Venture capitalists do not want to openly encourage competition. They would like to have you all to themselves. Another way of approaching the issue is to ask: "Would any other venture firms that you have worked with before be interested in reviewing my proposal at the same time you work on it?" Most venture capital firms work with other venture firms that have a similar approach to investing. They probably welcome having you send your proposal to their friends, and since most venture firms syndicate their investments, you will be one jump ahead of the syndication process.

Background Information on the Venture Capital Company

In order to verify that you have contacted a reputable venture capital firm, you will want to obtain the name of its banker. You will want to ask the banker a number of questions, your main purpose, of course, being to verify that the venture capital firm has money to invest. After you have determined that the banker believes that the firm has money to invest, you will want to ask about the reputation of the venture capital firm. In a similar vein, you may ask your own banker to ask the venture capitalist's banker about the venture firm. Some bankers will talk more openly with bankers. You may want to ask your accountant about the venture firm's accountant, and you may want to ask your lawyer to ask about the firm's lawyers. If your banker, accountant, and lawyer, tell you that the venture capital company's bank, accountant, and lawyers, are all of poor quality and have a poor business history, then you may not want to deal with the venture capital firms. Guilt by association is not necessarily true, but, birds of a feather do fly together.

In talking with the venture capital firm, you want to obtain a list of companies they have invested in. You want to call the entrepreneurs of these portfolio companies because soon you will be stepping in their shoes. You will want to ask some questions along the following lines:

- How long did it take to get your money from the venture firm?
- Is the venture firm reasonable?
- Are the managers of the venture firm honest?
- Can you trust them?
- What type of negotiators were involved?
- Were they difficult to deal with?
- What is the management of the venture firm like to "live with?"
- What have they done for you besides invest the money?
- Have they given you any assistance that you didn't have to pay for?
- Do they act like they are your partner or do they act like they own you?
- What is there attitude toward you and how do they treat you?
- How active are they in your business?
- Do they try to tell you how to run your company?
- Are they helpful?
- Do they hinder the operations?
- What is the relationship between you and the venture capitalist?
- If your company has had some operating problems, how did the management of the venture firm act during the period of difficulties?
- Would you say their contributions were helpful or did they create greater problems?
- If you could sell your company and go out and start over again, would you do it with the same venture capital company?

All of these questions are oriented toward the relationship between the venture capitalist and the management of the portfolio company. If you decide during your discussions with portfolio companies that the venture capitalist is unethical, and overbearing and tries to take over portfolio companies, you may wish to switch to another venture capital firm.

Timing Questions for the Venture Capitalist

You should question the venture capitalist about the status of the legal papers necessary for closing. Ask him, "What is the procedure for closing so the legal documents can be signed?" This question should be asked without trying to push the venture capitalist over the brink. Usually venture capitalists are already pressed for time, so that adding one more deadline that needs to close "tomorrow" might create difficulties for the venture capitalist. However, it does not hurt to ask about the procedures and the timetable before closing.

Objective

Your objective during the visit by the venture capitalist will be to give him an extensive tour of the plant, and to answer the thousand questions he will ask you about your business proposal and about the business in general. You should finalize any negotiations left undone. You should also try to make him feel at home, and try to become his friend on a first-name basis. The more you can become friends and partners, and the more he feels at home with your business, the more successful his visit will be. The more successful the visit, the quicker the venture capitalist will want to have a legal closing, as covered in Chapter 8.

You also need to complete your homework on the venture firm. You must determine if the firm will be a good business partner. If you do not take the time to do this, you may end up in business with a gorilla.

8

The Closing

Will We Ever Learn To Live with Lawyers?
Getting It All Down in Legal Terms.

S ometime after the due diligence is completed and the visit to the business is past, the venture capitalist's lawyer will contact you about closing the investment. You may even hear from the lawyer before the due diligence is completed. This will be your first exposure to the lawyer who is looking out for the interest of the venture capitalist. It is important that you have a lawyer of your own to look after your interests.

The venture capitalist's lawyer will draw up the legal documents that are necessary for closing. The legal documents should follow the commitment letter. He will forward a copy to you and your attorney. Sometimes there will be oral changes to the commitment letter that will be incorporated in the closing documents. You should read the legal documents to determine if the documents are in agreement with the business deal. The legal documents will contain standard paragraphs known as "boiler plate" paragraphs. Your lawyer can explain these to you. There are many boiler plate paragraphs in every set of legal documents. A set of actual legal documents appears in Appendix 1.

In this chapter we discuss two types of closings: first, a loan with options to own stock, and later on, an agreement to purchase common stock.

First Closing: Legal Documents For Loans With Options

It would be wonderful if you could sign an IOU and receive your money. You cannot. There must be adequate legal documentation before the loan can be closed and the proceeds of the loan disbursed. Three fundamental legal documents are involved in a loan with an option to buy stock: a loan agreement; a note; and a stock purchase option. Each document has specific objectives and each covers separate ground. It is important for you to realize that these documents will govern the legal relationship between you and the venture capitalist. Please read all legal documents carefully. There is nothing frightening about legal documents. They are written in English, not a foreign language. As you read the documents, make sure they say precisely what you and the venture capitalist have agreed upon. There can only be two reasons why they may not. Either the venture capitalist has changed his mind and instructed his lawyer to change the documents, or there has been a mistake. In either event, you should discuss the changes with the venture capitalist. This will head off any expensive arguments between you and the venture capitalist's lawyer. Now, let's examine each of the three basic legal documents in the first closing.

Document One: The Loan Agreement

By far the largest document will be the loan agreement. It will contain fifteen to fifty pages, and possibly more if the investment is a complicated one. To some extent, the loan agreement will include the items in the commitment letter plus items standard for loan agreements. There are ten sections to the loan agreement and each is discussed below.

1.   Purchase and Sale

In this section the lawyer will use specific language to describe the loan with all its terms and conditions. He will describe the equity option with all its terms and conditions. This section will describe in detail the securities to be purchased and will specify the following:

- The interest rate per annum.
- When repayment of principal will begin and over what period it will be repaid.
- Dates payments are to be made, such as the first day of each month.
- Delivery date of the funds by the venture capitalist to you.
- Description of the venture capitalist's stock option.
- Ownership in the company by the venture capitalist.
- Cost of ownership.

Also, this section will establish that the company has authorized and empowered its management to enter into the sale. It will discuss any other venture capital participants and the amount that they will be purchasing in your company.

2. Collateral Security and Subordination

This section will describe the collateral for the loan in great detail and it will refer to a collateral security agreement that will be an exhibit to this agreement. Normally, the lawyer will describe each piece of collateral as set forth in the summary terms below:

- A second mortgage on specific land and building.
- A third secured interest in machinery and equipment of the company.
- Personal guarantees of certain individuals.
- Assignment of certain leases.
- Assignment of life and casualty insurance.

3. Affirmative Covenants

This section covers all the items you agreed you would do as long as this loan or option to own stock is outstanding. Your company will do the following:

- Provide the investor with detailed financial and operating information on a monthly basis.
- Provide the investor with any documents filed with the Securities and Exchange Commission or other government agencies.
- Provide an annual budget by a specific date each year.
- Advise the investors of any adverse changes in the company's status.
- Maintain certain current ratios, working capital amounts, or net worth amounts.
- Maintain life insurance on certain executives of the company.
- Maintain property and liability insurance in sufficient amounts.
- Notify the representative of the venture capital company when board meetings will occur so that the venture capital representative may attend the meetings.
- Provide access for the venture capitalist to the premises and to the books and records of the company.
- Keep all equipment and property in good repair and in working order.
- Comply with all applicable laws and regulations.
- Pay all taxes and other levies of taxes against the company.
- Maintain its corporate existence and other business existences.

- Give the venture capital firm the right of first refusal on new financings in the future.

- Maintain a standard system of accounting in accordance with generally accepted accounting standards.

- Notify the venture capitalist if you are in default on any loans or leases.

The items above will be spelled out in their own separate small paragraph in the Affirmative Covenants section of the Loan Agreement. Be sure you agree with each covenant because once you sign the agreement you must perform or the loan will be in default. If a new covenant is brought up as a "standard" covenant, discuss it with the venture capitalist, not the venture capitalist's lawyer.

4.   Negative Covenants

As you can imagine, this is the section where you agree not to do certain things. Some typical negative covenants are:

- There will be no change in control of the company.

- Management will not sell, assign, or transfer its shares.

- The company will not change the basic business it is in.

- The company will not change its current business format; that is, change from being a corporation to a partnership.

- The company will not invest in other companies or unrelated activities.

- The company will pay no cash or stock dividends.

- The company will not expend funds for capital improvements in excess of certain amounts.

- The company will not pay nor loan to any employee money in excess of a certain amount per year.

- The company will pay no brokerage fees and the like in excess of a certain amount.

- The company will not transact any business with members of the board of directors or management or its officers or affiliated individuals.

- The company will not dissolve, merge, or dispose of its assets.

- The company will not change its place of business.

- The company will sell no additional common stock, convertible debt, or preferred stock.

Each item above will be covered by a short paragraph in the legal documents. Violation of any of the above items will be considered a default, as set out below. Each item should have been discussed with the venture capitalist. If a new item appears, you need to discuss it with the venture capitalist because it will have an impact on the way you conduct business. If material new covenants appear in this section, you may need a meeting with the venture capitalist to negotiate the terms in the legal documents.

5. Events of Default

This section describes items that will cause a default of the loan. A default may mean you have to repay the loan in full on the day of default. A default is usually called on any of the following items:

- If you do not carry out the Affirmative Covenants.
- If you violate any of the Negative Covenants.
- If the representations and warranties you made in the legal documents are not true.
- If you do not make timely payments on the loan.
- If you do not pay other debts as they come due.
- If you have any other loan called in default.
- If you have any lease called in default.
- If a final judgment is rendered against the company by the creditor.
- If bankruptcy or reorganization of the company should occur.

In this section the lawyer will also specify what remedies are necessary to remove the default. As an example, suppose a default is called because you have not made a payment; making the payment within ten days of written notice of the default may be the solution to remove the default. Some defaults can happen easily, as with the case of a payment that is not made on the due date. If you miss the payment date by only one day, the venture capital firm can call the loan in default. A grace period should be provided in the legal documents. This refers to the amount of time you have to correct a default once notified. In negotiating grace periods from the venture capitalist, remember that the longer they are, the better for you. Do not be unreasonable because you will lower the venture capitalist's opinion of you and may make him think twice about closing the loan.

6. Equity Rights

Here the agreement may cover a wide range of items relating to the equity of the company, the equity of the venture capitalist, or option to own equity held by the venture capitalist. These items include:

- The right of the venture capitalist to force the company to register the venture capitalist's shares in a public offering, free of charge.
- The right of the venture capitalist to include his shares in any registration of the company's shares, free of charge.
- Any restriction on the transfer of the shares being received by the venture capitalist.

- A section referring to certain Securities and Exchange Commission regulations to which everyone must conform.
- An indemnification of the venture capital company against any violations on your issuing the stock.
- Representations on your part about the number of shares and options outstanding.
- Any rights the venture capitalist may have to require you to repurchase the shares held by him. This is the put.
- Any rights you have to repurchase the shares at a later date. This is the call.

This section covers all the equity rights that the venture capitalist will have. This part of the document should cover all matters that you and the venture capitalist have agreed upon with regard to the equity rights he will have in your company. These equity rights are the mechanism whereby the venture capitalist will someday realize a profit on his equity position. It is his exit. Be sure you understand how the venture capitalist will realize a profit on his equity. Be sure it is in concert with your agreement with him. This section is particularly critical to the venture capitalist and you should exercise caution about trying to remove provisions from this section. As you can understand, the venture capitalist wants to exit from your deal some day and these equity rights will be his mechanism for doing so.

7.   Representations and Warranties

In this section you are representing and warranting to the venture capitalist that certain things are true:

- Your corporation is in good standing.
- You are in compliance with all laws.
- There is certain capitalization of your company.
- There are no subsidiaries.
- The financial statements are correct.
- There have been no material adverse changes since the last financial statements.
- There is no litigation going on, or if there is, a description of it is attached as an exhibit.
- The company is in compliance with all government regulations.
- There are no defaults on current borrowings.
- The company is current on all taxes.
- The company has rights to any patents that you own.

Paragraph after paragraph of these types of representations and warranties can be expected in the legal documents. Each one has a specific focus and meaning. Your lawyer should be able to substantiate most of the claims. Read each one and be sure that on the closing date all representations made by you are true. A false representation can mean a legal problem for the company and for you personally.

8. Fees and Expenses

This section will explain who pays the fee to the lawyers for drawing up the documents, who pays the fees for filing any legal documents at local courthouses, who gets notices, and so on. Normally, you, the borrower, will pay all the lawyers and closing costs.

9. Definitions

In this section the lawyers will define every technical or legal term appearing in the document. You should understand the definitions because they are an integral part of the entire document.

10. Conditions of Closing and Miscellaneous

This last section includes items such as indemnification, waivers, notices, and addresses. In this section, too, the lawyer will list all the conditions for closing. Condition-of-closing items are things such as:

- Certificate of incorporation.
- Copy of bylaws.
- Certificate of incumbency.
- Opinion of entrepreneur's lawyers.
- Certified audit.
- Certificates from secretary of state.
- Copies of all corporate action taken by the company to authorize its execution of these documents.
- Copy of letter from senior lender consenting to this transaction.

There will also be a final page for your signature, the venture capitalist's signature, and the signatures of any guarantors.

This is a general overview of the loan agreement. You should find that the loan agreement follows closely the terms and conditions set forth in the commitment letter. If it does not, something is wrong.

Document Two: The Note

Usually the note will be written on one to five pages. The note will be an in-depth, detailed statement of the terms of the loan. It will specify:

- How much money is being loaned.
- When it is to be repaid.
- The interest rate.

- What day of the month it is to be paid.
- Guarantors.
- Conditions of prepayment of the loan.
- Collateral for the loan.
- Subordination of the loan to other loans.
- References to covenants in the loan agreement.
- A complete list of defaults.
- Waivers and amendments.

It will be signed by the president and usually the secretary of the corporation, plus any guarantors of the note. The corporate seal will usually be affixed to the last page.

Document Three: The Stock Purchase Option

Finally, you can expect a four- to ten-page document describing the stock options to purchase stock in your company. It will provide details such as the following:

- Duration of the stock option.
- Any covenants of the company during ownership of the stock option.
- The mechanism for securing the option in exchange for stock.
- The exact price that must be paid when the option is exercised.
- Adjustments to the exercise price; that is, the formula that will be used in case shares are sold at a low price or additional shares are issued by the company.
- The availability of shares owned by the company to be issued if the option is exercised.
- Any written notices that must be given.
- A definition of common stock.
- Expiration date of the stock option.
- Transferability of the option.

Normally this option will be signed by the president and the secretary of your company on the final page of the stock purchase option.

Other Documents: Exhibits

As few as five but usually about ten exhibits will be attached to every financial agreement. Most of these were listed above when we discussed the sections of the loan agreement. Be sure you understand what each exhibit states because you will be agreeing that it is true and correct. Some typical exhibits listed for a closing are:

1. Security agreement describing the collateral security for the loan. Be sure you have given the venture capitalist only the collateral agreed upon.
2. Financing statement that includes UCC-1 forms that will be filed in the records of the courthouse. This statement will let all creditors know who has a claim on your assets.
3. Opinion of your counsel on the validity of the transaction.
4. Copy of all corporate actions taken by stockholders to effect the transaction.
5. Copy of certificate of incorporation.
6. Copy of the bylaws of the company.
7. Certificate from the secretary of state evidencing good standing.
8. Copy of a certified audit from your accounting firm.
9. Any forms necessary for government-related financing.

The description above is a simple overview of the documents and exhibits. Appendix 1 contains a set of documents from an investment made by a venture capital company. When you receive the real documents, you should read each one in detail to make sure you understand what you are signing. Some presidents of companies rarely read the legal documents. Some entrepreneurs ask their lawyers if everything is all right, and if the lawyer nods a yes, the entrepreneur signs it without reading the legal documents. The lawyer's nod only means that the legal documents are in legal order. His nod does not indicate that the business deal is correctly presented in documents. Only you can determine that. Some venture capitalists do not read legal documents, but most take the time to read the documents before they sign them. Be smart; read your legal documents. Ask questions if you do not understand the legal descriptions.

Simple Is Good

The complexity of legal documentation has baffled American businessmen for decades. The simpler the legal documents are, the better it is for all parties. If there is a simple way to say something in a legal document so that everyone will understand it, that should definitely be the order of the day. Some lawyers are carried away with a great deal of verbiage. You should ask them to refrain from following this practice. In legal documents, simple equals good.

The best legal documents are those that you never refer to after the closing. If, during your relationship with the venture capitalist, you never have to look at the legal documents, then the deal has worked well. If you or the venture capitalist are constantly referring to the legal documents and questioning the meaning of every word, then something is wrong. You and the venture capitalist have a problem.

Unethical Venture Capitalist

When the legal documents arrive, you may find them quite different from the commitment letter or the understanding you have with the venture capitalist. Rather than wasting legal time, you should immediately take the documents to the venture capitalist. Determine if he is trying to renegotiate a better deal. If you find that the venture capitalist is fairly rigid and will not come around to the original understanding, then you should have your commitment deposit refunded so that each of you can go your separate ways. You should not deal with a venture capitalist who pulls a surprise punch by writing the legal documents to suit his new position.

One venture capitalist is known to obtain excruciatingly binding conditions from many of his entrepreneurs. When asked how he was able to obtain such onerous conditions from his entrepreneurs, he explained the technique. At the last minute at closing, he merely walks into the closing room with a set of pre-printed forms and says to the entrepreneur, "Of course, you will want to sign our Form 406." Most entrepreneurs seeing this preprinted form assume it is a standard document that the venture capitalist uses on every deal and merely sign the several copies presented before going on to the other legal documents. The entrepreneurs do not realize that the provisions they have signed virtually tie them in knots. Only the smartest entrepreneurs have read and questioned each item on this preprinted form. Do not get caught signing "Form 406!" Read everything before you sign it!

Second Closing: Legal Documents for the Purchase of Stock

You would think that the purchase of stock would be a simple transaction—that the venture capitalist would write you a check and you would issue him some stock certificates. As it turns out, that is far from the truth. There will not be a note and there will not be a stock option (unless options are an additional part of the stock purchase), but there will be a fairly lengthy stock purchase agreement. An example of a stock purchase agreement is given in Appendix 1. The stock purchase agreement will be similar to the loan agreement described above, but let us discuss the points again from the perspective of a stock purchase.

Stock Purchase Agreement

The stock purchase agreement has ten to twelve sections. Many of the sections will be similar to the ones covered below.

1. Purchase and Sale

In this initial section the lawyer will describe the sale of stock and the price being paid, as in the corresponding section of the loan agreement above.

2. Affirmative Covenants

Many of the affirmative covenants that were covered above in the Loan Agreement will be set forward in this section.

3. Negative Covenants

Again, many of the same negative covenants will appear in this section for the sale of stock.

4. Equity Rights

In this section the lawyer will carve out the liquidation rights of the stock: Are the shares sold to the venture firm on the same basis or do the shares get preference in liquidation? What dividends do they receive? What rights do they have to elect directors? It is typical for the venture capitalist to have the right to elect one to three directors, as long as they do not elect a majority? Although they may have the right to elect as many as three directors, they often elect only one. This single director will follow your company, attend the board meetings, and if things become critical, he will ask you to elect two additional directors who will then have more to say about the operation of your business.

Covered in this section are the many equity rights of the venture capitalist, including the right to register his shares in any public offerings, and the right to require you to register his shares free of charge. Be sensitive to the fact that these equity rights are the primary exit for the venture capitalist. He will be reluctant to change any of these equity rights.

5. Representations and Warranties

A full set of representations and warranties similar to the ones in the Loan Agreement will appear here.

6. Fees and Expenses

Again, this section explains who will pay all the legal fees; usually it is the seller of the stock.

7. Definitions

There may be a short definition section, but usually there is none.

8. Restrictions

Some restrictions may be placed on your operation of the company. You may have to operate under certain guidelines as long as the venture capitalist owns his shares. This section will describe any operating restrictions.

9. Voting Trust

A voting trust may be involved in a sale of stock. If so, this section will discuss the voting trust in detail. Here is how a voting trust works. Usually a trust is set up at a bank trust department with a bank trust officer as trustee. Your shares and the shares of others are put in the trust. The venture capital firm controls the voting trust, but only under certain conditions can the venture capital firm vote the shares in the trust. In all other circumstances you vote the shares that are in the trust, even though you do not hold them. This section will give you the precise details on what the venture capitalist has in mind when he sets up a voting trust.

10. Employment Agreement

Many times the venture capital firm will want to insure that key employees continue to work for the company, at least for a specific period of time. The venture capitalist may therefore ask key employees to sign one-way employment contracts insuring that the key people will be with the company as long as the venture capital is an investor. As part of the agreement, the employee may be asked not to reveal confidential company information if he is permitted to leave the company.

The employment agreement can be turned around, of course, to the advantage of the entrepreneur. It can insure that his job is secure during a period in which the venture capitalist firm may have an opportunity to take over the company. Usually this security is overshadowed by the one-sided nature of the contract. A venture capitalist told me of three young M.B.A.s who signed employment contracts. The contracts provided that these gentle souls be paid a reasonable sum despite their brief experience in the business world. However, the contracts were for five years. As fate would have it, the business failed. Among the "assets" of the business were the three employment contracts. The institutional investor who had invested the funds foreclosed on all the assets of the business and picked up the employment contracts of the three M.B.A.s. For the remaining four years of their contracts, these men were virtually the slaves of this corporate giant. You may wish to avoid having an employment agreement.

11. Consulting Contract

Many venture capital firms play an active role in the management of the company in which they invest. They may help the company to establish marketing or financial controls or to address any number of problems that may arise in a new or small, growing company. They will want compensation for the time and attention their consultants take to help the new business get off the ground.

Compensation is usually arranged through a contract with the venture capital firm for management consulting services. This agreement will recite the description of the services to be rendered, and the terms and the amount of payment that will be made to the venture capital firm for these services.

12. Conditions to Closing

Again, there will be a section on indemnification, waivers, and notices. There will be a list of items that must be completed before closing can occur. At the end there will be a page for you, the venture capitalist, and other parties to the agreement, to sign.

Lawyers as Businessmen

Many lawyers will take it upon themselves to tell a client not to enter into a business arrangement because it is a bad business deal. All venture capitalists want to know if something is wrong from a legal perspective, but they become upset by lawyers who jump into the business fray in order to "save" their client from signing a bad business deal. Some good lawyers are certainly good businessmen. However, very few *practicing* lawyers are good entrepreneurs or venture capitalists. It's difficult for anyone to carry on two professions successfully. Every venture capitalist can tell you about a lawyer who killed a business deal because he felt his client was not getting a good deal. If lawyers would stay in the legal profession and leave the businessmen to the business profession, the world would be a better place.

You should encourage your lawyer to refrain from trying to renegotiate the deal for you. Your venture capital partner will appreciate it. If your lawyer tries to renegotiate the deal, the venture capitalist will assume that you have directed him to do so. He will believe you are trying to change the deal, or find a way to get out of it. Needless to say, this will take his attention away from closing the deal, and move him away from investing in your company. Be very careful before you instruct your lawyer to openly negotiate with the venture capitalist. If there is something you do not like about the legal documents, go to the venture capitalist and negotiate for yourself. Do not use a surrogate who is not familiar with the business deal.

Experienced Lawyers Are Best

A lawyer experienced in drawing up legal documents for venture capital investments is worth his weight in gold. A lawyer trying to bluff his way through this type of investment agreement will destroy your chances of a quick and successful closing. Usually, you will be better off to have the venture capital company's lawyer complete the first draft of the proposed legal documents and to have your lawyer review them. If your lawyer prepares the first draft, you may end up paying him a large fee for drafting the documents and paying the venture capital's lawyer a large fee to undo the mess made by your lawyer. Remember, you will pay all legal costs unless you do not go through with the agreement. Be economical in your use of lawyers; they are expensive.

One of the main factors to slow down the legal process is the lack of time that lawyers have to work on legal closings. Legal documents sent by a venture capitalist's attorney to the entrepreneur's attorney can sit on the desk of the entrepreneur's lawyer for weeks before he gets around to reviewing them. It is incumbent upon you to find out when the legal documents have been sent by the venture capitalist's lawyer, and to remind your lawyer daily, if necessary, that you cannot close until he reviews the documents. Do not expect anyone else to ride herd over your lawyer.

You may not realize it, but your lawyer may have incurred a liability if he doesn't perform quickly and reasonably. Any lawyer who does not close a deal that should have closed, could be held liable for whatever damages are caused to your company. Certainly a lawyer who does not act on legal documents sent to him for review within five days is courting disaster, especially in a deal that must close quickly because the company needs the funds.

Legal Fees Keep Going Up

Legal fees are rarely low. In fact, of all the fees that businessmen complain about, legal fees probably top the list. The question is not whether legal fees are too high. The question is whether a specific legal fee is fair, in view of the work that has been performed by the lawyer. Some attorneys are unethical in their billing practices. They think nothing of padding a legal bill with ten or twenty hours of work, and mail the bill to the client without a great deal of explanation. Most legal bills consist of a single line, "for services rendered," followed by a dollar amount.

Because legal bills have become such a large part of business life, most businessmen are attempting to manage the fees. The most common method of managing legal fees was introduced by large corporations, many of which now require a detailed legal bill. The bill must include hours worked, the specific project on which the time was carried out, the bliling rate of the individual working on it, and the name of the individual authorizing work on the project. Besides these detailed bills, many smaller businesses are requiring the law firms to give them advance estimates of the time it will take to complete a project. They ask the lawyer to call them once he reaches a certain amount of time expended. By doing this, the small business keeps track of the law firm's hours and does not let it run up a big bill.

If you have agreed to pay the legal fees for both your lawyer and for the venture capitalist's lawyer, it is incumbent upon you to manage the legal fees. This means contacting the venture capitalist's lawyer and discussing fees. You must discuss the procedure for working on your deal and how the bill will be rendered. Do not be surprised when you arrive at the closing table and see the legal bill. If you are surprised by the amount of the legal bill, then you have not been managing your lawyers very well. All too often, entrepreneurs receive a shock at the closing table. The venture capitalist may be in a poor position to help you negotiate these fees. If the lawyer for the venture capitalist has a close relationship with the venture firm, the venture capitalist will have a hard time questioning his friend about legal fees, even if they seem too high. The venture capitalist cannot be expected to manage your legal fees. It is important that you manage all your legal fees so that you are satisfied with the amount that you are charged at the closing table.

How Lawyers Run Up Your Legal Bill

Besides the unethical padding mentioned above, watch for the many methods employed to run up your legal fee. Listed below are five of them.

Disagree on Legal Points

Your lawyer or perhaps even the venture capitalist's lawyer will often disagree on many points. This means that they will have to spend innumerable hours discussing these points and working each one out to their satisfaction. If you have agreed to pay legal bills, remember that when these two lawyers disagree, you are paying the bill on both sides of the table, even as they argue about miniscule points. There is a fairly simple way to cure this problem. When your lawyer has reviewed the papers drafted by the venture capitalist's lawyer, tell him to make a note by each item in the documents where he sees a problem. Before he discusses these points with the venture capitalist's lawyer, ask him to discuss each one of them with you. Many of them may have no material business significance and therefore you will be willing to let the venture capitalist's lawyer put them into the agreement. Each time you knock out one of these small points for discussion, you save yourself some money.

Rewrite Sections

Some lawyers increase their fees by rewriting sections of the documents over and over again. Suppose the venture capitalist's lawyer presents his written version of the document. Your lawyer may rewrite the documents completely. He will run up secretarial time and drafting time in order to redo entire sections. You should instruct him, from the beginning, that there is to be one writer of the documents and one commentator on the documents. The venture capitalist's lawyer should be the writer and your lawyer should be the commentator. This arrangement will reduce your legal fees.

Research Points of Law

Often lawyers will disagree violently over points of law. The disagreement will send them scurrying to the library, or to other research sources, in order to clarify various points of law. This research can burn up many hours of time. Each lawyer is trying to show which one is the best legal scholar. You should instruct both lawyers that you do not wish them to research various points of the law without your permission, and that you will not pay for such research.

Legal Style

Lawyers will correct each other on usage, style, grammar, and even spelling. They will use up your time for the purpose of "clarifying the language." Tell the lawyers that you are not interested in matters of style. Stress that you want a clear document and that is all.

Arguments

Most lawyers are by nature argumentative. They spend three years in law school arguing points back and forth. Once they enter the real world, they continue to argue with one another. You should remember that you are paying for all of these arguments. If you have two lawyers arguing with each other, and they are each billing you at the rate of $150 an hour, you are paying $5 per minute to hear them eloquently debate the merits of a legal point. Act as a moderator and get to the heart of the argument. Ask your lawyer what the consequences will be if you agree to the words being proposed by the venture capitalist's lawyer. If these consequences are quite modest, or if the consequences are extremely unlikely, you may wish merely to sign the document rather than fight to remove the words. On the other hand, if the consequences appear to be drastic, you must adjourn the legal meeting and call a business meeting with your venture capital partner to iron out the problem.

Questionable Legal Practices

In some instances, the venture capitalist's lawyer may be too close to the venture firm. The lawyer may be on the board of directors, or he might be part of management. If either is the case, and the venture capitalist's lawyer does the work, you are in a poor negotiating position. If, at the last minute, the venture capitalist's lawyer shows up with a legal fee two or three times larger than you expected, you have little negotiating power. Since he is part of the company, he can keep the deal from closing unless you agree to pay his fee. I remember one syndicated closing where a participant arrived at the closing with his lawyer. The lawyer had performed very little work, except to review the documents, but when closing started he presented a legal bill for an exorbitant amount. Everyone felt embarrassed by the amount; however, since the lawyer was an integral part of the venture capital company, he demanded that his fee be paid. The venture company refused to close on its part of the deal unless the bill was paid, and said the entrepreneur would not receive the entire funding!

There are not many ways to handle this type of problem before closing. You could, at the closing, try to give the lawyer a promissory note and after closing you might be in a better position to negotiate with him. However, if the lawyer is an integral part of the venture capital firm, then you are starting your relationship with the venture capital firm on unsure footing.

Syndications and Lawyers

When you are dealing with a syndication of venture capitalists, each venture capitalist's lawyer may want an opportunity to review legal documents. You should agree to pay for the legal fee, but only for the lead investor's lawyer, not for each participant's lawyer who wants to look at the documents. If you agree to pay for all the lawyers, and if four or five venture capitalist's lawyers look at the documents, you are opening up your cash register. When you ask the lawyers to take out what they need to cover their time and effort in reviewing the documents, the "review" may go on indefinitely.

Many lawyers tell an interesting story about the young lawyer who began working in his father's law firm. His father took a much needed vacation to Europe and left his son behind to continue the legal practice. The first case the young lawyer worked on was a railway right-of-way case. The young lawyer noted that his father had been working on the case for almost twenty years. In several days, the young lawyer assembled the parties in a room and negotiated a settlement. The case was closed. When the young lawyer's father returned from his vacation, the young lawyer explained with glee that he had settled that long outstanding railway right-of-way case. Needless to say, the father was extremely upset as he explained to his son that the railway case sent all of the young lawyer's brothers and sisters to college, and the annual fees from the case had even sent the young lawyer to law school. Remember, lawyers receive fees while cases are open. They do not receive fees from cases that are closed.

Another factor to watch for in sydications is the tardiness with which other venture capitalist's lawyers may review the documents. Invariably one of the venture capitalist's lawyers will be slow and not get around to the documents for days. You must obtain the names of all the venture capitalist's lawyers and constantly put pressure on each lawyer to submit his comments so that closing can take place. You alone can manage this process. The lead venture capitalist's lawyers cannot do as much as you can.

The Closing: A Moment of Truth

Once the lawyers have drawn up and examined the documents and once the businessmen have ironed out the business problems, a big pile of legal documents will be ready for signing. Normally, three to ten copies of each document will have to be signed. The closing usually takes place in a conference room. Every closing seems to have its crisis. Usually the entrepreneur's lawyer will bring documents, such as incorporation papers or life insurance, that are not in the proper form. If all the documents required are not present at closing, the venture capitalist's lawyer will not be able to close the loan. In large deals the lawyers will get together the day before the closing date to see if all the papers are in order and if it is possible to close the loan. An inexperienced lawyer for the entrepreneur or venture capitalist may try to have a closing without reviewing all the documents beforehand. To just pick a date and show up for a closing is almost a sure way to abort the closing.

A closing is an extremely exciting moment, because it is the moment when the venture capitalist parts with his money and the entrepreneur's business gets an injection of capital. The physical process can take hours and be extremely boring. Documents are signed, shuffled around the table, looked at by lawyers, and verified by lawyers. It is, to say it most simply, a lawyers' environment.

Closing Fees That You Pay

Lawyers can spend considerable time on the actual closing itself. Many hold a preclosing the day before the actual closing. This dress rehearsal, as well as the actual event, can be costly. Envision the entrepreneur who has agreed to pay the lead venture capitalist's lawyer, the lawyer of the bank giving him a loan, as well as his own lawyer. These three lawyers may charge as much as $250 per hour each. On top of these fees are those of the junior attorneys, paralegals, and secretaries, which can run from $50 to $90 per hour. All in all, the entrepreneur is probably being billed at the rate of $900 to $2,000 per hour. If the deal is extremely large and complicated and involves additional people, that figure can be multiplied by two or three. But for the moment, assume the minimum is $1,500 per hour. Assume the lawyers spend five hours in preclosing and seven hours in the actual closing, for a total of twelve hours. Twelve times $1,500 is $18,000, just for the closing, quite apart from what you will pay for the drafting, research time, and other document gathering.

There is only one way around the expense of closing, and that is to be absolutely ready when a closing date is set. Your lawyer should have reviewed all the documents in detail with the venture capitalist's lawyer to assure himself that when closing occurs and everyone is sitting around the table, everything that is needed to close will be at the table. There will be no last-minute scurrying for any documents and there will be no last-minute changes. If you can impress upon your lawyer that you do not want the closing set until everyone is absolutely ready, then you will be doing yourself a big favor. Do not go to the closing table prematurely. It will cost you a lot of money if you do. What is worse, you will have to do it again if the investment does not close.

What to Remember About Lawyers

You should remember that lawyers are merely specialists in a specific area and have knowledge of an area in which you do not. They are professionals. Just as you are a professional businessman, they are professional lawyers. Remember, too, that they are providing a service and that you hire them just as you hire any other employee. Tell them what you want them to do and you will have a satisfactory relationship with your attorneys.

Also remember that lawyers make money by charging for time and they are disposed to spend a great deal of time working on something. Most of the problems lawyers work on are not legal problems. They are simply problems which lawyers have been left to solve by businessmen. Many business problems turned over to lawyers can easily be solved by two businessmen in a "head-to-head" discussion. Before you try to solve a problem from a legal standpoint, be sure you have exhausted all other remedies. Legal solutions are expensive. In one case in New York City, a venture capitalist lost $50,000 when the lawyer, who was a member of one of the large prestigious law firms in New York, had been negligent in his closing of the loan and clearly was open to a suit. Once the venture capital firm looked into suing this pretigious lawyer in New York, he soon found that it would probably cost him at least $50,000 to sue the lawyer. He was told that he would be lucky if he recouped any of his legal fees, much less the $50,000 that the lawyer had lost for the venture capital firm.

Also remember that the number of lawyers in the United States is higher than ever before. By many counts there is a surplus of lawyers. If you do not like the lawyer you are working with, find a new one. There are hundreds of good lawyers seeking work with a growing company.

Objective

Your objective through this entire process is to obtian legal documents acceptable to the venture capitalist's lawyer, and to the venture capitalist himself. As soon as that process is complete, you and the venture capitalist can sign the documents. At that point, you will have your money. The quicker you can go through the legal documents, and the harder you can push your lawyer to re-view them and get them back to the venture capitalist's lawyer, the sooner you will have your funds.

Your role throughout the entire process is to be in touch with the lawyer and the venture capitalist. You should be in charge of getting together as many documents as possible in order to avoid any delays. You should be in touch with all lawyers in order to determine what might be holding up the process. When a problem arises, you must be involved in the solution in order to keep the process moving. You should review the documents and understand them completely, and you should not try to renegotiate the deal. If you can do all of these things, your closing will be an easy one.

9

Working Together

How Can You Both Make Money?
Operating Your Company To Make the Most Money.

Raising money from a venture capitalist has been compared to getting married. The closing has been compared to the wedding ceremony. After the wedding, when the honeymoon is over, the two of you must make a life with each other. During the next three to ten years you will be working with the venture capitalist, not so much on a day-to-day basis, but indirectly, for your relationship will be one in which he is or has the option to be a major stockholder in your business. The venture capitalist will be your business partner.

Most venture capital firms are not completely passive. A few large venture capital firms are very active in the management of companies and have a consulting staff to perform this task. These consultants may supply marketing expertise to help improve your marketing effort. They might also supply production expertise to help you with production or financial expertise to help you with financial matters. Furthermore, consultants can help with your overall management by implementing a management by objective (MBO) system.

Most venture capital firms are not staffed with consultants. Many will not invest in a company unless it has full management team that can run the company on a day-to-day basis. By and large, venture capital firms do not have expertise in marketing, nor do they have expertise in production or administrative matters. Most managers of venture capital companies are heavyweights in the area of finance, and, if they have been in the business for an extended period of time, they will have considerable knowledge of small business practices. You should rely on them extensively when talking about financial matters, and should use them as a sounding board for general policy questions. If you need a bank loan, they can help you determine which bank to approach and how to approach it. They may be able to help you with an industrial revenue bond (IRB). Sometimes they can suggest the person to talk to about an insurance company loan. These and other financial matters will be part of the venture capitalist's general knowledge. He is a financial expert and in many cases can save you hundreds of hours of time and effort in seeking additional financing. You should tap this store of knowledge often.

Major Policy Decisions Should Be Joint Ones

All major policy decisions should be discussed with the venture capitalist—first, of course, because he is your business partner, but second, because most venture capitalists have at hand, or have access to, a great deal of business knowledge. An experienced venture capital firm will have seen many small companies go through the development cycle. It will have encountered many problems similar to yours. The venture capitalist's accumulated knowledge can be used to solve some of your problems. Many venture capitalists have been trained in business schools. They have excellent analytical minds. You can use this resource to help analyze your business problems, or the potential business problems that you contemplate for the future. Keep your partner informed about your business and use his mind to help solve your problems.

Most venture capital companies are extremely busy places. A telephone call from you every day or so is totally unnecessary, unless you are in a crisis situation. Most venture capitalists would like to hear from you every week or two, and you should contact the venture capital firm at least twice a month. If you have a loan or convertible debenture, be sure to send the payment that is due. Most venture capital firms think a monthly payment is a useful way to track a company. Send the monthly financial statements as they are due, and always send a written report with the financials.

The point to be emphasized is that you are keeping your partner, the venture capital firm, apprised of what is happening in the company. You need not discuss the day-to-day routine. You should discuss items such as the progress being made, the backlogs that exist, projections if they have changed, or the hiring of a new controller or other key employees. Also discuss problems you foresee in the future, such as market changes and new competition. The venture capitalist, like most investors and lenders, does not like to be surprised. As a minimum, an accurate, written report is necessary to avoid surprises.

Monthly Financials

Monthly financial statements are usually required by venture capital firms when they invest in a company. Receiving timely monthly financial statements is second only to receiving timely monthly payments on debts owed venture capital firms. You can be sure the venture capital firm will call you if you have not made your monthly payment on the convertible debenture or loan. You can also be sure that if you do not send in your monthly financial statements, the venture firm will think that you are not running a strong operation. No firm can be managed without accurate, timely, monthly financial statements. If you are not receiving monthly financial statements on a timely basis, you cannot possibly make reasonable decisions about your business. Tardy monthly financial statements are a red flag to every venture capitalist. Do not make the mistake of getting off to a bad start with the venture capital firm. Send the payment that is due, and send the monthly financial statements as they come due.

The accuracy of monthly financial statements is also very important. Every venture capitalist has now and again been surprised at year end when the audited financial statements came in. There are various types of surprises. Usually the surprise is lower earnings; that is, a profit is shown for eleven months and then a whopping loss for the year end. Typical excuses for the surprise are failure to accrue enough for accounts payable, an inventory write-off, or a difference in standard cost items in the costing system. Neither you nor the venture capitalist should be surprised at year end by the financial statements. Everyone can accept some accounting adjustments for year end. It is the magnitude that we are talking about and the reasons for large changes in financial statements at the end of the year. You will destroy your credibility with the venture capital firm as a competent manager if you have a big surprise on the financial statements at year end.

A Monthly Report Is Mandatory

A monthly report can be a letter, a report, or a memo. A typical monthly report is exemplified by the following:

MEMORANDUM

TO: A. V. Capitalist
FROM: J. Entrepreneur
SUBJECT: Monthly Report for October

Attached are the monthly financial statements for the nine-month period ending September 30. The profit-and-loss statement is understated in that our company will probably not pay taxes at the rate of

50 percent this year because of our net operating loss carried forward from last year. This should put approximately 95 percent of the pre-tax dollars to the bottom line.

As we near year end, it is evident that next year will be an extremely busy year. Our backlog has increased fivefold over last year. You should also note that inventories have increased approximately 40 percent more than our forecast. This is due to three very large orders that are now working their way through our production line. We have had to add people to the second shift to make sure that the items come through on schedule. None of these three orders will be completed and shipped by our year end, and therefore we will start out the year with an extraordinary amount of sales in the first several months.

We have talked to four people since we began looking for a controller to relieve some of the duties of our vice-president of finance. However, as of today we have not found a suitable candidate, but may be able to find one within the next ten to twenty days.

Finally, I am happy to say that the second generation of our product has now been completely designed and developed, and should be ready for introduction into the marketplace within six months at the national convention/trade fair. It will be an important milestone for our company; we introduced our first prototype only two years ago, and have since built many of these products. At our next board meeting we may be able to see a second generation unit.

The monthly report above mentioned several key items, each of which has a bearing on the future of the company. It also included a brief discussion of the financial statement, which are fairly self-explanatory. The discussion of the financial statements brought out a point that probably was not obvious to the venture capitalist reviewing the financial statement for ten minutes. It is incumbent upon you to highlight in the monthly report any negative, or in this case, positive developments.

Hold Board or Investor Meetings at Least Monthly

It is important that you have regular board meetings or investor meetings. You can keep your venture capital partner informed with memos and telephone calls, but a face-to-face meeting in which you discuss material items related to the business is an absolute must. Many venture firms meet with their portfolio companies two to four times per month. At a minimum, the venture capital firm should visit you once per quarter. You should prepare for these meetings. There should be an agenda and you should go through the agenda as if you were holding a formal meeting of the board or stockholders.

The first thing on the agenda should be the financial statements. A review of the financial statements compared to the statements of prior periods and compared to projections is a must. If you are presenting new projections, then you should explain them in detail. Generally speaking, these meetings should have a financial orientation rather than a marketing or production orientation. Numbers speak louder than words to a venture capitalist. As part of the financial discussions, mention the cash you have, plus credit available from your bank line. The amount you have borrowed should be set out. Keep the venture capitalist up to date on backlogs.

You may want to take the venture capitalist on an abbreviated plant tour to show him any new improvements, or changes that you have made since he made his original or prior plant tour. You will also want to discuss with him in detail the next round of financing that you need or a bank line of credit you are trying to negotiate. If you are planning an acquisition or have been discussing an acquisition, now is the time to lay out the figures and let the venture capitalist know what you are trying to accomplish. Other members of the management team should be present at this meeting and should participate in the discussions. Questions asked by the venture capitalist will often make people think about their business differently. It is important that you all get to know each other well.

If this is an initial or second meeting, you should present the venture capitalist with a cash reconciliation to show where his cash has been applied, and precisely how it was used in the business.

Other Discussion Items for the Venture Capitalist

If you have completed some market research or customer surveys, you may want to relate the results to the venture capitalist, especially if they are significant for your company. If you have reviewed the competition and their activities, you may want to pass along this information. Also, if suppliers have changed policies, or if you have found new suppliers, discuss this information with the venture capitalist. If there have been any industry studies or articles about your company or the industry in general in trade journals, you may want to make copies of these and give them to the venture capitalist as background information so that he can continue to learn and understand all of your business particulars.

If you have hired some key people or if you have fired some important people, you should tell the venture capitalist. Hiring a new director of marketing, or changing your controller, is a material action and you should keep your venture capital partner informed about your personnel situation. Any changes in overhead, additions or subtractions, should be explained to the venture capitalist. If you are opening a regional office or just hiring a regional representative, you may want to mention it in one of your monthly reports or in your formal board of directors or investors meeting.

Any large capital expenditure should be brought out. Any material changes in the backlog, either up or down, should be highlighted to the venture capitalist. If your audit is going to be late, you should explain why. If your research and development completion dates will not be met, you should also have an explanation. Target dates for introducing a product to the marketplace should be given to the venture capitalist, and if they are not kept, you should explain why.

Your venture capital partner is always seeking material information about your company. He will be more receptive to financial information than any other information. You need not inundate him with statistics and detailed information, but should keep him up to date and should highlight any material changes in your business or in the industry. You are doing all this so that your venture capital partner can assist in promoting your company's growth. Remember, the venture capital company is a resource for money and it is also a resource for brain power. The more you keep the venture capitalist involved and interested in your company, the more you will be able to use his brain power to help solve your problems.

You Are Building Confidence

In the relationship with the venture capital partner, as in any other human relationship, you are trying to build confidence. Being honest and informative with your business partner will build that confidence. Always do what you say you are going to do. If you intend to change something, explain why you will be going in a different direction. Do not make a statement and then fail to live up to it. Call the venture capitalist if there is a major decision to be made. Normally he is only one phone call away. Do not wait until you have a quarterly or monthly meeting to let him know that you have a problem, or that you have some good news. If you are behind in developing your product, make sure you let him know ahead of time with a phone call or a small note. If there has been a major change in your financial condition, be sure to tell him. The venture capitalist should receive no surprises.

By being open, straightforward, and informative with your venture capital partner, you will build additional confidence. The benefit of this open door policy can be stated succinctly: the more confidence you build with your venture capital partner, the less he will bother you for information, and the more he will rely on your judgment. As with any new relationship, he will be uneasy in the beginning of the relationship. The more confidence you build in demonstrating your management style and ability, the more the venture capitalist will relax and allow you to run the show completely without his influence.

Warning Signals to the Venture Capitalist

Generally speaking, entrepreneurs are unrealistic in evaluating problems. They often fail to recognize the early stages of failure. Entrepreneurs are optimistic. They cling to their dreams until the doors of their business are locked tight and the auctioneer has sold off the last piece of equipment.

In all probability, the venture capitalist will be the first to react to warning signals he receives from your business. These are commonly referred to as "red flags." The venture capitalist will be the first to point out the problems and perhaps burst the dream bubble of the entrepreneur. Many times an entrepreneur will be very antagonistic to the accusations of the venture capitalist. It will be in your interest to be cooperative, and to determine if the venture capitalist has a valid point. If the venture capitalist sees a problem, maybe there is a problem. Listed below are a number of red flags that a venture capitalist will react to.

Late Payments

If you are late in making payments on your convertible debenture, the venture capitalist will see that tardiness as a sign of very tight cash flow. You might think it is acceptable to leave the venture capitalist short and use the money in the business as working capital, but this will only bring suspicion of internal operating problems. You should make the payments to the venture capitalist on time, and keep his mind at rest. If you must be late, tell him before the payment is due that it will be late.

Losses

If your monthly financial statements show losses, the venture capitalist will be concerned. Losses as such are not bad. They may be the result of a temporary abberation, or you may have presented losses in your projection for a certain period of time until you break even. The venture capitalist will become more upset if you miss the monthly projections that you have presented to him. This will be a very large red flag indicating that the business is not going well.

Late Financial Reports

Tardiness in sending in the financial reports and other items you are supposed to supply to the venture capitalist will be considered a sure sign that your business is not operating well. It may be thought that you are trying to hide bad news from the venture capitalist, or that you are so disorganized and are running the business so poorly that you cannot get a financial statement out.

Poor Financial Reports

Even if you produce the financial statements but they are poorly prepared or somewhat unreliable, it will be a warning to the venture capitalist that your company is not well managed. Receiving inaccurate financials is worse than receiving no financials. There was an entrepreneur who sent in a financial statement that showed the company was marginally profitable. This was good news to the venture capitalist since the business had been losing money. Then the venture capitalist discovered that several line items had been excluded from the statement—the rent and interest payments. Even worse, when the venture capitalist added up the expense column, he found it was understated by 20 percent!

Large Changes in Your Balance Sheet

If your accounts payable increase drastically, the venture capitalist will suspect that you are not paying your bills. The venture capitalist will soon spot such changes and want to know why they have taken place. On the other side of the balance sheet, if your inventories become very large, the venture capitalist will believe that you are not making the needed sales and you are producing too many items for inventory. In the same vein, ballooning accounts receivable may mean you are unable to collect some of the receivables that you have booked as sales. Any of these developments will be red flags to the venture capitalist.

Unavailable Entrepreneur

Repeated telephone calls to the entrepreneur that are not returned are a tell-tale sign. Why would the entrepreneur not return phone calls unless he is afraid of being asked questions about the business? Also an entrepreneur's failure to schedule regular board meetings is perceived as a warning signal by the venture capitalist.

Large Thefts

Unexplained large thefts of inventory may be an indication that the entrepreneur himself is stealing from the company and covering it up by a reported theft. More revealing is a theft that the insurance company does not cover. This normally means the entrepreneur is unwilling to pursue the case with the insurance company because he does not welcome the insurance company's investigation. An unexplained fire falls in the same category. Entrepreneurs in trouble often try to cover up their problems with a large fire. In the south, a large fire that destroys a business is called "selling out to a northern concern." As the story goes, a "good ole boy" will insure all his assets through a northern insurance company; then a mysterious fire will wipe them out and he will collect from the northern insurance company.

Major Adjustments in Figures

A large year end adjustment in financial numbers is an indication that management is not running the company well. If you have to write off a large part of inventory or if your accounting firm is not willing to capitalize some expenses, the impact on the profit-and-loss statement will be disastrous and a sure indication that management is not running the shop well. This will be a red flag to every venture capitalist.

Why Entrepreneurs Have Financial Problems

When you ask a venture capitalist, "What makes a good company?" he will always say, "Good management." But, in a sense, that goes without saying. If the company shows strong growth and the venture capitalist makes money, then it had good management. If the company gets in trouble and loses money for the venture capitalist, then the company had poor management. So what did the venture capitalist mean by good management? He meant good management recognizes that the two most critical problems for an entrepreneur running a small company are: (1) lack of financial monitoring and control; and (2) undercapitalization.

The Financial Control Problem

Most entrepreneurs can put together a good business plan and solid projections, and can understand the cost of the required capital from banks and venture capitalists. However, only a few will set up a system to monitor progress and analyze the information they are receiving. As an entrepreneur, you should want to know what the sales figures are on a weekly basis. Some retail operations want to know on a daily basis. Every entrepreneur should be watching the figures closely. When cost figures do not coincide with those projected, find out why. When sales do not match projected figures, find out why. When the projections do not work out precisely, revise the future projections in order to determine how much capital you are going to need to go where you are going.

The most successful entrepreneurs have been "cash flow freaks." These are people who know exactly what is going on in their company from a numerical standpoint. They know when they will run out of cash, the so-called "drop dead date." They know what they have to do in order to increase cash flow. When things get rough, they know how much money they need to carry them through the next stage. They know precisely what they are doing in allocating their scarce resources properly. A monthly profit-and-loss statement is almost an afterthought for them. They ride herd on the company's cash on a weekly and sometimes daily basis.

The Undercapitalization Problem

Undercapitalization has always been a serious problem for small businesses. Too often the entrepreneur will fail to raise the amount of money he needs. He will raise $200,000 when he really needs $500,000. He does this so he won't have to give up as much equity to the venture capitalist. This approach is shortsighted. Most businesses need more money than originally projected in order to reach profitability. When the entrepreneur needs the extra money, the venture capitalist may charge a high price. Always raise enough money.

Smart management recognizes the need to have sufficient capital in the company. It does not tie up excess capital in accounts receivable or inventory. It seeks ways to increase the capital in the company. When the company grows, management knows the company must increase its capitalization. Be a good manager and maintain adequate capital for your company.

Why Entrepreneurs Have People Problems

Many an entrepreneur can run a company well when it consists of a small intimate group, but cannot manage the business when it begins growing into a larger company. The failure often relates to the selection and management of people. As can be expected, no business can grow and remain a one-person operation, nor can an entrepreneur remain a chief with many Indians. In order for a company to grow, the business must attract top-notch middle management to the team. There are five basic reasons that many small businesses fail to build a strong middle management team.

Poor Job Definition

Senior management often fails to understand precisely what job needs to be filled. Entrepreneurs are accustomed to dealing with undefined job responsibilities. They expect the team to join in and work. However, as a company grows, specialization becomes important. Certain jobs must be segregated and defined so that certain individuals can be hired to do those jobs specifically. As manager of the company, you must define jobs.

Poor Selection Process

Once the job has been defined, top management may use a poor selection process. It is easy, for example, to let "good ole" Joe continue to be controller of the company since he has been the bookkeeper from the beginning. Or hire a relative out of loyalty rather than because of his ability to manage the job that needs to be done. These practices do not ensure strong middle management.

Poor Incentives to Management

In order to attract middle management to your company, you need an effective incentive plan. The members of the entrepreneurial team have a high incentive because they own a large share of the company. Their egos are submerged in the business and they want to make it a success. New members of the management team won't have the same rewards. In order to motivate them, top management should consider the various traditional methods of compensating top-notch middle management. These include stock options, stock performance rights, good pension and profit-sharing plans, bonuses based on formulas of sales or accomplishments, and the like. If you do not set up a proper reward system for your middle management people, they will not perform.

Poor Review Program

Because middle managers do not get the same satisfaction out of the growth of the company as entrepreneurs, they need to be rewarded through traditional review programs that let them know when they are succeeding and when they are failing. A good review program will give you an early warning of any problems with middle managers. It will also give you an opportunity to correct the problem. You must have a review system that is in concert with your incentive system.

Poor Development Program

Sometimes a company outgrows the abilities of the initial middle management team simply because the managers are not given a chance to develop their skills through seminars, and other educational methods. This situation can be avoided by having all the middle management team come together to share their ideas and discuss the problems they are having within the company. This interaction permits marketing to become acquainted with what is happening in production, and allows finance to better understand the problems of marketing, as well as other aspects of your business. This kind of internal professional development program is necessary for any growing company, and should supplement a regular development program.

The Protean Entrepreneur

As the entrepreneur, you will be expected to move from operating a one-man show to managing a team of people. You will be delegating responsibility and holding your managers accountable for their actions. You must be able to use a variety of management styles to keep your team motivated. In some situations you will have to be a tyrant, and in others, democratic. If you are unable to make this transition, it will be difficult for your company to grow. If you cannot manage people, the venture capital company may suggest that a chief executive officer is needed, and that you should play more of a figurehead role. Many entrepreneurial companies outgrow their scientific or technical founder. It is no disgrace for the entrepreneur to become chairman and to hire a hard-charging manager as president.

Why Do Some Entrepreneurs Succeed?

Why do some entrepreneurs succeed while most fail? There are many explanations of success and failure. Venture capitalists spend a great deal of time discussing why one entrepreneur failed and another succeeded, and they think that most successful entrepreneurs have certain things in common. The characteristics most often mentioned by them are as follows.

Problem Solvers

Every successful entrepreneur is an excellent problem solver. Venture capitalists agree that this is a predominant trait of the successful entrepreneur. Rarely do entrepreneurs waste any time placing blame on others. They try to determine what the problem is, solve it, and go on to the next situation.

Able to Grow Personally

Successful entrepreneurs can transcend their accomplishments and move on to the next level of objectives. One accomplishment seems to create a desire to accomplish the next task. Thus, the successful entrepreneur never seems to dwell on his past accomplishments, only with the current objectives. Once these entrepreneurs have accomplished their task, and seem to be living on Easy Street, they move on to the next task. They are unable to rest, and they must constantly be planning and striving for continued growth of their company.

Set Internal Goals

Successful entrepreneurs seem to be driven by their own internal goals. They love to set goals and then surpass them. The process of achieving goals seems more fun to them than actually surpassing goals. They love to run the race. Hitting the tape and winning is not important. Winning in itself means nothing. It is the art of winning that drives successful entrepreneurs. Money is important, but more as a measure of success than an end in itself.

Understand Downside Risk

Every successful entrepreneur has sketched out, either in his mind or on paper, the absolute downside risk of any major decision. What catastrophic occurrence could be brought on by a decision that he has to make? He knows beforehand exactly what the worst case could be, and decides whether he can live with that outcome. If he can live with it, he moves forward with confidence. If he cannot, he does not move forward. Most unsuccessful entrepreneurs fail to determine the downside risk.

Rehearse Coming Actions

One of the biggest surprises to venture capitalists has been to learn that successful entrepreneurs rehearse coming events. A good entrepreneur imagines almost every aspect of what it would take to achieve something. He practices in his mind as if daydreaming. This is a time-honored technique in sports events, particularly in track and field, but it is surprising to find the same trait in successful entrepreneurs. An average entrepreneur might prepare himself for a presentation by setting out the facts in an agenda. An achieving personality would mentally rehearse a perfect presentation and prepare his psyche for the entire successful presentation.

If you do not exhibit all of the traits set out above, you may wish to modify your behavior. In the beginning, you will be involved in every aspect of the business, but later you will need to become primarily a people manager. You will need to become a master of delegating authority. You must be able to work through people to accomplish objectives. Rarely will you be bogged down in minor details.

When You Have Problems

When you have severe operating problems, the venture capitalist will be trying to make one basic decision: should he try to remove you, the president, and find a new president, or should he run the company himself for a while? Does he have enough confidence in you to work with you in the hope that you can turn the crisis situation around? Should you find yourself in a crisis situation, the best thing to do is to lay it all out before the venture capitalist. Tell him what the problems are, and how you are trying to solve them. If you lie or hide problems, the venture capitalist will have no alternative but to try to remove you. Remember, the venture capitalist's cardinal rule for entrepreneurs is that they must possess integrity.

There is a general rule in the venture capital community that "You only get one chance." This means that if you, the entrepreneur, lead your company into trouble, the venture capitalist will try to exercise his control rights and force you out. Presumably, he will then try to run the company himself as he searches for a new president. In practice, the venture capitalist does not always adhere. to the general rule. You will only be forced out if you are dishonest or stupid.

If you find yourself in the terrible situation of running a company in trouble, the best thing you can do is generate a plan to save the company. Present the plan to your stockholders and venture capital partner. If the plan is unacceptable to the venture capital company and your other stockholders, you may wish to bow out gracefully rather than embroil the company in a battle. Try to retain as much ownership in the company as possible while bowing out. You will probably make more money by walking away from the company and letting the venture capitalist run it, if he asks to run it, than you could gain by entering a mudslinging fistfight with the venture capital company.

In most instances where the entrepreneur is an honest, hard-working individual who is willing to make the sacrifices necessary to save the company, the entrepreneur has been retained. Many companies in trouble have been saved because the entrepreneur was an honest individual who had the "will to survive." He did what was prudent to save his company.

Analysis of the Situation

Another cardinal rule in the venture capital business is not to lose one's principal investment. When the venture capitalist determines that a company is in trouble, he will try to minimize his losses. He will try to determine how he can get his money back. Furthermore, he will try to determine what actions will return the greatest amount of money to him. In order to answer these questions, he will analyze the company from two different perspectives.

First, he will analyze the earning capacity of the company. Can the problems at hand be solved? How quickly can they be solved? How much will it cost to carry the company while the problems are being solved? If the problems are solved, do we have a salable asset? Before the venture capitalist will invest additional funds, he will analyze the company in much the same way he made the initial analysis. Each new dollar he invests will be like a new investment to him. It must have a return. Throwing good money after bad will not be a venture capitalist's method of operating.

The second type of analysis will be concerned with the bricks and mortar. The venture capitalist will look at all the assets and what they are worth in liquidation. He will reduce any asset by the amount of secured liabilities against it. He will look at the probability suppliers will offset against inventory. Mechanics' liens, taxes, and other items that have not been paid will be considered. On the positive side, he will try to analyze any intangible assets such as a franchise, a license to operate, patents, advantageous leases, and so on. These two analyses of your business will conclude with an assessment of the venture capitalist's options: fix the problem; sell the business; foreclose; seek bankruptcy; and liquidate the assets.

What the Venture Capitalist Will Do

The analysis made by the venture capitalist may not lead to a satisfactory conclusion. In fact, such analyses usually are inconclusive. Nonetheless, the venture capitalist will have to make a decision when faced with a company in trouble. Let's look at the five basic options open to him.

1. Fix the Problem

The venture capitalist can put additional money into the business, and try to keep it going. He may hire additional people, or do whatever else is necessary to solve his problems and save his investment. This solution may or may not include you as the general manager. Most entrepreneurs plead with the venture capitalist to go forward with the business. It is not always in the best interest of the entrepreneur to continue because the company may merely slide into deeper trouble and hurt more people. The entrepreneur often argues that the company should continue even though there may be no business reason for this decision.

In one venture capital situation, the company was in the cement business, which is a cyclical business based on the housing industry. In 1980 the housing industry was in shambles, but projections suggested a turnaround was about to take place. The entrepreneur and the venture group bought the company in the fall and used capital during the winter to carry the company. By spring, it needed an additional injection of capital, and the equity partners put in additional capital. By the end of the summer, the housing industry had not picked up and the equity partners were again called upon to place additional equity in the company. Only a few of them put up the additional money. By this point, the equity partners owned approximately 70 percent of the company and the entrepreneur owned 30 percent. Spring came and another capital infusion was needed to carry the company forward until the housing market began to expand. The expansion never took place. Finally, the company was sold for a pittance. Venture firms often feed a company month after month in order to keep it alive.

2. Sell the Business

The venture capitalist may try to sell the company, or merge it with a similar business. Invariably, every business is worth more as an operating entity than one that is shut down. This is especially true of service-oriented companies. Merging the company with a larger entity that can bring money and management to build the new company may be a plus for you and your investment.

In one venture situation involving retail tires the alternatives were to inject additional money in the company or sell the company. Since the venture capitalist had lost faith in the entrepreneurs, their one alternative was to sell the business quickly. As you can imagine, the tire business is made up of leased locations, inventory, and people. Without these three ingredients, you have nothing of value. It was necessary to move quickly to find another tire retailer who wanted to enter the marketplace in which this tire company was located. It was the only way to save the company.

3. Foreclosure

The venture capitalist also has the option of acting like a creditor, if he is in a creditor's position, and can foreclose against those assets. He can seize the assets and try to operate them himself, or sell the assets in order to generate enough money to pay back his investment. This is a very difficult move for venture capitalists, who are usually not operators of businesses.

Sometimes the venture capitalist, if he is in a secured debt position, has the option of foreclosing. In one business, the venture capitalist foreclosed on a radio station and took over the assets of the company. These assets were primarily a transmitter and studio on a lease site, and a Federal Communications Commission (FCC) license to operate a radio station. The FCC was petitioned to transfer the license to the venture capital firm on an interim basis, and it did. While operating the station, the venture capitalist always listened to it as he drove over to pay expenses. One day he heard many classy ads being broadcast. When he arrived, he asked the radio disc jockey how he had sold that many ads on the station. The disc jockey replied, "Oh, I didn't sell anything. I just like to listen to the ads so I put them on free!"

The venture capitalist soon shut down the radio station so he would not have to feed the losses. Then he went looking for a buyer. The venture capitalist was soon able to find a buyer who was willing to guarantee the repayment of the note in exchange for all the assets, including the FCC license. Most venture capitalists realize they cannot operate your business. In the case of the radio station, the venture capitalist knew he could not make money with free ads.

4. Bankruptcy

Some venture capitalists try to place the company in involuntary bankruptcy and have a receiver appointed. They seek bankruptcy in order to hold off creditors who may have a senior credit lien to the company's assets. If the senior creditors obtain the assets, there may be little of value in the remaining assets to pay the venture capitalist anything. Operating in bankruptcy until the business can straighten out its many problems may be the only way for a stockholder to receive anything. Often in bankruptcy stockholders are wiped out completely, and only creditors receive something.

The new bankruptcy code is quite lenient to business owners. It provides for creditors or the entrepreneur-owner to take the company into bankruptcy to hold off all creditors. Such action is frowned upon, however, and would probably reduce one's chances of receiving financing in the future. In one large venture capital situation, bankruptcy was used to hold off a senior creditor for three years while the company operated as "debtor in possession," meaning the management team continued to run the company. The senior creditor was unable to foreclose under its note. Three years later, the company was able to come out of bankruptcy, settle many of its accounts payable debts for several cents on the dollar, enter a long-term payout with the senior creditor, and go forward.

5. Liquidate

The venture capitalist can work hard to liquidate the company by selling off the assets, paying off any creditors who are ahead of the venture capitalist, and then receiving as much money as is left. Sometimes a business that is asset heavy may be worth more after liquidation than it would be as an operating entity, because as an operating entity, it is projected to lose money indefinitely. If the venture capitalist is placed in this position, he will definitely seek to liquidate the company in order to recover as much of his money as possible.

None of these choices is easy. You may find yourself at odds with the venture capitalist on which decision to make because he will be influenced by money matters—he is usually the one who has to put up additional money. The entrepreneur can easily represent that the business will be fine if it can just get to cash flow break-even. The venture capitalist must carry the company until it gets there. Once the decision is made, you are probably better off trying to help. Running counter to the adopted plan and the venture capitalist can only destroy the company's chances of recovery.

Ten Things Not to Say

In your long-standing relationship with the venture capitalist, there are ten things you probably should not say to him, if you do not want him to lose faith in you. Some of these items deal with your manner of speaking rather than with the context. Each item may sound humorous as presented below, but I personally have heard people say these things in one form or another.

1. My wife and I have decided to move to Florida where the weather is warm so that we can both enjoy the outdoors more. Even though the business is located in Massachusetts, I will be able to run it from Florida.

Obviously, the venture capitalist will be upset to see you moving away from the business. Most entrepreneurial businesses cannot be operated by an absentee manager, especially a start-up business or one in a high growth mode. When you decide to move, like the fellow above, check out the local employment scene, as you will soon be out of work. The legal documents usually will prevent you from moving. That is, a move may be a violation of the negative covenants. Your presence at the company is desirable for all members of the management team. Big failures have occurred when management was not present.

In one venture situation the company was located in Washington, D.C., while its president lived in Westport, Connecticut. He commuted to work. He rationalized his living in Westport by saying there was good transportation, and that the company was oriented toward marketing, which kept him on the road a lot anyway. In addition, the company's marketing manager lived in Houston. This meant neither of the top people in this marketing-oriented company lived in Washington, D.C. They were not constantly in touch with the people in the central office. The company failed and was merged with another large company. These two "flying officers" had their wings clipped.

> 2.   Some friends and I got together and we purchased the franchise to a doughnut operation. I am putting $25,000 of my money into the deal through a second mortgage on my house, and my wife and I are going to help operate the doughnut shop.

Taking on a second business when you are supposed to dedicate 100 percent of your time to the business at hand is a stupid move on your part. It will be viewed by the venture capitalist as a sign of poor judgment on your behalf. Getting involved in outside investments when you have to run an entrepreneur business is not acceptable. When you decide to open another business like the fellow above, make plans to proceed full-time, because if the venture capitalist has his way, it will soon be your only occupation.

Most legal documents have a provision saying that you must give your full time and attention to the business, so if you become part owner and operator of another business, you will be in violation of your agreement. There is a second danger in taking on another business. What if the second business were to develop tremendous operating problems? You would then have to spend a greater percentage of your time on the problem company, and of course, leave the first business backed by the venture capital company to run itself. Many venture capitalists know what can happen when one business venture pulls down another venture because management was spread much too thin. Be smart. Stay in only one business.

> 3.   We have been negotiating with another small business and have now entered into a final agreement to acquire it. We're going to give up about 30 percent of the stock in our company in a stock swap for their company. I didn't talk to you about it because it's such a good deal I knew you would like it.

Acquiring a business without consulting your venture capital partner is a mistake. Diluting his ownership in your company by 30 percent is a major move. Bringing in a new business, which may or may not have the same profitability chances as your business, will give the venture capitalist reason to think twice about your intelligence. In addition, any merger is usually a violation of your loan or stock purchase agreement.

One of the greatest problems in the game of mergers and acquisitions is the difficulty of merging one company with another. We are so accustomed to reading about acquisitions in the large financial newspapers that we think an acquisition only takes a small amount of time. In actuality, an acquisition can consume years of management's time as they integrate the new company into the old. Much time will be spent on learning about a new business. Most venture capitalists have been involved in a number of mergers and they know the tremendous amount of time small business management can spend on mergers.

4.   We came up with a new product. It is unrelated to our business but it's in the solar energy field. I have been meaning to tell you about it. We have spent about $200,000 developing the product and we are now producing it at the rate of about two hundred a week. We have a warehouse full.

Obviously, taking on a new line of business that is unrelated to your own is a major decision. Spending large sums of money to develop it is another major business decision. All of this should have been discussed with your venture capital partner before you embarked on it. Jumping into a new area without consultation, and without the approval of your partner is a bad idea. If you try something like this, watch out! If the product does not move quickly you, personally, will be moved out of your office into the street.

Any new product that you go into will be a violation of your investment agreement. On top of this, a new product will consume an inordinate amount of working capital. The risk you run of failure by taking on a product that has no close relationship to your own is extremely high. Ask the venture capitalist. He is constantly investing in new products and new businesses that may or may not be related to anything he has seen before. It will be wise for you to understand that investing in new, high-risk situations should be left to the venture capital professionals, and that you should invest your time and money only in the areas where you have expertise.

5.   We now have seven new regional offices that cost us about $80,000 each to set up. We wanted to set them all up at once in order to penetrate the market quickly. I didn't call you because I knew you would think it was a good idea to make a fast move.

Any fast move of this magnitude that would cost the company over half a million dollars should have been cleared with your venture capital partner. Marketing plans seldom require rapid penetration to ward off the competition. A slow rollout can eliminate some costly mistakes. The quick penetration plan is a drastic change in marketing strategy, and is a high-risk proposition. If sales do not pick up quickly, the entrepreneur can kiss his leadership position in the company goodbye.

6.   I sold 200,000 shares of the company's stock at $1.00 each to some friends of mine. I know this represents 20 percent of the company, but I just couldn't pass up the opportunity for a quick $200,000. After all, you and I only paid $.25 a share and we have been able to sell the stock now for $1.00 per share. That makes the company worth more.

Violating the loan agreement willy-nilly, without even a telephone call to the venture capitalist, is risking sure destruction of your relationship with your venture capital partner. Whenever you plan anything that is in violation of your loan agreement, you should obtain written authority. Giving up equity is always a touchy subject with the venture capitalist because it dilutes his potential ownership and return on investment. Do not treat your partner badly and he will not be a bad partner.

One venture capital firm tells the story of an entrepreneur who just could not stop selling shares in his company. All of his marketing talents had been tuned up and turned on for selling stock in his company. Even after receiving venture capital financing, he continued to line up additional investments for private placement and to work with several stockbrokerage firms for a public offering. It seems the public offering never came around and the entrepreneur spent so much time trying to arrange future financings for his company that he never really got the product off the ground. He was soon relieved of his duties and, what is not surprising, he became a stockbroker.

> 7.   Two of our accounts receivable customers who owed us a total of $200,000 declared bankruptcy on the same day, and it would seem that our claim in the bankruptcy court is probably worthless. This will lower our profits by $200,000 and, as you know, make the company a break-even operation for the first six months.

Without question, this type of action has great impact on your financial judgment, but it has an even greater impact on the venture capitalist. You never consulted with him about a major account, or about the risk you were running by shipping goods to the companies. Now they have gone bankrupt. Your credibility with the venture capital partner will be very low in these circumstances. You may also wind up bankrupt.

Some entrepreneurs building up a company become so excited about sales, projections, and backlog, that they forget to analyze fundamental credit risks. When you have large orders coming from companies that are not too well known, it is better for you to understand their financial strengths early. You should let your venture capital partner know what kind of risks you are taking when you ship a large order to a small client with a poor credit rating. Both of you should make the decision together to expose the company to a potential large loss.

> 8.   I am out of money and can't meet Friday's payroll. I know the cash flow projections showed that we had enough money to last another year, but in checking through my cash flow projections I found a $70,000-per-month mathematical error. I thought we were using cash awfully fast three months ago, but I thought it would turn around soon. I am sorry. What can I do?

For starters, this fellow should look for a new job. Any entrepreneur who makes a $70,000 per month cash flow *mathematical* error deserves to be kicked out. It may be possible to forgive a mathematical error, but to know three months ago that cash was being chewed up quickly, not to have looked into it, and not to have brought it to the attention of your business partner—that is a grave error. It will be practically impossible for you to recover from this stupid mistake.

> 9.   We just finished the prototype of our initial product. I immediately turned the engineers loose on four other products we should be developing. It won't take much time or money to sell our prototype and to get the manufacturing process going. Then we'll really be rolling in the money. Meanwhile I know there are other products that we can develop for the marketplace.

Your first priority, when you are in the development stage, is to develop the product you agreed to develop and develop it on schedule. It has been my experience that development of a product is easy, compared to manufacturing it within the projected cost, and marketing it to the new customers. By continuing to emphasize research and development rather than changing your company's focus to manufacturing and marketing, you will demonstrate to the venture capital firm that you are not an entrepreneur. You are, in essence, a research engineer. If you are to be the guiding light behind your business, you must determine at the outset what business you are in. Most venture capital firms have no interest in backing research and development companies. They are in the business of backing manufacturing and marketing companies. If you are not willing to make the step from research and development to manufacturing and sales, you should realize that the venture capital firm has no alternative but to replace you with a management team that will move the company into the manufacturing and marketing stage.

> 10.   This recession is killing us. Industry sales are off 35 percent. I don't want to cut anymore overhead because I am sure sales will turn around. I put on a television blitz for the last two months. However, it didn't work and now we are completely out of working capital. Can you invest some additional money?

Embarking on a television blitz in the middle of a recession is playing with fire. When you have a shrinking market, it is very difficult to hold your sales share, but this is not the point of the example. The point is, the entrepreneur's plan did not work. He took precious working capital and spent it on advertising. He did this rather than lay off additional people. Laying people off is difficult. I can remember every time that I have been involved in the process. But if you, as an entrepreneur, are to be a manager, you must manage in good times and in bad. In bad times laying off people is usually required. If you are unwilling to manage the company in bad times, the venture capitalist will have no alternative but to get someone who will.

Secret of a Successful Relationship

Every relationship is based on trust. If you have entered into a financial deal with a venture capital firm that you do not trust, you have made a grave mistake. You are sure to have some doubts about the venture capital firm in the initial months, but if your checking has been accurate, then the venture capital firm should prove trustworthy. Assuming you both trust each other, there must also be a desire to help each other. The venture capitalist wants to make money, and you want to make money. You both have a common objective. One should not be making money at the other's expense. You should be on the same level, and therefore, should have a desire to help each other. From time to time, you may ask the venture capitalist to help you with various problems encountered in your company. The venture capitalist may ask you to do some things that will enhance his profit position. Remember, you are partners.

More than anything, the secret to a successful relationship is the ability to talk to each other, and to communicate both the good and the bad news to one another. If two individuals can openly discuss the things they like and dislike about a relationship, as well as tell one another what things are good and what things are bad in a constructive critical approach, then the relationship will most likely be a successful one. In turn, the business will probably prosper.

I remember an entrepreneur who was highly motivated, well trained, and an achiever of the first order, but who was unable to admit failure. This flaw dominated his personality to such a degree that not only did he refuse to admit small errors, but he would not accept the fact that his company had lost $175,000 at the end of its second year. When he received the audit from a large accounting firm, he would not accept it. He made the accounting firm restate the figures, but give him a qualified opinion. The financials showed the company had made a profit and was in good financial condition. The accountants' opinion had a section which said the financials were correct, subject to the adjustments made by the entrepreneur. The entrepreneur presented these financial statements to his board of directors, to his bank, and to his investors. He seemed to think that if he could somehow get through the year without anyone except the accountant knowing his true condition, then he would have time to turn the company around and cover up past mistakes.

This entrepreneur was unsuccessful in his cover-up. The company was liquidated. Many people lost a great deal of money. In your relationship with your investors, your board of directors, and your employees, be open and speak your mind. Save all of your connivings and devious actions for your competition, as long as your actions are legal and acceptable in the marketplace where you sell your products.

Venture Capitalist as Board Member

Most venture capitalists want to be a member of your board; in fact, they may want several people from the venture capital group to be on your board. Some venture capitalists will not sit on your board of directors because of the liability involved, but they will attend board meetings. Sometimes, you may find a young venture capitalist monitoring your business and may feel as though you are training him in the ways of business. Many young venture capitalists are oriented toward "strategic planning" of the type promoted in business schools. They review your business plan as if it were a strategic plan for the industry, and they look at you as if you were a large business about to capture a premier position in the marketplace. While it is important to have a long range and perhaps even a strategic plan for your business, it is more important to have a growth plan for your company during the early stages. A strategic plan for the marketplace in the early years is probably not necessary. However, managing tremendous growth takes a high degree of planning. You should emphasize your growth plan to your young venture capital board member, rather than your strategic plan. You should turn his attention to the early stage of growth.

When you have a syndication of venture capitalists investing in your company, make sure your relationship is a simple one by indicating that you will be responsible primarily to the lead venture capitalist. You should send reports to all the venture capitalists, but you should work with only one of them. Venture capitalists are familiar with the lead investor situation in which they conduct business with the lead investor rather than the small businessman. This does not mean you should ignore them. From time to time, you may want to talk to one of them about specific subjects relating to your business and their specific skills. You should have semiannual or quarterly investor meetings in which you bring them all up to date on the company. Your lead investor can help you with these meetings.

Degree of Involvement by the Venture Capitalist

The amount of time the venture capitalist will spend with your company will depend on a number of factors.

Amount Invested

The amount the venture capitalist has invested in your company, compared to other investments, will determine how much time he spends with you. If he has invested $50,000 in an early stage, he may not spend nearly as much time as if he had invested several million dollars. The larger the amount invested, the more upset the venture capitalist will be if he loses it. The more the invested funds mean to the venture capitalist, the more attention you will receive.

Need for Assistance

If you have a complete management team, and do not need assistance, the venture capitalist will usually stay away. If you need a financial adviser or someone to discuss marketing, then the venture capitalist may perform that function. The more help you need, the more the venture capitalist will be concerned, and the more time he will give your company.

Management's Willingness to Accept Advice

If management is willing to accept advice, most venture capitalists are willing to give it. If management resists every suggestion, obviously the venture capitalist will not waste his time making suggestions to tell management. There is a fine line for you to walk here. You should be hungry for advice on major decisions, but not on day-to-day operations.

Experience in Certain Areas

If the venture capitalist is not experienced in a certain area where you have a problem, he will not try to advise you on the matter. If the venture capitalist has good financial information and the entrepreneur is not a financial whiz, the venture capitalist will try to help with financial decisions.

Lead Investor

If the venture capitalist is the lead investor, he will probably spend more time than if he was the sole investor. This arises from his feeling of responsibility to the other venture capital investors. While he is under no legal obligation to ensure that they make money, his reputation is on the line with his friends. He wants you to succeed so he will probably spend more time with your company.

Distress of Company

If the company is operating in distress circumstances, then the venture capitalist will try to play an active role. Every venture capitalist works on whatever problems threaten his investment. Many venture capitalists spend most of their time working out problems, rather than reviewing new deals. In fact, most venture capitalists say they are not in the venture capital business at all, but rather that they are in the business of working out bad deals. They are always trying to avoid losing their money. It seems the good companies take care of themselves.

Relationship with Entrepreneur

Often a strong bond will unite entrepreneur and venture capitalist. A certain chemistry that exists among people in venture situations draws them together. Great friendships have arisen from these relationships, even in dire circumstances.

Time Availability

As mentioned many times before, venture capitalists are extremely busy. They work on the most pressing problems first. If yours is a small problem or if you are operating well, you can expect the venture capitalist to invest most of his time in more serious problem situations. You should not interpret the venture capitalist's lack of attention to your business as a lack of interest in your company. The amount of time spent on an investment is usually inversely proportionate to the success of the investment. In general, a venture capitalist cannot make a company a success, but he can often save his investment when there is trouble.

Venture Capitalist's Objectives

During this period of time, when you are working together, the venture capitalist will have one objective: growth. He wants to see your company grow as fast as possible, and to see it become as large as possible. He wants to see sales go up, and he wants to see profits go up. Those are his basic objectives for being an investor in your company. The venture capitalist also wants to see you become a leader. He wants to see that you no longer have to be involved in every detail, that you have found good employees, and that you can work through them.

If your company has grown sharply and is now becoming large, the venture capitalist will be looking toward liquidity. The venture capitalist wants to be able to see part of his investment when the time is right. He receives no bonuses because of your growth and success. He receives his rewards when he is able to see part or all of his investment and make a large profit. You will find that every venture capitalist has a desire to sell part of his investment. The only drawback in selling is the matter of price.

During this period of time the venture capitalist will avoid all lawsuits. He will advise you not to involve the company or yourself in lawsuits. The rationale behind this is simple; during the growth phases, a small business cannot afford to allocate its man power or monetary resources to lawsuits. If the company has lost money because it was cheated, then a lawsuit is in order, but if less important problems are at issue, a lawsuit will be the last thing the venture capitalist will want. A venture capitalist can be counted on to vote against lawsuits.

Objective

Your objective during this period of time will be to build the company. Make it strong so that you can either: (a) buy out the venture capital partner by refinancing the company; (b) go public so that the venture capitalist and you, the entrepreneur, can cash in some of your ownership; or (c) sell the entire company so that you and the venture capitalist can realize a large capital gain. Also, you should consult the venture capitalist. He can help you with information that can be of help in making tough decisions. Putting your time and effort into running a good strong business, rather than concentrating on how quickly you can get rid of the venture capitalist, will make life more bearable for you. In the next chapter we discuss how you can move the venture capitalist out of your life.

10

The Exit

How Can You Remove the Venture Capital Company?
The Way To Own It All.

There has always been a love-hate relationship between the venture capitalist and the entrepreneur. Most venture capitalists are frustrated entrepreneurs. They will watch you make a great deal of money and sometimes, they will be envious of your success. Most entrepreneurs, on the other hand, love their venture capitalist the day they receive an infusion of cash from him, but some years later, when the venture capitalist is able to cash in his equity ownership and make ten times his money, the entrepreneur is apt to believe the venture capitalist made too much money. After all, the only thing the venture capitalist did was put in his money. Another source of friction arises in the company that operates poorly. The venture capitalist may take actions to remedy the situation, and the entrepreneur, thinking the actions are wrong, may try to resist them.

Instead of reacting negatively, both parties should remember that each one took a substantial risk. There were many times when both wondered if the company was ever going to make it. Each party had a great deal to lose: the venture capitalist's reputation and money were on the line; and the entrepreneur's reputation and one chance were on the line. Both should respect each other's position and continue to work together as mature adults.

Nevertheless, there comes a time when every entrepreneur wants to be completely free of his venture capital partner. He does not want to be under the influence of the venture capitalist. He wants to have complete operating authority over his business. When this time comes, the venture capitalist will sell his equity ownership in the business.

Every ownership position in every company held by a venture capitalist is for sale. Do not ever think that a venture capitalist wants to own a minority interest or even a majority interest in your firm forever. Venture capitalists are not in the business of owning and operating companies. They are in the business of investing for a period of time and cashing in on those investments. They receive no kudos from the owners of the venture capital fund when they say they own 30 percent of a dozen small companies. The only time the venture capitalist is rewarded is the day he converts the ownership in your company into cash. Most venture capital managers receive a bonus in proportion to the cash capital gains they generate. Every venture capitalist wants to sell the ownership position in your company and generate capital gains so he can receive a bonus.

It's All a Matter of Price

Now that you understand what the venture capitalist wants to get out and needs to get out, you have reduced the argument to one of price. The price at which the venture capitalist will sell depends on the value of the company, which in turn depends on the stage of development of the company. If it's early in the game plan for the company, you may have to pay dearly to buy out the venture capitalist. He is prepared to wait for the business to mature. He will not sell short if he sees that the company will be twice as large next year. If your company is mature, the venture capitalist will want out soon and his price can be negotiated more easily. The venture capitalist will be taken out in the four ways discussed below.

First Method: Going Public

Most venture capitalists will spend a great deal of time talking about the virtues of going public. You and the venture capitalist will like the idea of going public. By establishing a public market, you can cash in some of your chips. The public market gives the venture capitalist an exit for part of his holdings and a method of selling additional shares as time goes on. In a publicly-owned company in which the venture capitalist merely has an investment, his role in the policy-making activities is relatively small.

When to Go Public

Many brokerage houses will tell you that there is a time to go public and there is a time not to go public. They will discuss the marketplace in terms of being hot or cold for new issues or for the concept behind your company. They may tell you that your company has not achieved an equity value, enough sales, and earnings to permit it to go public. Generally, they will want a growth record of 30 to 60 percent or more. Most stockbrokers are reluctant to take companies public unless they have at least $1 million in net after-tax income. From your standpoint, the entire discussion is not material. There is only one time to go public for you and that is when a brokerage house will take the company public at the price you think is reasonable. If one brokerage house says it cannot take you public, go to another one.

Entrepreneurs usually ask if they should sell any of their shares in the initial underwriting. They ask this question because they believe if management is selling any of their shares, new stockholders who are being asked to purchase shares will be leery. The answer, of course, is that it is a matter of percentages. If you are selling 2, 3, or even 5 percent of your holdings, or perhaps even 10 percent if you hold a large percentage of ownership in the company, then it is perfectly all right for you to sell some of your shares in the initial or secondary underwriting. Every entrepreneur is advised to sell some of his shares in the initial public offering if the underwriter will permit it. This makes sense for you as the entrepreneur because it allows you to diversify your own investment.

You should take some of your capital gains as soon as possible and invest them in some other medium, such as tax-free bonds. You want to diversify your own holdings rather than tie them up in one company. Nothing will give you greater happiness and satisfaction than to have half a million or a million dollars parked in a tax-free money market fund that pays you a handsome income each year, tax-free. This type of money from the entrepreneur's standpoint is often called "screw-you" money. It is called screw-you money because if everything were to blow up and the company were to fall on hard times, the entrepreneur would have some money with which to survive. He can in essence say to the business world, "screw you!" When your time comes, do not forget to obtain some screw-you money.

Why You Should Have a Public Offering

There are a great number of reasons to go public.

- Generally speaking, selling shares in the public market will allow you to sell them at a higher price than they can be sold for in a private placement of the shares. The reason is simple. Public shares have liquidity that makes the shares more valuable. By selling shares at a higher price, you will have much less dilution in your company. Everyone's ownership will be diluted less by the new shares.

- Once your company is public and the shares are traded, it will be much easier to raise additional equity capital.

- Having the shares of the company in the public hands will establish a market for the company's shares. It will allow you to attract new management talent and to motivate them with stock options. A publicly-held company has greater credibility with customers and suppliers as well as lending institutions.

- The most important reason is that a public market creates liquidity through which you as a large stockholder and the venture capitalist as a stockholder can exchange shares in the company for cash. Nothing is sweeter for the entrepreneur or venture capitalist than to take a few shares and exchange them for $500,000 or $1,000,000, or more, in cash.

Why You Should Not Have a Public Offering

Unfortunately, several serious drawbacks have to be considered before one goes public.

- A public company has to disclose a great deal of information about itself. The data can be used by your competition, by customers who deal with you, and by your employees who, when they learn how much money you make, may want pay raises. All your friends and neighbors will be able to buy one share of stock in your company just to keep track of you. Unless you like living in a goldfish bowl, you should not be a public company.

- All public companies are subject to reporting requirements established by the government, primarily the Securities and Exchange Commission, and in addition must file certain information with their stockholders. This will mean increased time and expenses to your company in the form of reporting, audits, and so on.

- Once you are a public company, your new pubic shareholders will be desirous of strong performance. They will want the earnings per share to increase each year. If you do not perform, they will sell your shares and drive the price down.

- Particularly troublesome are the cost and management time necessary to accomplish the public offering itself—management will be kept from performing day-to-day duties, and the costs of going public will be very high. The legal fees, the accounting fees, and the underwriter's charges, by any standard, will be exorbitant.

- Finally, in a public company you will be severely constrained from insiders dealing with the company. That is, you will no longer be able to use the company to increase your own personal fortune at the expense of the company's. All transactions must be at "arm's length." If insider transactions are not proper, stockholder suits and an audit by the Securities and Exchange Commission are sure to follow.

Underwriter's Fees and the Public Offering

Your stockbroker will charge you a fee for acting as an underwriter of your stock. Part of the fee will go to the stockbrokers who join the syndicate, but most of the fee will go to the firm you choose to be the underwriter. The underwriter's fee can range from 5 to 10 percent. Eight percent seems to be the standard for new, high-growth companies. The fee for high-risk companies, the high fliers, is 10 percent.

Sometimes you can reduce the underwriter's fee substantially by offering him options to buy stock. For example, rather than having the underwriter receive 10 percent on all the funds he raises for you, you might negotiate a fee of 6 percent of all the funds raised, plus an option to own 3 percent of the stock in your company. As icing on the cake, you might offer the underwriter the right of first refusal for the next underwriting of your stock. In a $5 million underwriting, the 4 percent that you have saved is $200,000. Your company will receive the $4.7 million cash, the underwriter $300,000, and the underwriter will have the option to purchase 3 percent of your company in place of the extra fee of $200,000.

The fees you will pay out to other professionals in your underwriting may shock you. Legal fees can range from $75,000 to $400,000. It is not unusual for a complicated underwriting to cost $300,000. Printing the prospectus may cost anywhere from $25,000 to $150,000, depending on the number printed, the color photographs used, the paper quality, and so forth.

Accounting bills seem to be lower. Expect to pay $25,000 to $100,000 to your accountants for their certification of the financial statements and their review of your prospectus. Do not forget your own attorney. He will want a substantial fee for working with the lawyers of the underwriter, and your special SEC lawyers. His fee could range from $20,000 to $50,000. In total, a full-blown public registration and offering may cost you $400,000 to $500,000. You should factor this into the amount that you are raising. Thus, if you are raising $5 million and you pay an underwriting fee of 8 percent or $400,000, plus $300,000 in professional fees, then the cost of the money will be 14 percent. Your net will be $4.3 million.

You will have to negotiate a letter of intent from your underwriter for this public offering. One of the points of intense negotiation will be the price range being set in the letter of intent. The initial price for the stock is usually related to market valuations of issues similar to yours. The initial price will also be related to how hot your new company will be perceived to be by the public. Generally, if an underwriter says the range is $13 to $16 per share, he means $13 per share.

Selection of a Brokerage House for the Public Offering

As you talk with stockbrokerage firms, friends, accountants, and bankers, the name of a local brokerage house that has participated in underwriting new issues for many smaller companies will be mentioned by more than one person. As you widen your sphere of discussion, you will hear the names of three or four national firms that specialize in new issues. Just as you did when raising venture capital, you should contact a few of these firms and determine if one is interested in taking your company public. Once you have found a brokerage firm that is interested, you should stay with it until you have reached an agreement. If you cannot reach an agreement, move to the next firm.

In selecting your brokerage house, look for one that has an excellent reputation and a professional status in the underwriting community. You should also look for experience in underwriting new issues, particularly in companies such as yours. You should determine the brokerage's ability to distribute the shares to its clients. If it has a small number of retail customers, the brokerage may not be as effective as one with a large number of customers or one with an institutional client base. You should determine the brokerage's market-making ability. Once the initial offering is over, will it be an active market maker in your shares in order to maintain the price of the stock, or will it step aside and let the price of the stock drop significantly? Finally, determine if the brokerage firm can take the entire issue or if it will have to syndicate the issue through numerous other brokerage houses.

As you can see a public company has its share of problems. Going public will be a method for you to remove the influence of your venture capital partner and perhaps even encourage him to go away completely. In his place, however, will be a number of outside stockholders who will be as interested in your company as the venture capitalist was.

Second Method: Purchase by the Company or Entrepreneur

Obviously the company or entrepreneur can negotiate a price for which the venture capitalist will sell his stock ownership. If the company does not have the cash, it can borrow the money from the bank and buy the stock owned by the venture capital company. This sale leaves the entrepreneur and any other stockholders owning 100 percent of a company, but the company now has increased liabilities in the form of the bank loan. The venture capital company might accept part or all of its payment in the form of a long-term note. Whenever possible, you should give the venture capitalist a note for a long-term payout at a medium interest rate in return for his equity position, or his option to own an equity position. This gives the venture capitalist an exit and solves his liquidity problem.

There is also the remote possibility that you may have some asset such as an investment in another company or stock in some subsidiary that would be more meaningful to the venture capitalist than his ownership in your company. You might arrange for a stock swap—the stock you hold in another company for the stock he holds in your company. Or, you may own the land and building in which the business is housed. You could swap the land and building for the stock in your business. These types of swaps are uncommon but they have been discussed by venture capitalists and entrepreneurs on numerous occasions.

Purchase by Employee's Stock Ownership Trust

A method used by some entrepreneurs to buy out the venture capitalist is to set up an employee's stock ownership trust (ESOT). The ESOT is like a pension and profit-sharing plan, except that it buys stock in your company rather than stock of large traded companies. The ESOT obtains money through contributions by the company and therefore builds up cash. The ESOT can also borrow from the bank on the basis of the projected future contributions by the company. The ESOT uses the money to buy the stock that is owned by the venture capital firm. This is a relatively painless way for the company to buy back the equity ownership held by the venture capital firm. Contributions by the company to the ESOT are tax deductible. In essence, the company can use pretax dollars rather than after-tax dollars to purchase the stock. This excellent method of removing the venture capitalist puts the entrepreneur in a complex tax situation. Anyone contemplating this method should contact an expert in the field of employee stock ownership trusts.

Exit by Puts and Calls

When the investment was negotiated, you may have set up a formal arrangement that provides for exit for the venture capitalist. This may be in the form of "puts" and "calls." As we noted earlier, a put is a right given to the venture capitalist to require you or the company to buy the venture capitalist's ownership in the company at a predetermined formula. The call provision gives you, or the company, the right to purchase the venture capitalist's ownership by the same or similar formulas.

There are probably as many put-and-call formulas as there are minds thinking about how to structure deals. However, there are seven popular ones that you should consider.

1.   Price-Earnings Ratio

Probably the most popular is a price-earnings ratio formula that treats your company's stock like the stocks traded on national stock exchanges. The earnings per share are figured for the shares owned by the venture capitalist. A popular price-earnings (PE) ratio is selected from public stocks in the same industry. That PE ratio is multiplied by the earnings per share to come up with a price per share that you or your company will pay to the venture capitalist for the stock he owns.

2.   Book Value

A less common formula is based on book value of the company. It's simple to compute the book value per share for stock owned by the venture capitalist. That would be the price you or the company would pay for the shares owned by the venture capital company. Book value per share is seldom used because in the early years of a company's development the company usually has a small book value. It's only in older companies that have been around long enough to establish a good book value that this becomes the method of valuing the venture capitalist's equity position.

3.   Percentage of Sales

Sometimes it is inappropriate to use the earnings of the company in a price-earnings formula because in the early years of development, particularly in a start-up company, the earnings may be low owing to heavy depreciation or research and development expenses. It may take several years for the company to become profitable. Using pretax earnings may seem to be more appropriate. However, pretax earnings are held low often because of heavy salaries or heavy expenditures for promotion. In such a case, it may be easier for you to take the normal profit before tax as a percentage of sales typical for the industry. You will find statistics on your industry in publications on business statistics. You may find that most companies similar to yours have a pretax earnings of 10 percent of sales. It would be simple, then, to take 10 percent of your company's sales and pretend that number is your profit before taxes. Then you would determine earnings per share by using the hypothetical profit before taxes. Using the industry price-earnings ratio, you could easily determine what the value of the stock owned by the venture capital company would be worth if the hypothetical earnings existed. This can be the method used for buying back the shares owned by the venture capital firm.

Using the percentage of sales formula to value and buy back the shares owned by the venture capitalist can be very expensive. If, for some reason, sales take off or you invest a great deal in advertising to push sales and market share up, your formula for repurchasing the venture capitalist's shares will become unbearable. On the other hand, if the formula were based on earnings, you would control the amount of earnings. For example, you might increase advertising in order to reduce earnings and build a name for the company in the future. By using the earnings formula, you will be reducing the value of the venture capitalist's shares. As the venture capitalist sees it, you cannot tamper with sales as easily, and therefore sales become a good indicator of the value of the company.

4.   Multiple of Cash Flow

In some industries cash flow is a more accurate barometer of how the business is doing than are profit-and-loss statements based on generally accepted accounting principles. Using an eight-to-ten-times cash flow formula, we might say a company is worth millions of dollars more than a price-earnings ratio of the profit-and-loss statement would indicate. If we assume a company is worth ten times cash flow, it is simple to compute the value of the percentage of the company owned by the venture capitalist. You can use this as the method for buying back his equity position.

The cash flow formula may work quite well for a stable company, but could be extremely expensive in an asset-heavy, leverage buy-out situation. For example, in a leverage buy-out you may have inflated the value of the assets in order to shelter income. However, when these heavily depreciated assets are removed in the calculation of cash flow, the cash flow number will be much higher than the profit before-tax figure. The price you have to pay for the equity of the venture capitalist can be high if it is based on cash flow.

5.   Multiple of Sales

The value of some companies in certain industries is based on a multiple of sales. Radio stations traditionally sell at two to three times gross sales. If you determine the value of a company to be two and a half times gross sales, it would be simple then to compute the value of the venture capitalist's percentage of equity ownership and pay him that amount for his ownership in the company. As in the percentage-of-sales calculation above, the multiple-of-sales valuation also means you will be paying for a company that may or may not have earnings. Many investors in the radio business buy a poorly-run station on a multiple-of-sale calculation knowing full well that the station's earnings cannot possibly pay back the investment. The investor who is buying the station must put in enough money to carry the station until its sales and earnings can be increased. In fact, the earnings must increase drastically if he is to pay back any debt and get an adequate return on the money invested.

6.   Appraised Value

It is often easy to find an expert individual or a stock brokerage firm to appraise the value of the equity ownership held by the venture capital company. The appraisal will probably be based on a combination of some of the items above. Appraisals are usually computed by two methods. First, the value of the company is determined by its earning power, both past and future. This formula is similar to the price earnings ratio used above. Second, the value of the assets (bricks and mortar) are determined as if they were sold at auction as part of an orderly liquidation. From this liquidation the appraiser subtracts all debts outstanding, and the remaining value is the appraised value. The bricks-and-mortar formula is similar to the book-value calculations, except there it includes an appraisal of the assets and a restated new book value based on their appraised value. When these two figures do not agree, the appraiser usually selects something close to the higher of the two. For example, if the bricks-and-mortar formula was higher than the earnings formula, the appraiser would assume that the highest and best use of the company was to sell all of its assets.

7.   Prearranged Cash Amount

Of course, a simple formula would be to base a put-and-call option on a single cash amount. That is, at the end of three years the venture capital firm would have the right to require the company to buy its equity ownership position for a certain amount, say, $200,000. Although this method saves a great deal of negotiating and appraising at the end of three years, people find it difficuilt to agree on a value at the beginning of the investment period.

Third Method: Sale of the Company to Another Company

Rather than having the venture capitalist sell his ownership position in your company, you and the venture capitalist may decide to sell the entire company to another individual or a large conglomerate. This will rid you of the venture capitalist as well as rid you of your own company. You may prefer to sell the company, receive a large amount of money, and dissolve your marriage to the venture capitalist. Then you can start a second company with the cash you received from selling the first company, but this time without venture capital financing.

When the entire company is sold to a conglomerate, the venture capitalist and you will be paid in one, two, or three different kinds of payments for the purchase of the stock in your company or the assets of the company. There are six basic ways in which a company may be sold. You should understand each so that you will be ready to negotiate with the buyer of your company.

Selling Stock for Cash

The simplest of all methods is to sell the stock in your company to someone else for cash. This triggers capital gains and is a straightforward method of selling your company.

Selling Stock for Notes

Rather than take cash for your stock, you may wish to take a note from the buyer. That is, the buying company may buy the stock you own in your company by giving you a note that pays off over a certain period of time, say five years. In the venture capital community these notes are called paper, so when you "take back paper" you have taken notes in place of cash. Although cash is made out of paper as well, only the notes are called paper. Maybe the word paper is used here because it suggests something that is worthless. Many people have taken notes that later became worthless.

It is common to give notes in order to establish a deferred purchase and give you, the seller, tax advantage. Most venture capital companies expect to take some deferred payment for their investment. Receiving a note for stock that you are selling can create complications in that you will have a note from an unrelated third party, which may be strong if it's a big conglomerate, or may be weak if it is a group of individuals. A way around the weak note is to have your company buy back all the stock you and the venture capitalist own except for several shares. Your company pays you and the venture capitalist for the stock with a note, and the note is collateralized by the assets of your business. Then it is very simple to sell the remaining several shares of stock for the cash down payment amount to whomever is buying the company. The buying group will be the sole stockholder. You will have collateral for the note that you have received for your stock.

Selling Stock for Stock

At times you may wish to take stock in a very large conglomerate for the stock that you own. This will give you the advantage of not paying taxes until you sell the stock received from the conglomerate. As a tax-free exchange you will not pay the tax until the day you sell the shares of the large conglomerate. Of course, it will be much more dangerous to take stock in a smaller company. It might be ludicrous for you to swap the stock in your company for stocks of another private company since you still will have neither liquidity nor income from the stock you receive. When dealing with large companies, you should try to obtain *registered* shares so that you will be free to sell your stock whenever you wish.

In another twist, you may wish to take a dividend-paying preferred stock from the large conglomerate that is convertible into the conglomerate's common stock. In this way you can have income until you decide to convert your shares into common stock and sell them in the open market.

Selling Assets for Cash

In this situation your company agrees to sell all of its assets for cash. Then all the operating assets and all the operating liabilities are assumed by the buying corporation for a specified cash amount. Your company is left with only cash as its asset. It is quite easy afterwards for you to file a tax plan to liquidate the corporation and distribute the cash to stockholders of the company, including you and the venture capital firm. If you have a larger company and your stock is more widely held, you may wish to offer any individual stockholder who wants to sell the opportunity to take cash for his shares. Then you could file as a registered investment company (mutual fund) with the Securities and Exchange Commission. Now you, and any remaining stockholders, no longer own shares in an operating company, but you own stock in a mutual fund. If the cash is invested in tax-free securities, then you can sit back and collect your tax-free dividends for your remaining years and pay no taxes on the transaction.

Under the current tax law the sale of assets is a taxable event, even if you liquidate the company shortly thereafter. Therefore, if you sell the assets for more than book value, the corporation will have to pay a tax on the difference between book value and the price you sold the business for. When you liquidate the company and distribute the cash to the stockholders, the stockholder will have to pay a tax on the difference between their cost of the stock and the amount of cash they received from liquidating the company. This means that there is a double tax on the sale of the company. As you can see, selling the assets for cash and liquidating the company can be a very expensive method of selling the business.

Selling Assets for Notes

Sometimes the acquiring company may not have the cash necessary to pay for the assets it is buying from your company. In that situation, your company may have to take notes, secured by the assets being sold as payment. Once you have sold your assets for notes, these notes will be the only asset of your company. As the payments on the notes are made, your company may distribute them to the stockholders in a liquidation plan. The notes must be for the short term. If there are many stockholders, this is a tricky situation. Someone will have to manage the collection of the notes and the payments to stockholders in order to retire their shares. You may wish to have the buyer issue the notes in small denominations. This will allow you to distribute the notes directly to the stockholders and they can collect principal and interest directly on the notes. Such a multiple-note plan may be appropriate for large conglomerates that are acquiring your company, since their credit is good. But it would be inappropriate for a small company that is acquiring your company because it would be hard for you as a group to get back together and file suit against the small company for nonpayment under the many notes. If there are only a few stockholders— for example, a few key managers, and the venture capital company—then the multiple notes can be transferred into proper denominations to the appropriate parties upon sale of the assets without much danger.

Be aware that the sale of the assets of the company for notes can be a taxable event and can require the double tax payment as discussed above, as if the company had received cash. You need a good tax lawyer or tax accountant to review the transaction before you sign the document to sell the assets.

Selling Assets for Stock

If you are receiving as payment for the assets, registered shares (or even shares that are restricted), it is quite easy for you to exchange the assets of your company for stock in a large conglomerate. Then you can file a plan of liquidation and distribute these shares to the stockholders of your company. This too can be a taxable event and you should consult your tax expert.

Other Forms of Payment

Many other forms of payment can be used in concert with the above structures. For example, you could structure the payment on an "earn-out basis." An earn-out involves paying you an additional amount for the stock that you own in the company, which is based on the earnings of your company over the next few years. As an example, the company that purchases your company might agree to pay you an additional amount (earn-out) of 25 percent of pretax income in excess of $2 million for each of the five years succeeding its acquisition of your company. This would mean you would get some cash up front, but the bulk of your earnings would come as a percentage of the earnings. Many buyers like to do this because it gives the entrepreneur who is selling the company an incentive to spread earnings over several years.

Another form of compensation to entrepreneurs who sell out is known as the "W2" method. This method is used when the company is not in good shape. It is used when assets are sold and there is not enough money to pay creditors. In this situation the entrepreneur tells the creditors that as a stockholder he is not receiving anything and that, therefore, they should compromise their debt and receive only a partial payment. This arrangement will permit the assets to be transferred to the buyer. What the entrepreneur has failed to tell the creditors is that he is being paid for his stock through his W2—that is, his employment contract with the large acquiring company. They agreed to pay him what they normally pay managers, say $50,000 a year, but at the same time they agreed to pay him an additional $50,000 per year in salary to compensate him for not making anything on the transaction. This type of exercise is called a W2 because an employee's reported salary is part of his W2 government form. What the entrepreneur lost on his stock he made up in his paycheck.

Obviously, the selling entrepreneur can be rewarded with a consulting contract or an employment contract as part of the payment. Of course, this takes something away from the stockholders that they would have received. To use an absurd example, the entrepreneur might agree to sell the assets of the company for one dollar and at the same time sign an employment agreement with the buying company providing that he be paid $1 million per year for the next three years. In this instance the entrepreneur received $3 million and the existing stockholders received virtually nothing. You can be sure the venture capitalist will be upset if you are selling out and part of the overall consideration is your compensation through an employment contract. You will have to reduce the amount that you are being paid for your stock in order to compensate for a large employment contract.

Negotiating the Sale of Your Company

Negotiating with large companies for the purchase of your company will be an exasperating experience. Big companies rarely move quickly. There are reports, projections, analyses, discussions, and so forth. Negotiating with the acquisition team from a large conglomerate can be a harrowing experience. These people are usually sharp. They frequently play "good guy and bad guy." That is, one or two individuals in their negotiating team will be the good guys and one or more will be the bad guys. The bad guys will tell the good guys, and you, what a bad deal this is, what a terrible thing to do, how overpriced the deal is. At some point the bad guys may scream and walk out of the room. Then the good guys will saddle up to you and tell you they believe they can bring the bad guys into line if you can just agree on some of the remaining minor issues, such as lowering the price by 20 percent. Many individuals on the corporate acquisition team will resort to any method to obtain a good deal. You should be on your toes when negotiating with the team trying to buy your company.

One of the main conditions that you will have to determine at the outset is whether you will stay with the company after the acquisition. The acquisition team will want you to stay. Unless you have an outstanding middle management team, a condition of the purchase will be that you stay long enough for the corporate giant to understand your business. The new owner will need time to prepare somebody to run your company. The transition from running your own company to becoming a wholly-owned subsidiary or a division of a large company will be quite a change for you if you are not ready for it. The number of reports, the memorandums, the auditors, the cash disbursements—all these and more will create a great change when you become a subsidiary of a large company. Your entrepreneurial spirit may be broken by the bureaucracy in large companies. In many respects, there is no difference between a large conglomerate's bureaucracy and the bureaucracy of any state or national government. Be sure you reach an understanding about the operation of your business before you sell. If that understanding is not satisfactory to you, make sure the price paid for your company is sufficient so that you can walk away happy when the time comes.

Buy—Sell Arrangement

The sale of the company may have been triggered by a buy-sell arrangement. That is, you have agreed with the venture capitalist that if a bona fide offer is made to purchase your company and you do not wish to take it, then you must buy out your venture capital partner on the same terms and conditions as the sales offer. If you cannot buy out the venture capitalist, then you have agreed to sell the company on the same terms and conditions as the bona fide offer. A buy-sell arrangement is useful in any agreement. It offers you the same option. If someone offers to buy and your venture capital company does not want to sell, then you have the right to require them to buy you out on the same terms and conditions or they must sell the company. It gives you both the opportunity to look at any bona fide offers that may arise and have either party (you or the venture capitalist) accept the offer.

An example of a more drastic form of a buy-sell arrangement is a deal in which at the end of four years the venture capital company can market all of the stock of the company to the highest bidder. That is, in year four the venture capital firm can approach anyone. It may try to sell all the stock of the company in order to trigger a long-term capital gain for the venture capital firm and for the entrepreneur stockholder. This is a more severe version of the buy-sell arrangement in that the venture capitalist has a built-in exit for all of the shares. You might wonder why the venture capitalist has the right to sell all of the shares rather than just his own. Obviously, a buyer of the stock will pay a premium for owning all the stock, or at least control of the company. It is worth more per share than the same buyer would pay for a minority stock position in a small company. In short, control is worth more than a minority position on a share-by-share basis.

Fourth Method: Finding a New Investor

Sometimes you may be able to find an investor who will buy the ownership position of the venture capital firm. Perhaps the new owner can become a working partner with you. You may have a close personal friend who has enough money to purchase the position held by the venture capital firm. On the other hand, you may find a passive investor who wants to be a long-term investor in your company, and who is willing to buy the position held by the venture capitalist. Sometimes you can make a better deal with this second investor. You can have the passive investor buy stock in your company, which you in turn use to retire the options and the note of the venture capital company. This is somewhat unusual but it has been used by entrepreneurs to remove venture firms.

Corporate Partners

When your company has grown substantially and is moving along at a good pace, you can sometimes find a corporate partner who wants to own part of your company. The corporate partner's objective may be to own all of your company at a future time. It may make good sense for you to have the corporate partner buy out the venture capitalist. The corporate partner may make a better partner than the venture capitalist because he will know more about your marketplace and how to produce your product. The corporate partner will be the logical company to buy your personal stock when the time comes for you to cash in your ownership. As an example, one venture capital firm was an investor with a large international conglomerate. As the company began to grow, the conglomerate decided it wanted to buy the venture capitalist's position and a bargain was struck. No sooner had that acquisition taken place than the conglomerate decided it had to own the rest of the shares and bought them after strenuous negotiations with the entrepreneur. The entrepreneur made a lot of money. It was a happy ending.

Having a corporate partner can be dangerous if your company has enough shares scattered around to give the corporate giant the opportunity to buy those shares and squeeze you into a minority stockholder position. You should be careful about taking on a corporate partner for this reason, and everyone's intentions should be on the table before the transaction occurs.

There once was an entrepreneur who owned part of a small publicly-traded company. The company needed additional cash in order to grow. The entrepreneur located a corporation that traditionally had invested in small companies. He raised the necessary cash from them by giving up 20 percent ownership of the company. He then owned 20 percent of the company and the public owned 60 percent. However, the entrepreneur had not looked into the real motives behind the corporation's investment in his company. After one year, when everything seemed to be going well, he woke up one morning to find that his corporate partner had made a tender offer for all the shares outstanding. The price was approximately 50 percent more than market value. Not only did the corporate partner offer a 50 percent premium over market, but he offered stockholders 5 percent of the tender offer price for rounding up shares of the company. The entrepreneur saw the writing on the wall. He tendered his shares along with everyone else. He made a substantial profit on the investment but within three years the company had grown to three times its original size. He had missed making his fortune. Meanwhile, his corporate "barracuda" partner made millions.

If the company is public but has a thin market and if there is every intention to have an additional public offering so there will be a wider market for the company's shares, then the venture capitalist may be able to sell his block of stock to a large institutional investor like an insurance company or a pension fund. These institutional investors will be interested in buying such a block at a discount from the current market prices. The institution may think long-term growth is available and it can obtain a higher return on investment with a block of stock in your company than with a small position on a large New York Stock Exchange company. The institutional investor will probably not be interested unless the venture capitalist's position is worth more than $1 million.

New Venture Capital Partner

In certain circumstances it is possible to find another venture capitalist to purchase the position held by your venture capital partner. Your first venture capital partner may be an equity-oriented venture capital fund that invests in early stage investments. This partner will invest for a medium term, so that once your company reaches a certain stage he will be delighted to exit. The new venture capital firm will be oriented to third- or fourth-round financing. This venture capital partner may loan you the money and have an option to buy a small amount of equity in your company. You can then use that money to buy out your first venture capital partner. This happens in the venture capital community from time to time, but it is not a common practice. It typically happens in the venture capital business when a venture capital group that has backed an individual becomes impatient with his performance. To put a stop to such harassment, the entrepreneur will try to find a new venture capitalist to take their place.

Fifth Method: Liquidation of the Company

More venture capitalists than you would imagine have made their exit by this method. If the business performs poorly, it may be easier to liquidate the company and sell off the valuable assets than to find a buyer for the company. Some companies that grow to a certain stage are worth more dead (liquidated) than alive. That is, the land, building, machinery, equipment, and other assets are worth more in liquidation than they are as a going business. A good example of this situation has been drug wholesalers. For some years these wholesalers were quite profitable and built up a large book value, but, as wholesaling became more competitive, their profits dropped. Several conglomerates began to buy up drug wholesalers; however, they were paying only 50 percent of book value because the earnings were so poor that the book value did not represent true value for the company. As a result, some drug wholesalers sold off the inventories and customers lists of their businesses to the conglomerate. Then they liquidated the land, building, machinery, equipment, and other assets. All of these in liquidation were worth more than the company by itself as an operating entity.

In the venture capital business, liquidation usually comes about because default provisions in the loan agreement have been violated. This makes all the funds due and payable immediately. Of course, this action puts an intolerable cash demand on the company and usually forces it into liquidation. In a forced liquidation, all assets are worth much less than their value on the balance sheet. Accounts receivable and inventory may be sold in liquidation for 50 percent of their cost. Machinery, equipment, furniture and fixtures may be sold for twenty to thirty cents on the dollar. Obviously the best way to sell assets is not through liquidation but through orderly liquidation.

Liquidation can also be accomplished at a high price when the company requires a large amount of cash in order to generate income from the assets. As an example, think about oil and gas drilling. It takes a large amount of money to purchase mineral rights and to drill several sample wells. The investor hopes one will strike oil or gas. But it takes an inordinately large amount of money to drill many wells over a large acreage of mineral rights. As a result, many independents will sell these partly proven mineral rights to large companies in order to avoid having to raise large amounts of cash for drilling.

Negotiating With the Venture Capitalist

Negotiating to purchase the venture capitalist's shares (option two above) or have him sell to someone else (option four above) will remind the entrepreneur of the day he tried to persuade the venture capitalist to invest his money into a new company. Now you are on the other side of the argument. You are trying to tell the venture capitalist that his investment in your company has reached a peak. It is time for him to sell his position. You may tell him some discouraging stories about the company and about its future. You might even downgrade the forecasts and the projections. However, your best strategy at this moment will be to tell the venture capitalist that it is a good time for him to sell, that it is a reasonable price, but do *not* downgrade your company. Remember, if your attempt to purchase the venture capitalist's ownership falls through and your company continues to progress, you will have impaired your credibility with the venture capitalist. Do not mislead the venture capitalist who does not sell his ownership and make him distrust you.

Objective

Your objective during this period is to find a way to rid yourself of the venture capital company. You should be reminded that it is possible to end up with an investor who is worse than a venture capitalist. The new partner looking over your shoulder may be worse than your venture capital partner. Helping the venture capital firm find an "exit" may be beneficial to you as a stockholder of the company because it means you have larger stock ownership.

A secondary objective during this point in your life may be liquidity of your own investment. Having a marketable security in a public company that has raised a sizable amount of equity can make you rich on paper. Putting a few dollars in your own pocket as a result of selling some of your shares in the public offering (or the sale of your company) can make you sleep well at night. If this is your objective, you will find it totally in concert with the venture capital firm's. The venture capitalist, too, would like liquidity and realization on his investment.

11

Using Brokers

Are Financial Brokers or Consultants Worth Anything?
A Broker Could Destroy Your Chances.

Most venture capital firms do not have a great deal of confidence in financial brokers. Of the thousands of people who call themselves financial brokers, only a few are competent ones. At the top of the financial brokerage list is the corporate finance department of major banks and stockbrokerage houses. Second are those at smaller stockbrokerage firms. After that, it's difficult to find more than a few competent financial brokers.

There are very few financial brokers in the United States who understand venture capital financing. Of the thousands of people who call themselves financial brokers most are merely packagers of paper, meaning that they will help you assemble some of the information about your business and send it off to a venture capital firm. These packages have no similarity to the business proposal discussed in this book. They are usually a copy of some of your existing documents put together in a haphazard way. The broker usually looks up the venture capital company in a guidebook on venture capital. (The names and addresses of venture firms are listed in the back of the book.) Then he mails the package. The inexperienced financial broker may call the venture capitalist. The telephone conversation usually proceeds as follows:

Broker: Hello, Mr. A. V. Capitalist. My name is Barney Broker. I am a financial broker and I have a number of clients who are in need of venture capital financing. I would like to send you a package on these good investments, but before I send over these packages I would like to talk to you to see if you have an interest in them.

Venture Capitalist: All right. Why don't you tell me about the business?

Broker: I have a company that's in chemical solvents and it does a great job of making solvents in New Jersey. They have a nice operation and they are growing like Topsey.

Venture Capitalist: What are the gross sales on the company today?

Broker: Just a minute, and let me look that up. [Shuffling of papers heard in the background.] Here it is. Last year they had gross sales of $800,000 and it looks like they had about $700,000 the year before and they are projecting $2.3 million this year.

Venture Capitalist: What profits have they had?

Broker: Uh, uh [more shuffling of paper in the background], uh, it looks like they didn't make any money last year, but the year before they had a $25,000 profit. I don't know why they're not profitable this year.

Venture Capitalist: About how much money do they need?

Broker: They need $1 million to finish building a new plant and buy some new machinery and equipment, and at least $200,000 in working capital. If they get all that money they can build this into a nice operation.

Venture Capitalist: How much money does the owner have in the company?

Broker: I'm not sure that's in the business package, but I can find out for you. But rather than go through this business package with you, I would really like to send it to you.

Venture Capitalist: Oh no. [Under his breath]. Well, that will be fine. Send it on down to me and we will let you know in the next day or two after we receive it whether we have an interest.

As you can see from the above, the business broker had no idea of what he was talking about. He had a poor business proposal in which he could not find basic information. He left a poor impression of the entrepreneur and the business proposal. After receiving one of these phone calls, the venture capitalist knows exactly what kind of business proposal he will receive. It will be worthless. It will not set out any of the key elements covered in our summary in Chapter 2, and it will not come close to providing the detailed information required in a business proposal, as discussed in Chapter 3. The broker in these cases will receive what is known in the venture capital business as a "standard no" letter. Most standard no letters are as follows:

Mr. Barney Broker
Brokers Plus Unlimited Money, Inc.
123 Fifth Avenue
New York, NY 12345
Re: Chemical Solvent Plant
Dear Mr. Broker:

I have discussed your proposal with my associates and at this time we do not wish to make an investment in the chemical solvent plant. We appreciate your considering our company for this investment.

Sincerely,

A Venture Capitalist

If you do not wish to receive a standard no letter, you should complete most of the work yourself or hire a competent professional to help you. Some financial brokers are excellent assistants to entrepreneurs. Some brokers can help you prepare a good business proposal, but you need to know how to use their services as well as those of lawyers, accountants, and any others who offer you assistance.

Accountants: How to Use Them

Most venture capitalists have great faith in the accountants who prepare the financial portion of the business proposal. Accountants spend considerable time on the numbers to make them believable. However, accountants usually lack in-depth knowledge of your business, so they cannot prepare the remainder of the business proposal on marketing, production, and administration, as discussed in Chapter 3. The accountant can help you write those sections but cannot do it without you.

The best way to use an accountant is to have him check the numbers after you have prepared the financial statements on your own. He will make sure that the math is correct. The accountant should ask enough questions to test your assumptions. If you do not have the time, you may wish to have the accountant prepare the numbers first. Then you can review the numbers in detail with him. All the assumptions should be yours, and the accountant should merely pull together the numbers or check them.

Many accounting firms do not wish to make projections for new businesses or for entrepreneurs. They believe it may lend their name to an otherwise uncreditworthy financing. The accountants believe that if you obtain financing and fail, you will tarnish their name before the venture capital firm. You may have to employ some strong arguments to convince the accounting firm to prepare your financial projections, but the firm will be willing to review them.

Sometimes the entrepreneur will bring his accountant to the meeting with the venture capitalist. In one such meeting, the entrepreneur was being questioned intensely by the venture capitalist about the projections. After stumbling through some of the projections for several minutes the entrepreneur turned to the accountant and asked for some assistance. It was obvious to the venture capitalist that the accountant was responsible for completing the projections. What was more obvious was that the entrepreneur had no idea of the meaning of the projections. If you want to display your ignorance about the projections, do it alone with your accountant in the accountant's office. Once you have become fully knowledgeable about the projections, then go to the meeting with the venture capitalist without your accountant.

Investment Bankers: What They Can Do

Perhaps the people who can help you with your business proposal best are the investment bankers of stockbrokerage firms and large banks. Most of them have seen many private placements and understand what goes into a business proposal. They usually know many sources of financing and can help you with many of the written items in the business proposal, although they may be weak on the numerical aspects of the proposal. They can give you informed guidance in selecting a financial source. It is appropriate to ask the investment banker to attend the meeting with the venture capitalist. Most brokers, and especially investment bankers, will insist on going with you. They believe they should be in the meeting to help you as much as possible. Sometimes an investment banker can be a bit overbearing. When the venture capitalist asks the entrepreneur a question, he expects the entrepreneur to answer. He does not expect the investment banker to answer. It is all right for the investment banker to contribute to the conversation, but he should not be the main individual answering the questions.

As a small businessman you may receive more service from the small independent brokerage houses than you will from the large brokerage firms. Large brokerage houses are geared to massive underwritings, and your financing will be too small. Small regional brokers are more knowledgeable in financing businesses through the financial sources in that region. Sometimes their fees are lower, but you should not count on lower fees. All brokerage fees will be much higher than you expect.

Lawyers: Are They O.K. as Financial Brokers?

Generally speaking, lawyers are not good financial brokers. They should not be consulted when you are writing your financial proposal, except to review it as a friend. If you use a lawyer to help you write your business proposal, it will be filled with legalese. It will be sanitized and devoid of any excitement. It will read like a legal document and will not help you sell your company to the venture capitalist.

Your lawyer may be long winded and argumentative when negotiating with the venture capitalist. If the lawyer is a litigator, he may find a dozen ways to kill the deal for you. Venture capitalists recommend that you never bring your lawyer with you during negotiations for the business part of your proposal. Lawyers should be introduced to the process after the businessmen have agreed on the terms and conditions. Some lawyers are well connected in the financial community. They know various venture capital firms in town and they also know bankers and other financial sources. Your lawyer may help you obtain a list of people to contact; however, he is not the person to write your business proposal. He is not the one to negotiate the deal for you.

Generally speaking, venture capitalists will not be happy to see your lawyer at the meeting. They know that the lawyer will try to negotiate every point. They have seen too many lawyers try "grandstand plays" by issuing ultimatums such as, "I won't permit my client to sign that kind of agreement." It is difficult to achieve consensus when you have third parties interacting in the process. It is better to negotiate your own business deal and then discuss it with your lawyer rather than include him in the negotiation.

Independent Financial Brokers: What Do They Want?

Above all, you should be cautious about hiring independent financial brokers as advisers for your company. Some independent financial brokers are outstanding, but many are not well regarded in the venture capital business. By independent one means not connected with an accounting firm, stockbrokerage firm, bank, or other institution. Every venture capital company and thousands of small businesses can tell you horror stories about independent financial brokers. Usually the small business has paid fees to an independent financial broker and received nothing in return, as illustrated by the following.

First the financial broker sets up an office and orders some stationery. He contacts people around town, small businesses, accountants, and so on. He may run ads in the newspapers, usually in the business or financial section of the newspaper. The small businessman learns of the broker and calls him. The financial broker visits the office of the small businessman. The broker does not want to meet in his meager office for fear of giving a poor impression. The broker discusses all the sources of financing that he knows. He boasts that he can obtain financing for the small business. Somewhere along the way the small businessman asks, "Well, how do we get started?" This will be the invitation for the scam.

The financial broker will indicate that he needs to spend time studying your business. He needs to pull together a financial plan and he must talk to a number of financial sources before he will be able to find financing for your company. In order to complete this process, he needs some money. His customary fee will be 2 percent of the amount you are seeking. It may be as low as 1 percent, but he will ask for it as an up-front fee. In most cases where an up-front fee is paid to an independent financial broker, the small businessman receives nothing in return. Once the small businessman has passed along the money, he is in a precarious position. The broker now has the money. He is a one-man, one-office operation and can disappear overnight. He may or may not have financial contacts in the community. Usually he will send out a few "packages" and seek "standard no" letters so he can prove he has worked on behalf of the sm 1 business.

Many thous nds and perhaps millions of small businesses have lost money in the form of an up-front fee to financial brokers. The U.S. government, through the Small Business Administration, has attempted to curtail the activities of financial brokers. Many local authorities have attempted to shut down these brokerage businesses. In many states financial and business brokers are licensed by the state. Be sure you understand your financial broker and his motives. Don't become a victim of this scam.

Qualities to Look for in a Broker

As in any business arrangement, you should look into the background of the person you are hiring. After all, this person will be working for you and representing your company, and he will be given some of your money somewhere along the way. The financial broker you hire should have the following qualities.

Experience

Extensive experience in helping finance small businesses is a must. Without such a background, the broker will not understand the problems that small businesses have in seeking finances, nor will he understand the sources of funds that usually finance small businesses.

Professional

Your business broker should be a true professional; that is, one who is knowledgeable about your company and about his own business of financing your company. He should be a full-time professional. There are many part-time financial brokers, but it is unlikely that a part-time assistant such as a lawyer or an accountant will be able to systematically help you locate venture capital financing.

Credentials

The broker should have a strong financial background. A degree from a recognized business school, either graduate or undergraduate, is a plus. Any experience as an investment banker for a brokerage firm is definitely a plus. Experience as a financial officer in a lending institution is also in his favor. If he's been responsible for buying into small businesses or lending to small businesses, he will understand what the loan officer and venture capitalist are looking for.

Operator of a Small Business

An individual who has operated his own small business successfully can be of help. If, during that period, he has raised money for his small business, then he may know what he is doing. Generally speaking, however, people who have operated a small business will not understand all the sources for financing a company unless their company was a heavy capital user. As a result, a past history of operating a business may not necessarily be helpful in the venture capital area.

Special Knowledge

If your company is oriented toward high technology, you may be better off with someone who has a technological background, an engineering degree, or experience in a high technology company. Capital sources that finance high technology ventures are a specialty. An individual with a high technology background may have helped finance other high technology companies and may be of more help to you.

The more your broker fits the qualities listed above, the more he will be able to point you in the right direction for the financing of your company.

Agreement With the Broker

You should enter into a formal written agreement with the broker. To rely on an oral agreement where the transfer of money is involved is to court disaster.

The arrangement between you and the financial broker should contain all of the elements of a contract. Below are the basic items of that contract.

Define the Service

In this section of the legal agreement you should spell out in detail the service to be performed by the broker. Establish what is expected of you in the way of financial information, data on your business, and so on. You should also clearly state the objective of this arrangement, such as, obtain $500,000 of venture capital financing.

Time Frame

Every legal document should specify the date that the relationship terminates. You and your broker should specify the final date for the agreement and, further, you should specify intermediate dates by which certain milestones are to be completed. If you or the broker do not meet these intermediate dates, then the contract can be cancelled by either party. You will be in a position to call the broker and ask what progress has been made. If none has been made, terminate your agreement with a letter to him stating that you are terminating it because specified progress has not been made. Also ask for a refund of any advanced fees. You are free to go to another broker, or better yet, do it yourself.

Termination Clause

Your agreement should provide for a termination subject to written notices from one party to the other party. This clause will state how, and for what reasons, the agreement can be terminated.

Amount of the Fee

State the amount of the fee in detail. It can be a flat fee that covers all out-of-pocket expenses or it may be a fee plus out-of-pocket expenses. If you are agreeing to the latter, make sure you have in writing an estimate of the out-of-pocket fees. Be sure to insist that the broker obtains your approval on any out-of-pocket expenses in excess of, say, $50 a week.

Reports on Progress

The agreement should state whether any progress reports are to be produced by the broker. Normally, the broker should report to you orally at least once every week and should give you a written report of the work completed frequently.

Ownership of Work Completed

Any work completed by the broker—such as charts or work on the business proposal—should be owned by your company. You have paid for it; therefore you should own it. If you do not have this clause in your agreement, any work completed by the financial broker may belong to him. If you should terminate this agreement for just cause, he may keep everything. This will force you to duplicate a great deal of work.

Nondisclosure Clause

There should be another clause in your agreement specifying that the broker will not disclose any of the information in your business proposal, or other information divulged to him, to any other persons without your prior written consent. This will prevent the broker, under any circumstances, from passing along information to your competitor. For example, if you disagree with him over his fee, he may try to make some extra money by selling your idea to a competitor.

Indemnification

The broker should indemnify you in the agreement against any misrepresentations or wrongful doings that he may perform while he is in your service. He should also indemnify you against violations of federal and state security laws. If he does not indemnify you for actions he has taken, he could conceivably misrepresent your situation to someone, and that person could sue you because of the misrepresentation. After all, he is your paid representative.

Complete Agreement

The agreement should state that this is the only agreement that the parties have entered into, and that any oral understandings are null and void. This written agreement should supersede any previous agreements, and all future modifications should be in writing.

Once you have a full, written understanding of the relationship between you and the broker, you will be in a better position to use his services.

Some Tips on Dealing with Brokers

The soundest advice anyone can ever give you is to urge you to check out the broker. Obtain references from the broker and determine if he is legitimate. Call any companies that he claims to have helped raise money. Call the presidents of those companies and ask about him. Also ask him for some names of companies that he was unable to help. Contact the presidents of those companies and ask them why he did not succeed. Any information you can develop about this individual will be useful in helping you to decide whether to hire him.

Do not believe any broker who tells you he can "guarantee" to raise money for you. No agent or intermediary can guarantee funds for your company. Anyone who gives you a guarantee is trying to impress you. Their influence is being overstated.

Amount and Type of Fees

If possible, you should not pay any significant cash up front to any financial broker. It may be unrealistic to hold to this idea. After all, brokers have to eat, too. The best arrangement is to pay the broker on the basis of performance once you have your money. If you must pay a fee, make a small down payment and pay the remainder when you are funded.

You can purchase various types of services from a financial broker. First, you may ask him to help you with your business proposal. He may charge you an hourly rate of $50 to $150 to supervise the assembling of a good business proposal. If he writes the business proposal using information presented by you, a one-time fee of $2,000 to $5,000 may be fair. Second, you may hire a financial broker to contact and work with the sources of financing. If the broker merely introduces you to a financial source, the customary fee is 1 to 2 percent of the amount you raise from the source. If he actually tries to sell your proposal to the venture capitalist, then his fee is higher. If he makes the rounds to help you sell it, then the formula has to be much higher, perhaps 3 to 5 percent. The fee is usually a percentage of the loan, and it can be as high as 10 percent.

The standard percentage of the loan or financing that is paid to the broker usually depends on the amount raised. The standard formula in the financial community is "five-four-three-two-one." This means that the broker gets 5 percent of the first million he raises, 4 percent of the second million, and so on. Smaller financings of $200,000, $300,000 or $400,000, may cost you more than 5 percent. However, anything greater than 8 percent is probably too much. As mentioned, some fees are as high as 10 percent of the amount being raised. Fees of this size will make the venture capitalist uneasy since 10 percent of everything he gives you will go to a broker. Sometimes the fee is partly in cash and partly in an option to buy stock. That is, the broker might receive 4 percent of the venture capital investment in a cash fee and an option to buy 2 percent of the stock of your company. This mixed fee is customary for new and untried companies that need every dollar of cash to make their company go. The best advice you can follow in this area is negotiate no up-front fee, or a very small up-front fee, and then pay the broker a fair and equitable amount when the loan closes. You should not pay the broker when the commitment is made, but only when the loan finally closes. Many deals fall apart between commitment and closing and you should not pay a fee if they do.

Some brokers promise to raise a large amount of money on very attractive terms. For example, one might say he can raise $1 million in equity for your company for 10 percent ownership. This will sound extremely good to you, but it may be quite unrealistic. What may happen is that you will raise $1 million, but it will be in the form of a high interest rate debt that forces you to give up 45 percent equity in your company. You still must pay the broker his percentage of the amount raised. Any broker who claims to be able to raise large amounts of money and give up a very small amount of ownership in the company should have his fee based on delivery of his promise. Your agreement should provide that you will pay him much less if you have to accept a deal that is not comparable to the one he has promised. By defining the terms of your contract in this manner, you can be sure the broker will give you a more realistic appraisal of what he can do for you.

You do not necessarily have to accept the first financial broker you meet. There are many of them around. You may want to talk to several before you select the one you think is best. After you have selected one and signed your contract, work closely with him and give him a chance to finance your company. Do not expect financing overnight.

Who Should Present the Plan to the Venture Capitalist?

No broker is prepared to sell your deal to the venture capital company the way that you can. Brokers should be used to advise you, but you should do the selling. After all, the venture capital company is not investing in a financial broker; it is investing in you. The most that the financial broker can do for you is to give you an introduction to the venture capitalist. Some skilled brokers can help move the negotiations along during an impasse. The venture capitalist knows that the broker works for you and will treat him accordingly.

As mentioned before, sometimes an entrepreneur will deliver a business proposal containing financial projections that were completed by an accounting firm. When questioned about the projections, the entrepreneur will behave as though he is not familiar with the numbers. This problem commonly arises when the entrepreneur asks his accountant to make projections from certain sets of assumptions, but he doesn't take the time to review the statements to make sure he understands them. You should understand the projections thoroughly—even better than the accountant who put the numbers together for you.

A similar problem can arise when a financial broker, or more likely the investment banking department of a large brokerage house, completes the business proposal for you. Unless you understand every word in the business proposal, you will not be able to answer questions from the venture capitalist. When the venture capitalist begins to ask his questions, he will be impressed only if you know what you are talking about.

Objective

Your objective in using financial brokers is to obtain leads to financial sources that you cannot develop yourself. You must check out any financial broker before you pay any amount of money. Be aware that most venture capitalists think that independent financial brokers have an anguine quality. Your objective in using accountants is to let them help you complete the numbers in the financial section of the proposal. The investment banking department of a large brokerage house can help you prepare the business proposal and help you find capital sources. Remember, all of the people can only lend a hand in completing the task. They cannot remove the hard work involved in preparing a business proposal and seeking venture capital financing.

12

Advice

Is It Worth All This?
How To Win.

Before you contact a venture capital firm, ask yourself the simple question, "Is it worth going into this business situation?" Many times when the venture capitalist is talking with an entrepreneur who wants business funding, he asks a simple question: "Why in the world does a smart person like you want to take the chances that you are about to take?" He might add, "Is it worth it?" In your mind, the answer is "Sure!" But think again.

You have probably heard a number of success stories about small business owners. Although some people have actually made millions in the small business field, you should not forget the thousands who have failed. The opportunities for failure in a small business seem to be infinite in number. The basic question for any entrepreneur is, "Are you ready to go through hell; and are you ready to undertake the tremendous amount of stress that will be involved in running a small business?" Every entrepreneur should engage in a moment of soul searching before he embarks on the road he has set out in his business proposal. Once he has completed this soul searching and if he has determined that he is right, then he should charge ahead.

Keeping Up With Venture Capitalists

In order to keep up with the venture capitalists in your area, or anywhere in the United States, you should write to them and ask them to place your name on their mailing lists. Ask for an annual report from all the publicly-traded venture capital firms. Some of the public firms are Allied Capital Corporation, Washington, D.C.; Biotech Capital Corporation, New York City; Greater Washington, Washington, D.C.; and Capital Southwest, Dallas, Texas. Some others are listed in Appendix 2. These companies, as well as a handful of others that are publicly owned, will send you a copy of their annual report. Other venture capital firms that are in your area will also be delighted to send you their brochures and information about the types of investments they make. Study the venture capital industry so that you will understand it better.

Seeking information about venture capital firms can be compared to taking a trip to a different state or a foreign country. You first obtain information about the country from the tourist bureau, the country itself, from the airlines, and from books written on the subject. You should do the same when searching for a venture capitalist. Study the field as much as possible in order to become knowledgeable about the type of business each venture capitalist is interested in, and his method of operation. This preparation will help you when you travel among the venture capital community.

Selecting a Venture Firm

In selecting a venture firm, you should investigate its business ethics. If the firm's operations seem to be shady in any way, you should not deal with it. Remember that if you deal with crooks, you will be the victim. Do not think you can outsmart them. Crooks know too many ways to hurt you. Life is too short to deal with crooks.

You should also be careful when you are dealing with rich individuals who have become venture capitalists. A rich venture capitalist is not averse to risk. He can shoot crap with hundreds of thousands of dollars without missing it. Although this attitude may help you in raising your money, it will not help you get out of trouble, as the rich person can walk away from your situation and not miss the cash. A rich person has no one to report to. He does not have partners or stockholders. He gets a tax break when he has a loss. When possible, take venture capital financing from a professional venture fund. If you have a choice, do not use rich people's money.

The best relationship between the venture capitalist and the entrepreneur is in isocracy. The entrepreneur should be on equal footing with his venture capitalist. If the venture capitalist is running the small business, then it is probably doomed to failure. If in operating the business the entrepreneur is inconsiderate of the investment made by the venture capitalist, then a struggle will inevitably arise and hurt the business.

Venture Capital Process

Remember that the process of raising venture capital and the relationship with the venture capital company will be a long, drawn-out one. If you expect a quick fix from the venture capitalist, you may be in for a rude surprise. Some venture capitalists work quickly, but they are few and far between. Most are interested in completing a full-blown, due diligence report to make sure they have found the right investment. After all, they invest for the long term. Be aware that the venture capitalist needs a long review period. Understand that few venture firms will be able to react in the time frame you may want. The diagram in Figure 12.1 will help you follow the list of events that must be accomplished. We have discussed them all in this book.

Venture Capitalists as Human Beings

This book has painted a picture of venture capitalists as wonderful people. Perhaps you have a completely different view. Venture capitalists are not saints. They are probably not as knowledgeable as this book portrays them. They are probably not as reasonable as you have been led to believe. Nor are they as professional as this book would indicate. But, in general, you will find the venture capital community a hard-working group. They will not try to cheat you, but they will try to get the best deal from you. They want to make money for their company. Most assuredly, there are some sharpies in the group, but most are good-hearted people. They are not trying to play the game of "I-got-you," whereby they use every opportunity to destroy your chances. They want you to succeed. They want to be your partner, and, if treated correctly, they will be a good partner.

Remember that the venture capitalist is just another human being. He is trying to do the best he can. Some venture capitalists like to think of themselves as the highly paid elite, standing at the pinnacle of capitalism, and determining which new companies are created. In reality, most of them are just part of the great middle class of businessmen who have helped make our country great. They can help make your company great too.

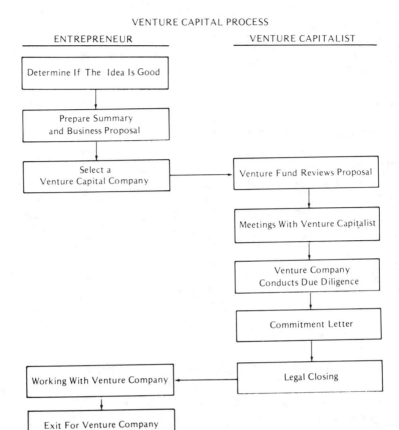

VENTURE CAPITAL PROCESS

ENTREPRENEUR

Determine If The Idea Is Good

Prepare Summary
and Business Proposal

Select a
Venture Capital Company

VENTURE CAPITALIST

Venture Fund Reviews Proposal

Meetings With Venture Capitalist

Venture Company
Conducts Due Diligence

Commitment Letter

Legal Closing

Working With Venture Company

Exit For Venture Company

Figure 12.1

Problem Companies Looking for Financing

Venture capitalists see many companies with problems that are seeking financing. As mentioned before, these are called turnarounds. Venture capitalists also see many turnarounds that are not presented as such by the entrepreneur. A company may have a significant flaw or a problem that the entrepreneur has covered up. The entrepreneur hopes that the venture capitalist will not uncover the flaw and will finance the company. He believes the new money will save the company. If you have a significant problem and do not tell the venture capitalist, and if he uncovers the problem, you have lost all chances of financing. On the other hand, if the problem is revealed, you still stand a chance of being financed, albeit less of a chance.

If you are operating a problem company, you are faced with a critical decision. Should you reveal the business problem to the venture capitalist and risk losing financing, or should you let the venture capitalist conduct his own investigation? If he does not find the business problem, maybe you will obtain the financing. You should think this one through carefully. If the venture capitalist does not find the problem and he invests his money, the problem will surface sometime after the financing. When the problem does arise, you will lose a tremendous amount of credibility with the venture capitalist. He will be out for revenge, and, quite frankly, you will deserve it.

Financing for Your Job or Your Ego

Sometimes an entrepreneur will dream up an idea in order to create a job for himself. Inventors will push an idea on a venture capitalist in the hope that the venture capitalist will put enough money into the company to guarantee the inventor a job over the next year or two. The inventor's reasoning is, "At least I will have a paycheck for eighteen months." Such an entrepreneur is unethical in his approach to the financing of his idea. His motivation for financing his idea is not to build a big company that will go public someday, but merely to use it as a vehicle to receive a paycheck for the next eighteen months. If you are caught trying to sell this type of idea, you deserve no respect whatsoever.

There is another type of entrepreneur who wants the venture capitalist to bankroll his acquisition of a company or his new idea in order to feed his ego. He wants to be president of a great new company that is doing wonderful things. The entrepreneur in this case may give the venture capitalist erroneous information in order to induce him to back his "great" new company. The entrepreneur's motivation is one of ego enhancement rather than one of making money.

Both of these examples show a divergence of interest between the entrepreneur and the venture capitalist that is bound to create trouble. In one case, the entrepreneur wants a job and he is merely looking for a way to finance it. In the other, the entrepreneur has a "big shot" complex and wants somebody to finance his ego trip. As you know from reading this book, the venture capitalist is interested in long-term capital appreciation. His interests do not coincide with those of the entrepreneurs described above. You can expect any venture capitalist to turn down your deal the minute he determines that his interests do not match yours, and he will be justified in doing so.

Too Much Information

Some entrepreneurs believe they should avoid giving the venture capital investor too much information. They believe too much information will confuse the venture capitalist and cause him to ask too many questions. Such an entrepreneur rationalizes that he knows the business will be successful so he will protect the venture capitalist from wasting time or being concerned with negative information about the company.

As an example, there was an entrepreneur who had invented a computer product. He had raised venture capital financing to manufacture the product. Soon after he began the manufacturing process, he found a problem that could not be corrected. He decided not to tell the venture capitalist. He delayed meeting with the investors, and when the meeting finally occurred, the entrepreneur indicated that some problems existed with the product but that he believed they would all be worked out. All the while, he worked feverishly to find a substitute product. Finally, after three months, he had a new product and it worked. He told the venture capitalist the entire story. The venture capitalist was furious. Credibility was reduced to zero. The venture capitalist felt he could not trust the entrepreneur. After all, what other information was being withheld? Their relationship was never the same again.

Do You Understand Credibility?

If you did not get the message from previous sections of this book, let me repeat it: credibility is the only firm basis on which the entrepreneur and the venture capitalist build a relationship. This relationship will be a close one for many years. If you enter it thinking that you will outsmart the venture capitalist by being dishonest, you are in for a rocky ride. Conversely, if you determine that the venture capitalist is entering the deal with ulterior motives, you should avoid his financing. No venture capitalist-entrepreneur relationship can be successful unless there is trust between the two.

Ten Commandments for an Entrepreneur

You should follow certain commandments in your quest for venture capital and during your working relationship with the venture capitalist. The Bible,. of course, has ten commandments. In order to be successful as an entrepreneur, you need to follow ten also.

Thou Shalt Be Truthful to Thyself

One of the hardest things for entrepreneurs to overcome is their belief in their own promotional material. It is usual for an entrepreneur to promote his ideas or business as strongly as possible. Gasconade is expected by everyone. After all, if the entrepreneur does not promote it, who will? However, after you have stripped away all the promotional items, ask yourself if the basic business is a good opportunity. The ultimate question for the entrepreneur is: "Do you really believe in the business you are undertaking?" Some entrepreneurs want to go into business for themselves so badly that they are blind to the bad points of the business. If you are not entirely confident about the situation you are putting together, you should rethink your decision. To make sure you are not eagerly accepting your own promotional information, you should go through the deal in detail, listing all the good points and all the horrible things you can think of. Now throw out all the promotional points and leave only the solid business reasons. Is it still a good deal?

In your heart you may think it would be a crime for you to miss such an opportunity. You may rationalize that the venture capitalist has reviewed and approved the investment. If he thinks it is a good deal, it must be good. Be realistic. A venture capitalist knows much less about the business than you do. He has made many mistakes. You should understand clearly that if you put together a deal that fails, it will be a disastrous experience for you. In being truthful to yourself, you will avoid making a mistake by not going into a poor deal. Even though you might be able to raise the money for the deal, it may not be the right deal. If you have any misgivings about a deal, you should discuss them with your venture capital partner to make sure you are both going forward with your eyes open. He may even have a solution for the problems that bother you.

There is the story of an entrepreneur who, during the last recession, had been analyzing and working with a small metal fabricator. By the middle of the recession he had negotiated a purchase price for the business on the basis of the financial statements for the prior year ending December 31. The price seemed fair, according to the company's status as of December 31. When the entrepreneur received the financial statements for the first six months, he saw that the figures had dropped significantly. In discussing this point with the venture capitalist, the entrepreneur made every possible excuse for the reduced earnings, which clearly showed that the company could not carry the amount of debt service needed to purchase it. Unless the earnings picked up quickly, the company would be in trouble shortly after the acquisition. The entrepreneur saw the venture capitalist becoming uneasy. He prepared a long analysis of the situation to convince the venture capitalist to go through with the deal. The venture capitalist did not invest. He was convinced the reduced earnings signaled a drastic slowdown. Others did invest. The company has been a poor performer and probably will not make any money for years. In this situation, the entrepreneur was willing to believe his own promotional material. As a result, he promoted himself into a very poor business situation. You should not make the same mistake.

Thou Shalt Recognize Reality

A basic theory about reality is that reality is real! Know reality, or you will lose. Consider the story of the entrepreneur who came upon a business to buy.

He began to study the industry. As he studied the industry, he saw that the basic economics of the industry were changing because of increased gasoline prices and increased interest rates. He could find no evidence that interest rates or the price of energy would return to previous levels. High gas prices and interest rates foreshadowed a sure reorganization of the industry in the form of reduced sales. The entrepreneur was unwilling to recognize reality, and instead he stormed ahead.

With venture capital money he purchased the business. Subsequently, industry sales dropped off sharply. The entrepreneur went through hell on earth. He couldn't make enough money to pay off the debt he assumed when he purchased the business. The venture capitalist was unhappy because this was turning out to be a poor investment.

Unless you are willing to recognize the facts as they exist, then you are doomed to failure. Do not let emotions interfere with sound business judgments. Seeing reality and disregarding it can only lead to disaster.

Thou Shalt Maintain Credibility

There is more to credibility than just being honest. Honesty is not telling lies. Credibility also means trying to do what you believe is right. You must maintain credibility with your venture capital partner, with banks, with suppliers, with employees, with all the other people who depend on you. If they find that you changed the meaning of your statements and you act like a Grade B lawyer trying to win a minor case in a small claims court, you will not fare well as an entrepreneur. When you give someone a set of projections and later are unable to achieve the projections, your credibility will suffer if you merely say, "Well, they were only projections and everybody knows projections are only a guess." When you say you are going to do something, projections or whatever, somehow, someway, make it happen. This is the only way to maintain your credibility with the venture capitalist and with all the other people who depend on you.

Thou Shalt Be Loyal to Those Who Have Helped You

Loyalty is another form of honesty. It means that you stick by your commitments. It means you are fair in your dealings with your venture capital partner, your employees, and all the others along the way who have helped your business. If somebody does you a favor, try to return the favor. This will build your business reputation. If you ask someone to help you, accept that help, and then later turn on that person, you will let the world know that you are disloyal to those who help you. You may make a few extra dollars in the short run by being disloyal, but in the longer term you must be loyal if you want to achieve greater results. Loyalty will carry you far in the business world. No business is built on one man's ability. It takes many people to build a business. You must be loyal to all the people upon whose shoulders you stand in order to reach the heights that you want to attain in your business.

Thou Shalt Be Prepared

Knowledge is power. Knowledge of your industry, of your own abilities, of your business, and of your venture capitalist's needs must be assembled in order to make a venture successful. Always be prepared for any outcome. Think through all decisions so you know the consequences. Be prepared for any reaction by competition. Be prepared for the transfer of a favorite loan officer at your bank. Be prepared for disasters such as fires or other catastrophes. Think about all the things that could destroy your chances of making this a successful business and be prepared for every one of them. Be prepared for your untimely death. Write a corporate "will" to ensure that everyone knows what you think should be done.

Thou Shalt Be Positive

The general mental attitude of an entrepreneur must be positive. Otherwise the entrepreneur will not be able to jump all the hurdles that stand in the way of success in the entrepreneurial world. You must always be selling the merits of your company, the merits of your people, and the merits of your products. A positive attitude is one of the outstanding qualities of a good entrepreneur. If you are positive, the people who follow you will be positive in all they do, even in solving problems. Self-confidence and a positive attitude generate respect from others. You must be self-confident, but not egocentric. Positive thinking means determining how to get the job done. Do not spend time blaming others. Determine what needs to be accomplished and adopt a positive mental attitude to achieving goals.

Thou Shalt Never Give Up

Never giving up is not the same as being stubborn. Never giving up means being an achiever and having a strong desire to win. You must have strong motivation to achieve the goals that you have set out. You need physical and mental energy to accomplish the tasks that have been set out. Without a tremendous amount of physical and mental energy, you simply cannot accomplish all the things in your business plans. Your drive, your ambition, and your desire to succeed are embodied in the phrase, "You shall never give up."

Thou Shalt Be Straight

This book has been a strong proponent of honesty and it has mentioned some situations in which entrepreneurs have not been honest. But it has not delved into the illegal activities of entrepreneurs. In a few publicized cases entrepreneurs have been involved with organized crime. In some other celebrated cases entrepreneurs have used illegal means to make their company grow faster. A few entrepreneurs have turned to crime in order to save their company. From the standpoint of risk and reward, crime does not pay. The rewards of saving your company or making your company grow faster are not worth the downside risk of a term in prison and a destroyed business life. It is better to be a straight entrepreneur.

Thou Shalt Be Lucky

When entrepreneurs are asked to account for their success as entrepreneurs, they invariably point to luck. They believe that luck as much as anything else has brought them to where they are. However, when one begins to analyze their careers more closely, the truth of Thomas Edison's statement about creativity comes shining through. Edison believed that creativity was 10 percent inspiration and 90 percent perspiration. It's the same for lucky entrepreneurs. Look at the track record of a successful entrepreneur and you will certainly find lucky breaks, but they seem to come when the entrepreneur is exerting a tremendous amount of energy in order to succeed. Being successful *is* 10 percent luck and 90 percent hard work. In other words, the entrepreneur constantly seeks success. He is doing whatever is necessary in order to achieve. Only in those instances where overwhelming odds have destroyed his chances, do you find an entrepreneur who is an achiever, but who is not "lucky."

Thou Shall Pray a Lot

I have been dealing with entrepreneurs for many years now. Some of them are religious and some are not so religious, but all of them have one thing in common; they pray a lot. In their prayers they ask that things turn out alright. They want to get that one critical sale that they need. They pray that the new machine that they purchased will work as it is supposed to. They give thanks that their employees are healthy and happy. While most of their prayers seem to be more material than spiritual, nonetheless they pray a lot.

I can tell you from first hand experience that prayer is not limited to entrepreneurs. Venture capitalists pray plenty.

Parting Shot

I have never been an entrepreneur in the traditional sense. I have met thousands of entrepreneurs and have backed hundreds of them in many different types of enterprises. This book should give you much of the knowledge you need to deal with the venture capitalist. If you will follow every item covered by this book, I assure you it will bring you good luck.

— Appendix 1 —

Actual Documents

What Do Actual Commitment Letters
and Legal Documents Look Like? Here They Are.

The following documents are facsimiles of actual documents used in a financing, except that they have been broadened in concept to include many of the standard "boiler plate" items used by most venture capitalists. After reading these documents, you will be well prepared for the ones you receive from the venture capitalist. All documents are for fictitious companies and people.

The following documents are covered in this appendix:

1. Commitment letter for a loan with options for stock on Ace Electromagnetic, Inc.

2. Legal Document 1: Loan Agreement on Ace Electromagnetic, Inc.

3. Legal Document 2: Promissory Note on Ace Electromagnetic, Inc.

4. Legal Document 3: Stock Purchase Warrants on Ace Electromagnetic, Inc.

5. Legal Document 4: Stock Purchase on Ajax Computer Genetics Corp.

6. Legal Document 5: Exhibits to Stock Purchase on Ajax Computer Genetics Corp.

Commitment Letter

Venture Capital Corporation
1666 K St., N.W., Suite 901
Washington, D.C. 20006

Mr. Joseph Entrepreneur, President
Ace Electromagnetic Incorporated
1234 Main Street
McLean, Virginia 22102

Dear Mr. Entrepreneur:

The Management of Venture Capital Corporation (Venture) has approved a loan to your company (the Company) in the amount of $300,000. The approval was based on the following representations made by you:

1.01   The Company is a corporation in good standing in Virginia. You will provide Venture with a Certificate of Good Standing and a copy of the Charter and Bylaws and minutes of the organization of the Company.

1.02   The Company is primarily engaged in the business of manufacturing electromagnetic equipment.

1.03   There are no lawsuits against the Company, its directors, or its officers, personally, nor any you know of that may be contemplated. If there are any suits outstanding or contemplated, your attorney will provide Venture with a letter stating the nature of such suits and a copy of the suits. You will provide us with a copy of all lawsuits you have filed against others.

1.04   The Company is current on all taxes owed and, in this regard, you will provide Venture with a copy of the last three years' tax returns for the Company.

1.05   You have presented financial information showing that the Company, for the twelve-month period just ending had: sales of $850,000 and pre-tax loss of $25,000; assets of $600,000; liabilities of $300,000; and a net worth of $300,000.

1.06   The money borrowed will be used as follows:
    A. $100,000 to pay First National Bank.
    B. $100,000 to pay accounts payable.
    C. $100,000 to pay fees and working capital.

1.07   Upon completion of Venture's loan, you will have approximately the following assets:

    A.   Cash, $100,000.
    B.   Accounts receivable, $100,000.
    C.   Machinery and equipment, $100,000.
    D.   Land and building, $100,000.
    E.   Other assets, $300,000.

1.08   With regard to leases, you will provide Venture with a copy of every major executed lease.

1.09   The information presented to Venture is correct and you believe the projections presented to Venture are reasonable.

1.10   You will pay no brokerage fees, legal fees, or other fees on this loan without Venture's written approval, and you will indemnify Venture against all such fees.

1.11   During the past ten years none of the directors has been arrested or convicted of a material crime.

2.   The terms and conditions of the loan shall be:

2.01   A loan of $300,000 for six years at 15 percent per annum, paid monthly on the first of each month.

2.02   The loan shall be interest only for the first 36 months and, beginning with the 37th month, you will pay principal and interest sufficient to amortize the loan over the remaining 36 months. All principal and interest outstanding at the end of six years shall be due and payable in full as a balloon payment.

2.03   The loan may be prepaid at any time in whole or part.

2.04   Take-down of the loan shall be $300,000 at closing.

2.05   Other terms standard for such loans.

2.06   In connection with this financing, Venture shall receive at closing separate options to purchase stock in the Company. Cost of the options to Venture will be $100. These options, when exercised by Venture and the other investment company, will provide stock ownership in the company of 35 percent at the time of exercise. The exercise price will be $100. The options will expire ten years from closing. Venture will share pro rata in any redemption of stock by the Company.

2.07   There shall be an "unlocking" provision whereby if there is a bona fide offer to purchase the Company and Venture wishes to accept the offer and you do not, then you shall acquire Venture's interest on the same terms or sell the Company.

2.08   There shall be a "put" provision whereby any time after five years from closing Venture may require the Company to purchase its options or the resulting stock at the higher of the following:

    A.   Ten percent of sales for the year just ended times a price-earnings ratio of eight less Venture's debt times 35 percent.

    B.   Ten times cash flow for the year just ended less Venture's debt times 35 percent.

2.09   Venture shall have full "piggyback" rights to register its shares any time the Company (or its management) is registering shares for sale and such registration of Venture's shares shall be paid for by the Company.

3.   Collateral for the loan shall be:

3.01   A second deed of trust on the land and building of the business, subordinated as to collateral to a mortgage of approximately $10,000, on terms acceptable to Venture.

3.02   A first secured interest in all of the tangible and intangible assets of the Company including, but not limited to, inventory, machinery, equipment, furniture, fixtures, and accounts receivable.

3.03   Pledge and assignment of all the stock of the Company and assignment of leases listed above.

3.04   Personal signatures and guarantees of you and your spouse.

3.05   Obtaining a life insurance policy on your life for $300,000 with the policy assigned to Venture and with Venture as the loss payee to the extent of its loan.

3.06   Adequate hazard and business insurance, which shall include federal flood insurance if your business is located in a designated federal flood area. All such insurance shall be assigned to Venture and Venture shall be listed as the loss payee to the extent of its interest. In this regard, you will supply Venture with a list of all business insurance and such insurance and coverage shall be acceptable to Venture.

4.   Conditions of the loan are:

4.01   Provide Venture with monthly year-to-date financial statements in accordance with generally accepted accounting standards (including profit and loss and balance sheet) within forty-five days of the end of the month.

4.02   The president of the Company will provide Venture with a certificate each quarter stating that no default has occurred in the Loan Agreement.

4.03 If requested in writing, provide Venture with an annual certified audit within ninety days after the year's end from an accounting firm acceptable to Venture.

4.04 Before each year end, provide Venture with projections of the next year in the same format as the financial statements.

4.05 Within thirty days after they are filed, provide Venture with a copy of all documents filed with government agencies such as the Internal Revenue Service, Federal Trade Commission, and Securities and Exchange Commission.

4.06 There will be no change in control of the Company, nor will there be a change of ownership without Venture's written approval.

4.07 Management will not sell, assign, or transfer any shares it owns in the Company without the written approval of Venture.

4.08 The Company will maintain in accordance with generally accepted accounting principles:
    A.   A current ratio of one to one.
    B.   Sales of $500,000 per year.
    C.   Sales of $30,000 per month.
    D.   Sales of $105,000 per quarter.
    E.   Net worth of $50,000 or more.

4.09 The Company will have board meetings at least once each quarter at the Company's business offices. While a Venture representative will not serve on the board, a Venture representative will have the right to attend each meeting at the Company's expense and Venture shall be notified of each meeting at least two weeks before it is to occur.

4.10 The Company will pay no cash dividends and the Company will not sell any assets of the business that are not part of the regular course of business without Venture's approval.

4.11 The Company will not expend funds in excess of $10,000 per year for capital improvements, and the like.

4.12 You will live in the general Washington, D.C., metropolitan area.

4.13 The Company will not pay, nor loan, nor advance to any employee money which, in total, is in excess of $25,000 per year, without the written approval of Venture. If (1) the Company is in default for nonpayment to Venture or any senior lien; or (2) the Company is not profitable for any quarter, then the Company will not pay, nor loan, nor advance to any employee money which, in total, is in excess of $20,000 per year, without written permission of Venture.

4.14   The Company will not pay any brokerage fees, legal fees, or consulting fees in excess of $5,000 per year without the written permission of Venture.

4.15   Other conditions standard for such loans.

4.16   You will pay all closing costs and recording fees, which include all attorney's fees. You may use any attorney to draw the legal documents; however, they must be reviewed and approved by Venture's counsel. A simple review by Venture's counsel will not incur a fee; however, if the work done by Venture's counsel is beyond a simple review, a fee will be charged and the fee will be paid by you.

4.17   In connection with this financing, Venture will receive a 2 percent ($6,000) fee. Upon acceptance of this commitment letter, you will pay Venture $1,500 of this fee and the remainder at closing. Should closing not take place owing to the fault of Venture, then the fee will be returned less out-of-pocket expenses; otherwise, it is forfeited.

5.   *This commitment is conditioned upon the following, which, if not attained, will make Venture's commitment void:*

5.01   Acceptance by you of this letter and the return of one copy to Venture fully executed by you, with the fee set out in 4.17 above, within 15 days.

5.02   Closing on the loan before the year end.

5.03   All legal documents being acceptable to Venture.

5.04   A favorable credit check of you and your business and no material adverse occurrences before closing.

5.05   A favorable visit by Venture to your business.

Sincerely,

A. V. Capitalist
President

VENTURE CAPITAL CORPORATION

AGREED: ACE ELECTROMAGNETIC, INCORPORATED

By: _____ DATE:
　　　 Joseph Entrepreneur, President

_____ DATE: _____
　　　 Personally: Joseph Entrepreneur

Legal Document 1
Ace Electromagnetic, Incorporated
McLean, Virginia

Loan Agreement

WHEREAS, Venture Capital Corporation, a District of Columbia corporation (hereinafter "*Venture*") has committed under terms of a letter of _____ (date) to lend to Ace Electromagnetic, Incorporated, a Virginia corporation (hereinafter "Company") the sum of Three Hundred Thousand dollars ($300,000);

WHEREAS, the Company will issue *VENTURE Stock Purchase Warrants (hereinafter "Warrants") for a total of 35* percent of the common stock of the Company.

NOW THEREFORE the Company and Venture agree as follows:

I. Parties

This agreement shall bind and accrue to the benefit of the Company and its successors, the undersigned shareholders of the Company, Venture, and any subsequent holders of the Note, Warrants, or the stock issued thereunder (who are collectively referred to herein as "Holders"). The Note issued hereunder may be held by different persons, as may the Warrants. The terms of this Agreement as of the day the Company receives notice that a new party is holder of a Note or Warrant shall be binding between the Company and such new party, regardless of modifications that may subsequently be made between the Company and another holder.

II. Loan

The Company will borrow and Venture will lend the sum of Three Hundred Thousand Dollars ($300,000) to be repaid according to the terms of the Promissory Note of even date herewith, (hereinafter "Note").

III. Use of Proceeds

The Company will use the proceeds of the loan only to fund commercial electromagnetic operations with approximately $100,000 to repay a line of credit at the First National Bank, $100,000 to pay accounts payable, and $100,000 for fees and working capital.

IV.   Collateral

The Note and the Holders' rights herein shall be secured *pari passu* against the collateral below, provided that future advances in addition to the original $300,000 advanced to the Company shall not be considered in determining the secured parties' shares from sale of collateral. In regard to the items in subparagraph 2., the Company grants Holders a security interest to attach when the Company has signed this instrument and acquired rights in the property, and when Venture has made whole or partial disbursement of loan funds to the Company, the Company's designated payee, or an escrow agent. Although other parties may become holders of the instruments secured hereby, all security interests of record will remain in the name of Venture Capital Corporation, which will hold such interests in trust for the benefit of all Holders. The collateral shall be as follows:

1. A second mortgage on the Company's real estate in the Commonwealth of Virginia subject to a first mortgage to a financial institution according to terms of a separate instrument;

2. A second security interest in the furniture, fixtures, machinery, equipment, inventory, contract rights, licenses, and all tangible and intangible personal property of the Company subject to credit lines from financial institutions;

3. Assignment of accounts receivable, pledge of all the outstanding stock of the Company subject to bank lines of credit according to the terms of separate agreements therefor;

4. Collateral assignment of the policy number 1234567 issued by ABC Life Insurance Company insuring the life of Joseph Entrepreneur in the amount of $300,000.00;

5. Personal guarantees of Mr. and Mrs. Joseph Entrepreneur according to the terms of a separate instrument.

V.   Representations and Warranties

To induce Venture to enter this transaction the Company represents and warrants that:

A.   It is duly incorporated, validly existing and in good standing under the laws of Virginia, having Articles of Incorporation and Bylaws (all of the terms of which are in full force and effect) as previously furnished to Venture; it is not and does not intend to become an investment company or passive investment vehicle;

B.   It is duly qualified to conduct business as proposed by it and is in good standing as a foreign corporation in all states in which the nature of its business or location of its properties requires such qualification;

C.   It has full power and authority to enter into this Agreement, to borrow money as contemplated hereby, to issue the Warrants and upon exercise thereof to issue the stock pursuant thereto, and to carry out the provisions hereof; and it has taken all corporate action necessary for the execution and performance of each of the above (including the issuance and sale of the Warrants, the reservation of shares of stock, and the issuance thereof upon the exercise of the Warrants); and each document above-named will constitute a valid and binding obligation of the Company enforceable in accordance with its respective terms when executed and delivered;

D.   The authorized capital stock of the Company is as set forth below, and all such stock has been duly issued in accordance with applicable laws, including federal and state securities laws:

Class	Par Value	Shares Authorized	Shares Issued	Shares Outstanding
Common	zero	5,000	3,200	3,200

E.   The list of officers and directors of the Company previously submitted is complete and accurate. All representations made by the Company, its officers, directors, shareholders, or guarantors in any instrument described in this Agreement or previously supplied to Venture in regard to this financing are true and correct as of this date, and all projections provided are reasonable;

F.   The Company has no debts, liabilities, or obligations of any nature whether accrued, absolute, contingent, or otherwise arising out of any transaction entered into or any state of facts existing prior hereto, including without limitation liabilities or obligations on account of taxes or government charges, penalties, interest, or fines thereon or in respect thereof except the debts to be paid off by the use of proceeds of this loan, and debts on open account; the accounts payable and the debts to be paid herewith have not changed materially since the date of the June financial statement previously submitted; the Company does not know and has no reasonable grounds to know of any basis for any claim against it as of the date of this Agreement or of any debt, liability, or obligation other than those mentioned herein;

G.   The Company has not been made a party to or threatened by any suits, actions, claims, investigations by governmental bodies, or legal, administrative, or arbitrational proceedings except as set out in the Company counsel's letter (hereinafter "litigation letter"); neither the Company nor its officers nor directors know of any basis or grounds for any such suit or proceeding; there are no outstanding orders, judgments, writs, injunctions, or decrees or any court, government agency, or arbitrational tribune against or affecting it or its properties, assets, or business;

H.   Since the date of the Venture commitment letter the Company has not suffered any material adverse change in its condition (financial or otherwise) or its overall business prospects, nor entered into any material transactions or incurred any debt, obligation, or liability, absolute or contingent, nor sustained any material loss or damage to its property, whether or not insured, nor suffered any material interference with its business or operations, present or proposed; and there has been no sale, lease, abandonment, or other disposition by the Company of any of its property, real or personal, or any interest therein or relating thereto, that is material to the financial position of the Company;

I.   The Company has duly filed all tax returns, federal, state, and local, which are required to be filed and has duly paid or fully reserved for all taxes or installments thereof as and when due which have or may become due pursuant to said returns or pursuant to any assessment received by the Company;

J.   The Company is not bound by or party to any contract or instrument or subject to any charter or other legal restriction materially and adversely affecting its business, property, assets, operations, or condition, financial or otherwise;

K.   Except for matters set out in the litigation letter, the Company is not in breach of, default under, or in violation of any applicable law, decree, order, rule, or regulation which may materially and adversely affect it or any indenture, contract, agreement, deed, lease, loan agreement, commitment, bond, note, deed of trust, restrictive covenant, license, or other instrument or obligation to which it is a party or by which it is bound or to which any of its assets are subject; the execution, delivery, and performance of this Agreement and the issuance, sale, and delivery of the Warrant and other documents will not constitute any such breach, default, or violation or require consent or approval of any court, governmental agency, or body except as contemplated herein;

L.   The statements set forth in the *Size Stand Declaration* (SBA Form 480, Exhibit 4 hereto) and *Assurances of Compliance* (SBA Form 625D, Exhibit 5, herein), as previously provided, are complete and accurate; the Company is a small business concern as defined in the *Small Business Investment Act of 1958,* as amended ("the Act"), and the rules and regulations of the Small Business Administration (SBA) thereunder; there exists no agreement expressed or implied, no condition, state of facts or relationship between the Company and any other entity or entities which would prevent the corporation from qualifying as a small business concern;

M.   Neither the Company nor any of its officers, directors, partners, or controlling persons is an "Associate" of Venture as such terms are defined in section 107.3 of the Regulations as amended promulgated under the Act, nor an "Affiliated person" of Venture, as such term is defined in section 2(a)(3) of the *Investment Company Act* of 1940 as amended;

N.   To the best of the Company's knowledge, it has complied in all material respects with all laws, ordinances, and regulations applicable to it and to its business, including without limitation federal and state securities laws, zoning laws, and ordinances, federal labor laws, and regulations and the *Federal Occupational Safety and Health Act* and regulations thereunder, the *Federal Employees Retirement Income Security Act,* and federal, state, and local environmental protection laws and regulations;

O.   There are no material facts relating to the Company not fully disclosed to Venture; no representation, covenant or warranty made by the Company herein or in any statement, certificate or other instrument furnished to Venture pursuant hereto or in connection with the transaction contemplated hereby contains or will contain any untrue statement of or omits to state a material fact necessary to make the statement not misleading;

P.   The Company is primarily engaged in the business of commercial electromagnetic manufacturing and is not a franchise;

Q.   The Company for the twelve month period ending January 31, 1983, had: sales of $850,000; pretax loss of $25,000; assets of $600,000; liabilities of $300,000; and net worth of $300,000;

R.   After disbursement of the subject loan the Company will have approximately the following assets: accounts receivable $100,000, machinery and equipment $100,000, land and building $100,000, other assets $300,000;

S.   Copies of leases provided are true and correct;

T.   During the past ten (10) years no officer or director of the Company has been arrested or convicted of any criminal offense;

VI.   Affirmative Covenants

Until the Warrants are exercised and the Note repaid in full, the Company will:

A.   Promptly make all payments of principal and interest as due under the Note and furnish from time to time to each Holder all information it may reasonably request to enable it to prepare and file any form required to be filed by Holder with the SBA, Securities and Exchange Commission, or any other regulatory authority;

B.   Forward, or cause to be forwarded to Holders, its monthly accounting balance sheet and profit-and-loss statement within forty-five (45) days from the end of each month;

C.   Forward, or cause to be forwarded to Holders, its final year end accounting balance sheet and profit-and-loss statement within sixty (60) days of such accounting year end, which if demanded by a Holder in writing shall be prepared at Company's expense by an independent outside accounting firm acceptable to a Holder, according to generally accepted accounting principles uniformly applied;

D.   Maintain a net worth of $50,000 or more and a level of current assets (which shall be reflected in its books in accordance with generally accepted accounting principles) such that the amount of such current assets shall equal or exceed the amount of current liabilities; maintain sales of at least $500,000 per annum; $105,000 per quarter and $30,000 per month as reflected on its books in accordance with generally accepted accounting principles uniformly applied;

E.   Provide to Holders in writing each quarter the certification of the President of the Company that no default has occurred under the Warrants, Note or this Agreement, or any debt or obligation senior to the debt of the Holders hereunder; or if any such default exists, provide Holders with a statement by the President of the Company as to the nature of such default;

F.   Maintain such shares of its common stock authorized but unissued as may be necessary to satisfy the rights of the Holders of the Warrants;

G.   Perform all acts as required under the Warrants including without limitation, the re-issue of replacement Warrants to a Holder upon loss or destruction;

H.   Permit any authorized representative of any Holder and its attorneys and accountants to inspect, examine, and make copies and abstracts of the books of account and records of Company at reasonable times during normal business hours;

I.   Notify Holders of any litigation to which the Company is a party by mailing to Holders, by registered mail, within five (5) days of receipt thereof, a copy of the Complaint, Motion for Judgment, or other such pleadings served on or by the Company; and any litigation to which the Company is not a party but which could substantially affect operation of the Company's business or the collateral pledged for this loan, including collateral securing any guarantees, by mailing to Holders, by registered mail, a copy of all pleadings obtained by the Company in regard to such litigation, or if no pleadings are obtained, a letter setting out the facts known about the litigation within five (5) days of receipt thereof; provided that the Company shall not be obliged by this paragraph to give notice of suits where it is a creditor seeking collection of account debts;

J.   Prior to each accounting year end, provide Holders with projected financial statements for the coming year, in the same format as used for item C above;

K.   Hold a meeting of the Board of Directors of the Company at least once each quarter; give Holders at least two weeks prior notice of such meeting; allow one representative designated by each Holder to attend such meeting at Company's expense;

L.   Maintain all-risk hazard insurance on its assets, with mortgagee clause in favor of Holders, in such reasonable amounts and forms as required by Holders; this shall include federal flood insurance if any assets be in a designated flood plain; and supply Holders with a list of existing coverage prior to closing;

M.   Give Holders notice of any judgment entered against the Company by mailing a copy to Holders within five (5) days of entry thereof;

N.   Take all necessary steps to administer, supervise, preserve, and protect the collateral herein; regardless of any action taken by Holders, there shall be no duty upon Holders in this respect.

O.   Within thirty (30) days of filing provide Holders with copies of all returns and documents filed with federal, state, or local government agencies including without limitation the Internal Revenue Service, Federal Trade Commission, and Securities and Exchange Commission.

P.   Maintain an original or a true copy of this Agreement and any modifications hereof, which shall be available for inspection under subparagraph H. above.

VII. Negative Covenants

Until the Notes are repaid and the Warrants exercised, the Company will not without the prior written consent of all the Holders:

A. Declare or pay any cash dividend of any kind on any class of stock; make any material change in its ownership, organization, or management or the manner in which its business is conducted; authorize, issue, or reclassify any shares of capital stock except as required under the Warrants;

B. Become a party to any merger or consolidation with any other corporation, company, or entity;

C. Make expenditures for capital improvements or acquisitions in any fiscal year in excess of $10,000;

D. Make loans, advances, wage payments including salaries, withdrawals, fees, bonuses, commissions direct or indirect in money or otherwise, to any officer, director, shareholder, partner, or employee in excess of $50,000 per year, or $30,000 per year if there is a default under this agreement;

E. Transfer, sell, lease, or in any other manner convey any equitable, beneficial, or legal interest in any of the assets of the Company except inventory sold in the normal course of business, or allow to exist on its assets any mortgage interest, pledge, security interest, title repention device, or other encumbrance junior or senior to Holders' liens except for liens of taxes and assessments not delinquent or contested in good faith;

F. Permit any judgment obtained against the Company to remain unpaid for over twenty (20) days without obtaining a stay of execution or bond;

G. Incur any declared default under any loan agreement pertaining to another debt of the Company;

H. Pay or incur any brokerage, legal, consulting, or similar fee in excess of $5,000 per year;

I. Create or incur any debt other than that incurred hereunder, trade debt or short-term working capital debt normally incurred in the ordinary course of business;

J. Incur any lease liability or purchase any additional life insurance from business income or assets;

K. Become a guarantor, or otherwise liable on any notes or obligations of any other person, firm corporation or entity, except in connection with depositing checks and other instruments for the payment of money acquired in the normal course of its business.

VIII. Investment Covenant

By accepting a Warrant, the Holder thereof represents, warrants, and covenants that it is an "accredited investor" within the meaning of section 4(6) of the *Securities Act* or an "accredited person" within the meaning of Rule 242 of the *Securities Act*, or acquiring the Warrant and any stock issued thereunder for its own account for investment and not with the view to resale or distribution thereof except in accordance with applicable federal and state securities laws. Upon exercise of any conversion rights under the Warrant, this representation, warranty, and covenant shall be deemed to have been given with respect to the stock received.

IX. Fees, Expenses, and Indemnification

The Company shall reimburse Holders for reasonable expenses according to the terms of the commitment letter. The Company shall pay, indemnify, and hold any holders of the Warrants and Note harmless from and against any and all liability and loss with respect to or resulting from any and all claims for or on account of any brokers and from finder's fees or commissions with respect to this transaction as may have been created by the Company or its officers, partners, employees, or agents; and from any stamp or excise taxes which may become payable by virtue of this transaction or the issuance of any stock or modification hereunder. Venture warrants it has not contracted to pay any such fees.

X. Unlocking

If at any time after five (5) years from the date of this Agreement the Company or its shareholders receive a bona fide offer to purchase the assets of the Company or an equity interest in the Company, then the party receiving such offer (hereinafter offeree) will submit a copy of the offer and such information pertinent thereto as it may have to the Holders of the Warrants or the shares issued thereunder within three (3) days of receipt of said offer. Within ten (10) days of receipt of said copy each Warrant Holder will indicate in writing to the offeree its approval or disapproval of the offer. If a Holder approves the offer, then the offeree shall, within twenty (20) days thereafter or such shorter time if provided in the offer, accept or reject the offer. If the offeree rejects the offer then simultaneously with such rejection it shall be bound to purchase the approving Holder's Warrants or resulting stock in the Company under the same terms and conditions that such Holder would have received under the offer. If a Warrant Holder fails to communicate timely approval or disapproval, the Company may construe such failure to indicate disapproval.

XI. "Put" Rights

Beginning five (5) years from the date of this agreement ending ten (10) years from the date of this agreement, Warrant Holders may by written demand require the Company to purchase its Warrant or the shares of stock issued hereunder at a price of 35 percent of the higher of the following sums:

(a) Ten Percent (10%) of the Company's sales for the fiscal year immediately preceding the year of the demand times a price earnings ratio of twelve (12), less the aggregate principal balance of the Note on the day of demand; or

(b) Ten times the Company's cash flow for the fiscal year immediately preceding the year of the demand, less the aggregate principal balance of the Note on the day of demand.

XII.   Default

A.   If any of the below-listed events occurs prior to maturity of the Notes, then a default may be declared at the option of any Holder without presentment, demand, protest, or further notice of any kind, all of which are hereby expressly waived. In such event the Note Holder shall be entitled to be paid in full the balance of any unpaid principal of its Note plus accrued interest and any costs thereof, including reasonable attorneys' fees, and to any other remedies which may be available under this Agreement, the Warrant, the Note, or any applicable law:

1. Occurrence of any default provision as set out in the Warrants or Note;

2. Any material representation made by the Company in writing herein or in connection herewith shall be untrue and shall remain so for thirty (30) days after written notice to the Company thereof;

3. The Company shall fail to comply with the covenants in this Agreement and such failure shall continue for a period of ten (10) days after receipt of notice thereof from any Holder of the Note;

4. The Company shall make an assignment for the benefit of creditors, or shall admit in writing its inability to pay its debts as they become due, or shall file a voluntary petition in bankruptcy, or shall be adjudicated as bankrupt or insolvent, or shall file any petition or answer seeking for itself any reorganization, arrangement, composition, readjustment, liquidation, dissolution, or similar relief under any present or future statute, law, or regulation pertinent to such circumstances, or shall file any answer admitting or not contesting the material allegations of a petition filed against the Company in any such proceedings, or shall seek or consent to or acquiesce in the appointment of any trustee, receiver, or liquidator of the Company or of all or any substantial part of the properties of the Company; or the Company or its directors or majority shareholders shall take any action initiating the dissolution or liquidation of the Company;

5. Sixty (60) days shall have expired after the commencement of an action against the Company seeking reorganization, arrangement, composition, readjustment, liquidation, dissolution or similar relief under any present or future statute, law, or regulation without such action being dismissed or all orders or proceedings thereunder affecting the operations or the business of the Company being stayed; or a stay of any such order or proceedings shall thereafter be set aside and the action setting it aside shall not be timely appealed;

6. Sixty (60) days shall have expired after the appointment, without the consent or acquiescence of the Company, of any Trustee, receiver, or liquidator of the Company, or of all or any substantial part of the properties of the Company without such appointment being vacated;

7. The Company shall be declared in default under an agreement in regard to the debts described in paragraph VI. E. above;

8. Any guarantor or undersigned shareholder of the Company shall fail to comply with the terms of his undertakings to Holders;

B. No course of dealing between a Holder and any other party hereto or any failure or delay on the part of the Holder in exercising any rights or remedies hereunder shall operate as a waiver of any rights or remedies of any Holder under this or any other applicable instrument. No single or partial exercise of any rights or remedies hereunder shall operate as a waiver or preclude the exercise of any other rights or remedies hereunder;

C. Upon the nonpayment of the indebtedness under the Note or any part thereof when due, whether by acceleration or otherwise, a Note-Holder is empowered to sell, assign, and deliver the whole or any part of the collateral for the Note at public or private sale, without demand, advertisement, or notice of the time or place of sale or of any adjournment thereof, which are hereby expressly waived. After deducting all expenses incidental to or arising from such sale or sales, Holder may apply the residue of the proceeds thereof to the payment of the indebtednesses, under the Notes, subject to the terms of paragraph XIII below, returning the excess, if any, to the Company. The Company hereby waives all right of appraisement, whether before or after the sale, and any right of redemption after sale. The Company shall have the right to redeem any collateral up to time of a foreclosure sale by paying the aggregate indebtedness under the Notes;

D. Holders are further empowered to collect or cause to be collected or otherwise to be converted into money all or any part of the collateral, by suit or otherwise, and to surrender, compromise, release, renew, extend, exchange, or substitute any item of the collateral in transactions with the Company or any third party, irrespective of any assignment thereof by the Company, and without prior notice to or consent of the Company or any assignee. Whenever any item of the collateral shall not be paid when due, or any part thereof has become due, Holders shall have the same rights and powers with respect to such items of the collateral as are granted in respect thereof in this paragraph in case of nonpayment of the indebtedness, or any part thereof, when due. None of the rights, remedies, privileges, or powers of the Holders expressly provided for herein shall be exclusive, but each of them shall be cumulative with and in addition to every other right, remedy, privilege, and power now or hereafter existing in favor of the Holders, whether at law or in equity, by statute or otherwise;

E. The Company shall pay all expenses of any nature, whether incurred in or out of court, and whether incurred before or after the Notes shall become due at their maturity date or otherwise (including but not limited to reasonable attorneys' fees and costs) which Holders may deem necessary or proper in connection with the satisfaction of the indebtedness under the Notes or the administration, supervision, preservation, protection of (including, but not limited to, the maintenance of adequate insurance), or the realization upon the collateral. Holders are authorized to pay at any time and from time to time any or all of such expenses, add the amount of such payment to the amount of principal outstanding, and charge interest thereon at the rate specified in the Notes;

F.   The security interest of the Holders and their assigns shall not be impaired by a Holder's sale, hypothecation, or rehypothecation of a Warrant or Note or any item of the collateral, or by any indulgence, including, but not limited to:

1. Any renewal, extension, or modification which a Holder may grant with respect to the indebtedness of any part thereof, or,

2. Any surrender, compromise, release, renewal, extension, exchange, or substitution which a Holder may grant in respect of the collateral, or,

3. Any indulgence granted in respect of any endorser, guarantor, or surety. The purchaser, assignee, transferee, or pledgee of the Warrants, Notes, collateral, any guaranty, or any other document (or any of them), sold, assigned, transferred, pledged, or repledged, shall forthwith become vested with and entitled to exercise all powers and rights given by this Agreement to Holders, as if said purchaser, assignee, transferee, or pledgee were originally named in this Agreement in place of the Holders.

XIII.   Notice

All notices or communications under this Agreement of the Warrants or Notes shall be mailed, postage prepaid, or delivered as follows:

To Venture: 1666 K Street, N.W., Suite 901
Washington, D.C. 20006

To Company: Ace Electromagnetic, Incorporated
1234 Main Street
McLean, Virginia 22102

or, to such other address as shall at any time be designated by any party in writing to the other parties.

XIV.   Entire Agreement

The Warrants, the Note, and this Agreement and the documents mentioned herein set forth the entire agreements and understandings of the parties hereto in respect of this transaction. Any prior agreements are hereby terminated. The terms herein may not be changed verbally but only by an instrument in writing signed by the party against which enforcement of the change is sought.

XV. Controlling Law

This Agreement shall be construed in accordance with and governed by the laws of the District of Columbia.

XVI. Headings

The headings of the paragraphs and subparagraphs of this Agreement and the Warrants and Note are inserted for convenience only and shall not be deemed to constitute a part of this Agreement or the Warrants and Note.

IN WITNESS WHEREOF, the undersigned hereby affix their hands and seals on the year and day first above written.

ACE ELECTROMAGNETIC, INC.   VENTURE CAPITAL
                               CORPORATION

By: _____   By: _____
    Joseph Entrepreneur   A. Venture Capitalist
    President   President

Attest: _____   Attest: _____
    John Smith, Secretary   Joe Smith
                                   Assistant Secretary

Agreed:

_____   _____
    Mr. Joseph Entrepreneur   Mrs. Joseph Entrepreneur

Legal Document 2
Ace Electromagnetic, Incorporated
McLean, Virginia

Promissory Note

$300,000   Washington, D.C.

FOR VALUE RECEIVED the undersigned Ace Electromagnetic, Incorporated, a Virginia corporation (hereinafter "Company") promises to pay to the order of Venture Capital Corporation, a District of Columbia corporation (hereinafter "Holder") the principal sum of three hundred thousand dollars ($300,000) together with interest as set out herein at its offices in the District of Columbia or such other place as Holder may designate in writing.

Interest: From date of advance and thereafter until repayment, interest shall accrue hereunder at the rate of fifteen percent (15%) per annum.

Payments: Payments shall be due on the first day of each month after the day of this Note. Through the first thirty-six full calendar months after the date hereof, payments shall be for interest only ($3,750.00). Thereafter until maturity payments shall be $10,399.60.

Maturity: The entire indebtedness hereunder shall become due and payable in full six (6) years after the date the first payment is due.

Prepayment: Payment of any installment of principal or interest may be made prior to the maturity date thereof without penalty. Such prepayments shall be applied against the outstanding principal in inverse order of maturity.

Default and Acceleration:

A.   If any of the below-listed events occur prior to maturity hereof, then a default may be declared at the option of the holder without presentment, demand, protest, or further notice of any kind (all of which are hereby expressly waived). In such event the holder shall be entitled to be paid in full the balance of any unpaid principal amount plus accrued interest and any costs including reasonable attorney's fees, and to any other remedies which may be available herein in the Loan Agreement or under any applicable law:

1. Failure to pay any part of the indebtedness hereof when due;
2. Occurrence of any default as provided under the Loan Agreement pertaining hereto.

B.   No course of dealing between the Holder and any other party hereto or any failure or delay on the part of the Payee in exercising any rights or remedies hereunder shall operate as a waiver of any rights or remedies of the Holder under this or any other applicable instrument. No single or partial exercise of any rights or remedies hereunder shall operate as a waiver or preclude the exercise of any other rights or remedies hereunder.

C.   Upon the nonpayment of the indebtedness, or any part thereof, when due, whether by acceleration or otherwise, Payee is empowered to sell, assign, and deliver the whole or any part of the collateral at public or private sale, without demand, advertisement or notice of the time or place of sale or of any adjournment thereof, which are hereby expressly waived. After deducting all expenses incidental to or arising from such sale or sales, Holder shall apply the residue of the proceeds thereof to the payment of the indebtedness, as it shall deem proper, returning the excess, if any, to the Company. The Company hereby waives all right of appraisement, whether before or after sale, and any right of redemption after sale. The Company shall have the right to redeem any collateral up to time of a foreclosure sale by paying the aggregate indebtedness.

D.   Holder is further empowered to collect or cause to be collected or otherwise be converted into money all or any part of the collateral, by suit or otherwise, and to surrender, compromise, release, renew, extend, exchange, or substitute any item of the collateral in transactions with the Company or any third party, irrespective of any assignment thereof by the Company, and without prior notice to or any consent of the Company or any assignee. Whenever any item of the collateral shall not be paid when due, or otherwise shall be in default, whether or not the indebtedness, or any part thereof, has become due, Holder shall have the same rights and powers with respect to such item of the collateral as are granted in respect thereof in this paragraph in case of nonpayment of the indebtedness, or any part thereof, when due. None of the rights, remedies, privileges, or powers of the Company expressly provided for herein shall be exclusive, but each of them shall be cumulative with and in addition to every other right, remedy, privilege, and power now or hereafter existing in favor of Holder, whether at law or in equity, by statute or otherwise.

E.   The Company will take all necessary steps to administer, supervise, preserve, and protect the collateral; and regardless of any action taken by Holder, there shall be no duty upon Holder in this respect. The Company shall pay all expenses of any nature, whether incurred in or out of court, and whether incurred before or after this Note shall become due at its maturity date or otherwise (including but not limited to reasonable attorneys' fees and costs) which Holder may deem necessary or proper in connection with the satisfaction of the indebtedness or the administration, supervision, preservation, protection of (including, but not limited to, the maintenance of adequate insurance), or the realization upon the collateral. Holder is authorized to pay at any time and from time to time any or all of such expenses, add the amount of such payment to the amount of principal outstanding and charge interest thereon at the rate specified herein.

F.   The security rights of Holder and its assigns shall not be impaired by Holder's sale, hypothecation, or rehypothecation of this Note or any item of the collateral, or by any indulgence, including, but not limited to:

1. Any renewal, extension or modification which Holder may grant with respect to the indebtedness of any part thereof, or

2. Any surrender, compromise, release, renewal, extension, exchange, or substitution which Holder may grant in respect of the collateral, or

3. Any indulgence granted in respect to any endorser, guarantor, or surety. The purchaser, assignee, transferee, or pledgee of this Note, the collateral, any guaranty, and any other document (or any of them), sold, assigned, transferred, pledged, or repledged, shall forthwith become vested with and entitled to exercise all the powers and rights given by this Note as if said purchaser, assignee, transferee, or pledgee were originally named as Holder in this Note.

Definitions: The term indebtedness as used herein shall mean the indebtedness evidenced by this Note, including principal, interest, and expenses whether contingent, now due or hereafter to become due, and whether heretofore or contemporaneously herewith or hereafter contracted. The term collateral as used in this Note shall mean any funds, guarantees, or other property rights therein of any nature whatsoever of the proceeds thereof which may have been, are or hereafter may be hypothecated directly or indirectly by the undersigned or others in connection with, or as security for the indebtedness or any part thereof. The collateral and each part thereof shall secure the indebtedness and each part thereof.

IN WITNESS WHEREOF, the undersigned has caused this Note to be executed and its seal affixed on the day and year first written above.

Seal:

ACE ELECTROMAGNETIC,
INCORPORATED

Attest: _____

BY: _____

John Smith
Secretary

Joseph Entrepreneur
President

THE SECURITIES REPRESENTED HEREBY HAVE BEEN ACQUIRED IN A TRANSACTION NOT INVOLVING ANY PUBLIC OFFERING AND HAVE NOT BEEN REGISTERED UNDER THE SECURITIES ACT OF 1933. SUCH SECURITIES MAY NOT BE SOLD OR TRANSFERRED IN THE ABSENCE OF SUCH REGISTRATION OR AN EXEMPTION THEREFROM UNDER SAID ACT.

Legal Document 3
Ace Electromagnetic, Incorporated
McLean, Virginia

STOCK PURCHASE WARRANTS

I. Grant

Ace Electromagnetic, Incorporated, a Virginia corporation (hereinafter "Company") for value received hereby grants to Venture Capital Corporation, a District of Columbia corporation, or its registered assigns (hereinafter "Holder") under the terms herein the right to purchase that number of the fully paid and nonassessable shares of the Company's common stock such that upon exercise and issuance of stock hereunder the Holder will hold thirty-five percent (35%) of the outstanding common stock of the Company. On the present date such number is 1,724 shares.

II. Expiration

The right to exercise this Warrant shall expire ten (10) years from the date hereof.

III. Exercise Price

The exercise price of this Warrant shall be one hundred dollars ($100.00).

IV. Effect of Redemption

Regardless of the above provision, if the Company shall redeem or otherwise purchase for value any of its shares of common stock prior to issuance of shares under this Warrant, the Holder shall be entitled to receive hereunder the same number of shares it could have received had the redemptions or purchases for value not occurred.

V. Exercise Procedure

This Warrant may be exercised by presenting it and tendering the purchase price in tender or by bank cashier's or certified check at the principal office of the Company along with written subscription substantially in the form of Exhibit I hereof;

The date on which this Warrant is thus surrendered, accompanied by tender or payment as hereinbefore or hereinafter provided, is referred to herein as the Exercise Date. The Company shall forthwith at its expense (including the payment of issue taxes) issue and deliver the proper number of shares, and such shares shall be deemed issued for all purposes as of the opening of business on the Exercise Date notwithstanding any delay in the actual issuance;

VI. Sale or Exchange of Company or Assets

If prior to issuance of stock under this Warrant the Company sells or exchanges all or substantially all of its assets, or the shares of common stock of the Company are sold or exchanged to any party other than the Holder, then the Holder at its option may receive, in lieu of the stock otherwise issuable hereunder, such money or property it would have been entitled to receive if this Warrant had been exercised prior to such sale or exchange.

VII. Sale of Warrant or Shares

Neither this Warrant nor other shares of common stock issuable upon exercise of the conversion rights herein, have been registered under the *Securities Act of 1933* as amended, or under the securities laws of any state. Neither this Warrant nor any shares when issued may be sold, transferred, pledged, or hypothecated in the absence of (i) an effective registration statement for this Warrant or the shares, as the case may be, under the *Securities Act of 1933* as amended and such registration or qualification as may be necessary under the securities laws of any state, or (ii) an opinion of counsel reasonably satisfactory to the Company that such registration or qualification is not required. The Company shall cause a certificate or certificates evidencing all or any of the shares issued upon exercise of the conversion rights herein prior to said registration and qualification of such shares to bear the following legend: "The shares evidenced by this certificate have not been registered under the *Securities Act of 1933* as amended, or under the securities laws of any state. The shares may not be sold, transferred, pledged, or hypothecated in the absence of an effective registration statement under the *Securities Act of 1933,* as amended, and such registration or qualification as may be necessary under the securities laws of any state, or an opinion of counsel satisfactory to the Company that such registration or qualification is not required."

VIII. Transfer

This Warrant shall be registered on the books of the Company which shall be kept at its principal office for that purpose, and shall be transferable only on such books by the Holder in person or by duly authorized attorney with written notice substantially in the form of Exhibit II hereof, and only in compliance with the preceding paragraph. The Company may issue appropriate stop orders to its transfer agent to prevent a transfer in violation of the preceding paragraph.

IX. Replacement of Warrant

At the request of the Holder and on production of evidence reasonably satisfactory to the Company of the loss, theft, destruction, or mutilation of this Warrant and (in the case of loss, theft, or destruction) if required by the Company, upon delivery of an indemnity agreement with surety in such reasonable amount as the Company may determine thereof, the Company at its expense will issue in lieu thereof a new Warrant of like tenor.

X. Loan Agreement

This Warrant is subject to the terms of a Loan agreement dated today between the Company and the Holder, a copy of which is on file and may be examined at the principal office of the Company in McLean, Virginia, during regular business hours.

XI. Unlocking

The Holder or its registered assigns shall have certain unlocking rights as set out in the Loan Agreement above-mentioned.

XII. "Put" Rights

Beginning five (5) years from today and ending ten (10) years from today, the Holder may by written demand require the company to purchase this Warrant or the shares of stock issued hereunder at a price of thirty-five percent (35%) of the higher of the following prices:

(a) Ten percent (10%) of the Company's sales for the fiscal year immediately preceding the year of the demand times a price earnings of eight, less the aggregate principal balance of the Note on the day of demand; or

(b) Ten times the Company's cash flow for the fiscal year immediately preceding the year of the demand, less the aggregate principal balance of Note on the day of demand.

XIII. Registration

If the Company shall at any time prepare and file a registration statement under the *Securities Act of 1933* with respect to the public offering of any class of equity or debt security of the Company, the Company shall give thirty (30) days prior written notice thereof to Holder, and shall, upon the written request of Holder include in the registration statement or related notification such number of Holder's shares as Holder may request to be sold on a one-time basis; the Company will keep such notification or registration statement and prospectus effective and current under the Act permitting the sale of Holder's shares covered thereby to be sold on a time-to-time basis or otherwise; such inclusion, in any event, shall be at no cost to Holder and shall be at the sole cost and expense of the Company; in the event the Company fails to receive a written request from Holder within thirty (30) days after the mailing of its written notice, then the Company shall treat such failure with the same force and effect as if Holder's failure to respond constituted notice to the Company that Holder does not intend to include its shares in such registration statement or notification; the foregoing shall not apply to a registration relating to securities of the Company covered by an employee, stock option, or other benefit plan; in connection with any notification or registration statement or subsequent amendment to any such notification or registration statement or similar document filed pursuant hereto, the Company shall take any reasonable steps to make the securities covered thereby eligible for public offering and sale by the effective date of such notification or registration statement or any amendment to any of the foregoing under the securities or blue sky laws of Virginia and the Dictrict of Columbia; provided that in no event shall the Company be obligated to qualify to do business in any state where it is not so qualified at the time of filing such documents or to take any action which would subject it to unlimited service of process in any state where it is not so subject at such time; the Company shall keep such filing current for the length of time it must keep any notification, registration statement, posteffective amendment, prospectus, or offering circular and any amendment to any of the foregoing effective pursuant hereto; in connection with any filing hereunder the Company shall bear all the expenses and professional fees which arise in connection with such filings and all expenses incurred in making such filings, and keeping them effective and correct as provided hereunder and shall also provide Holder with a reasonable number of printed copies of the prospectus, offering circulars and/or supplemental prospectuses or amended prospectuses in final and preliminary form; the Company consents to the use of such prospectus or offering circular in connection with the sale of Holder's shares; in the event of the filing of any registration statement or notification pursuant to this Agreement or document referred to herein which includes Holder's shares, Holder shall indemnify the Company and each of its officers and directors who has signed said registration statement, each person, if any, who controls the Company with the meaning of the *Securities Act,* each underwriter for the Company and each person, if any, who controls such underwriter within the meaning of the *Securities Act,* from any loss, claim, damage, liability, or action arising out of or based upon any untrue statement or any omission to state therein a material fact required to be stated therein or necessary to make the statements therein not misleading, furnished in writing by Holder expressly for use in such registration statement or required to be furnished by Holder.

XIV. Covenants of the Company

The Company covenants that until this Warrant is exercised or expires, it will:

(a)   Reserve authorized but unissued 1,724 shares of its common stock or such additional number of such shares as necessary to satisfy the rights of the Holder;

(b)   Not pay any dividends in cash or in kind unless written authorization is received in writing from the Holder;

(c)   Furnish the Holder consolidated financial statements of the Company, which statements shall include and be rendered as follows:

(1)   Monthly year-to-date financial statements within forty-five (45) days after the close of the last previous month which statements shall include a balance sheet and a statement of profit and loss for the period in question, and

(2)   If requested in writing by Holder, within sixty (60) days after the close of each fiscal year a balance sheet and a profit-and-loss statement of the Company relating to such year, certified by a firm of independent public accountants of recognized standing in McLean, Virginia, and approved by the Holder, accompanied by any report or comment of said accountant made in connection with such financial statements, and with a copy of all other financial statements prepared for or furnished to the Company.

(d)   The President of the Company shall certify on each statement furnished to the Holder that no default exists hereunder, or, in the event a default does exist, the President shall submit his statement of such default;

(e)   Maintain an office in the McLean, Virginia, area, at which its books and records will be kept and notices, presentations, demands, and payments relating to this Warrant, the Note, and the Loan Agreement may be given or made;

(f)   Maintain books of account in accordance with generally accepted accounting principles;

(g)   Permit the Holder through its designated representative to visit and inspect any of the properties of the Company, to examine its books and records, and to discuss its affairs, finances, and accounts with and be advised as to the same by the Officers of the Company at such reasonable times and intervals.

XV.   Investment Covenant

The Holder by its acceptance hereby covenants that this Warrant is, and the stock to be acquired upon the exercise of this Warrant will be, acquired for investment purposes, and that the Holder will not distribute the same in violation of any state or federal law or regulation.

XVI.   Laws Governing

This Warrant shall be construed according to the laws of the District of Columbia.

IN WITNESS WHEREOF, Ace Electromagnetic, Incorporated, has caused this Warrant to be signed on its behalf, in its corporate name, by its President, and its corporate seal to be hereunto affixed and the said seal to be attested by its Secretary, as of this 31st day of January, 1983.

Seal: ACE ELECTROMAGNETIC,
                                              INCORPORATED

                                  By:_____
                                       Joseph Entrepreneur, President

Attest:

_____

John Smith, Secretary

Legal Document 4

Ajax Computer Genetics Corp.
123 Main Street
McLean, Virginia 22102

Venture Capital Corp.
125 Main Street
Washington, D.C. 20006

Dear Sirs:

Stock Purchase Agreement

You have informed us that, subject to certain conditions, you are prepared to subscribe for and purchase, at a price of Ten Dollars ($10.00) per share, two hundred fifty thousand (250,000) shares (the "Shares") of our authorized but unissued Common Stock, One Dollar ($1.00) par value (the "Stock"). In this connection, we hereby confirm our agreement with you as follows:

    1. *Representations and Warranties.* ("Ajax" or "we") is a corporation duly organized and validly existing in good standing under the laws of the District of Columbia and is duly qualified to transact business as a foreign corporation under the laws of Florida and California, the only jurisdictions in which the nature of the business currently transacted by us requires such qualification.

    1.1 The authorized capital stock of Ajax consists of 2,000,000 shares of the Stock, all of one class, of which there are outstanding on the date hereof 972,515 shares and 27,800 shares are reserved for issuance pursuant to options held by key employees of Ajax and subsidiaries. Other than the shares (1) so reserved for stock options, and (2) the shares being purchased by you.

    1.2 Ajax has no subsidiaries, nor does it intend to establish any subsidiaries.

    1.3 There have been furnished to you the consolidated financial statements of Ajax as of and for the years just ending. These financial statements are complete and correct and present fairly the consolidated financial condition of Ajax and the consolidated results of their operations as of the dates thereof and for the period covered thereby. Such financial statements have been prepared in accordance with generally accepted accounting principles applied on a consistent basis throughout the periods involved, subject to any comments and notes therein. Since the year end there has not occurred any material adverse change in the consolidated financial position or results of operations of Ajax, nor any change not in the ordinary course of business.

1.4   There are no actions, suits, or proceedings pending nor, to Ajax's knowledge, threatened, before any court, agency, or other body which involves Ajax, wherein Ajax is a defendant.

1.5   This agreement and the issuance and sale of the Shares pursuant hereto have been duly authorized by appropriate and all required corporate action; such issuance and sale and Ajax's compliance with the terms hereof will not violate Ajax's articles of incorporation, bylaws, any indenture or contract to which Ajax is a party or by which it is bound, or any statute, rule, regulation, or order of any court or agency applicable to Ajax; and the Shares when issued and sold as provided herein will have been duly and validly authorized and issued, fully paid and nonassessable.

2.   *Covenants.* We covenant and agree with you that:

2.1   Prior to your purchase of the Shares, we shall provide to you, your agents, and attorney access to the same kind of information as is specified in Schedule A of the Securities Act of 1933 (the "1933 Act"), and shall make available to you during the course of this transaction the opportunity to ask questions of, and receive answers from, ourselves and our officers necessary to your satisfaction to verify the accuracy of such information.

2.2   For a period of at least two years following the Closing Date, we will not apply more than twenty percent (20%) of the proceeds from the sale of the Shares to the business of any new products without the concurrence of all members of our Board of Directors who have been nominated by you pursuant to Section 2.3 or elected thereto pursuant to Section 5.4.

2.3   As long as you and your affiliates own combined a total of at least ten percent (10%) of the outstanding voting securities of Ajax, you and your affiliates together shall be entitled to nominate a total of two (2) persons for election as members of our Board of Directors and, if they are so nominated and legally qualify to serve in that capacity, our Board of Directors will support their election.

2.4   (a) If, at any time while you or your affiliates (collectively "you") hold any of the Shares, we shall decide to register with the SEC any issue of Stock (other than a registration of shares solely for the purpose of any plan for the acquisition thereof by our employees or for the purpose of a merger or acquisition), we will give you written notice of such decision at least twenty (20) days prior to the filing of a registration statement and will afford you upon your request the opportunity of having any Shares then held by you included in the registration if the request is made within ten (10) days after receiving such notice, to the extent and under the conditions upon which such registration is permissible under the 1933 Act and the Rules and Regulations of the Securities and Exchange Commission; provided, however, that we may exclude such Shares from a registration statement filed by us to the extent that, in the opinion of the managing underwriter of the issue being registered, the inclusion of such of the Shares or of more than a designated portion thereof would be detrimental to the public offering pursuant to such registration, and to the further extent that such exclusion is made applicable to sales by all holders of outstanding Stock, pro rata in proportion to their holdings. In the event in any registration we offer you the opportunity to sell such of the Shares which you propose to register to underwriters on a "firm commitment" basis (as opposed to a "best efforts" basis), you shall, as a condition of your participation in the registration, accept an offer to sell such of the Shares to the underwriters if the managing underwriter so requires or, in the alternative, agree not to sell such of the Shares pursuant to such registration within such reasonable period (not exceeding 120 days) as may be specified by the managing underwriter to enable those underwriters to complete their distributions; and in any event, shall enter into an agreement with us and such underwriter containing conventional representations, warranties, and indemnity provisions. You will comply with such other reasonable requirements as may be imposed by the managing underwriter to effect the offering and an orderly distribution of the shares, including your acceptance of the same offering price as shall be accepted by us for the Stock being sold by us pursuant to such registration statement. All expenses of such registration applicable to Shares offered by you shall be payable by us, to the extent permitted by Securities and Exchange Commission Rules or policy, except for your pro rata share of the underwriters' discounts and commissions.

(b)   Our obligation to accord you the right to register Shares pursuant to paragraph (a) shall apply to each and every registration which may be effected by us following your purchase of the Shares, except if at the time you shall otherwise be, both as to time and amount, free to sell all the Shares held by you. Without limitation, for the purpose of this paragraph (b), you shall be considered to be free, both as to time and amount, to sell all the Shares held by you if all such Shares may be sold within a period of ninety (90) days pursuant to Rule 144 promulgated under the 1933 Act.

(c)   In the event that any registration statement relating to any Shares shall be filed and become effective pursuant to any of the foregoing provisions of this Section 2.4, then at any time while a prospectus relating to such of the Shares is required to be delivered under the 1933 act, but not later than nine (9) months after the effective date of such registration statement, we will, at your request, prepare and furnish to you a reasonable number of copies of such prospectus and of such registration statements as may be necessary so that, as thereafter delivered to purchasers of any of the Shares, such prospectus shall comply with Section 10 of the 1933 Act.

(d)   In the event that any registration statement relating to any Shares shall be filed pursuant to this Section 2.4, we will use our best efforts to qualify such of the Shares for sale under the laws of such jurisdiction within the continental United States as you may reasonably request and will comply to the best of our ability with such laws so as to permit the continuance of sales of and dealings in such of the Shares thereunder. The filing fees with respect to such jurisdictions requested by you shall be payable to you. We shall not, however, be obligated to qualify as a foreign corporation or file any general consent to service or process under the laws of any such jurisdiction or subject ourselves to taxation as doing business in any such jurisdiction or qualify under the securities laws of any jurisdictions which we reasonably deem unduly burdensome.

2.5   If the sale and purchase of the Shares shall be consummated, we will pay the reasonable fees and disbursements of your special counsel in connection with this agreement and the transaction contemplated herein and, in addition, will pay to you, a fee of twenty thousand dollars ($20,000.00) for services in connection herewith.

2.6   We shall indemnify you and any of your affiliates against any claim for any fees or commissions by any broker, finder, or other person for services or alleged services in connection herewith or the transaction contemplated hereby.

3.   *Representations and Agreements of Investors.* By accepting this agreement you confirm to us that:

3.1   You and your officers have such knowledge and experience in financial and business matters that you and they are capable of evaluating the merits and risks of your investment in the Shares.

3.2   You represent that you will acquire the Shares for investment and without any present intention of distributing or otherwise reselling any of them.

3.3   You understand that the Shares will be "restricted securities" as that term is defined in the Rules and Regulations of the SEC under the 1933 Act and accordingly may not be reoffered or resold by you unless they are registered under the Act or unless an exemption from such registration is available, and you consent that any certificates for the Shares may be legended accordingly.

3.4   You represent that you have no knowledge of any fees or commissions due in this transaction, except those fees set forth in 2.5 above and any fee that may be due and payable to John Brown Brokers.

4.   *Closing.* Subject to the terms and conditions hereof, the purchase and sale of the Shares shall take place at our office in Washington, D.C. the last day of this month, at 11:00 *A.M.* (the "Closing Date") by our delivery to you of a certificate or certificates for the Shares, registered in your name, and your payment to use of the purchase price therefore by wire transfer to our account with The First National Bank.

5.   *Conditions.* Your obligation to take up and pay for the Shares on the Closing Date shall be subject to the following conditions:

5.1   Our represenations and warrantees herein shall be true on and as of the Closing Date as though made on such date; we shall have performed all of our covenants and agreements herein required to be performed on or before the Closing Date; and we shall have delivered to you a certificate to such effects, dated the Closing Date and executed by our President or Executive Vice-president.

5.2   There shall have been delivered to you a letter dated the Closing

Date, from our accountants to the effect that, (i) nothing has come to their attention which would require them to withdraw or modify their annual report, on your consolidated financial statements as of and for the two years just ending; and (ii) they have performed a review of the interim consolidated financial statement of Ajax as of and for the three months ending, in accordance with the standards established by the American Institute of Certified Public Accountants. Such a review of the interim financial statements consists principally of obtaining an understanding of the system for the preparation of interim financial statements, applying analytical review procedures to financial data and making inquiries of persons responsible for financial and accounting matters. It is substantially less in scope than an examination in accordance with generally accepted auditing standards, the objective of which is the expression of an opinion regarding the financial statements taken as a whole. Accordingly, no such opinion is expressed.

5.3   There shall have been delivered to you a favorable opinion, dated the Closing Date, of our general counsel, John Paul, Esquire, as to the questions of law involved in Section 1.1 through 1.4 and 1.5 and covering such other questions of law as you or your special counsel may reasonably request.

5.4   There shall have been elected as a member of our Board of Directors, subject to the purchase and sale of the Shares, your President, Mr. A. V. Capitalist.

5.5   The certificates, accountants' letter, and legal opinion delivered on the Closing Date shall be deemed to fulfill the conditions hereof only if they are to your reasonable satisfaction and to that of Mr. M. S. Smith, your special counsel for the purpose of this transaction.

6.   *Miscellaneous.*

6.1   All notices required or permitted by this agreement shall be in writing addressed, if to us, at our address appearing at the head of this letter and, if to you, as this letter is addressed. Either party may, however, request communications or copies thereof to be sent to a different address and you may direct us to pay any dividends on the Shares to a bank in the United States for your account.

6.2   All representations, warranties and covenants made by all the parties herein shall survive the delivery of and the payment for the Shares.

6.3   This agreement shall be binding upon and inure to the benefit of the parties hereto and their respective successors and assigns.

6.4   This agreement shall be construed in accordance with, and the rights and obligations of the parties hereto shall be governed by, the laws of the District of Columbia, U.S.A.

6.5   This agreement supersedes any prior agreement, written or oral, between the parties hereto or their affiliates regarding the subject matter hereof.

6.6   In the event the closing described in section 4 hereof has not taken place by mid-year, this Agreement shall terminate unless the parties agree in writing to further extend the same. In the event of termination, all rights, duties and obligations of each of the parties shall cease and terminate, and this Agreement shall be considered cancelled and of no effect or validity thereafter.

If the foregoing accords with your understanding of our agreement, please sign and return to us the enclosed copy of this letter.

AJAX COMPUTER GENETICS CORPORATION

By _____

Joseph Entrepreneur, President

ACCEPTED: VENTURE CAPITAL CORPORATION

By _____

A. V. Capitalist, President

Legal Document 5
Schedule A: Exhibits To
Stock Purchase Agreement

1. Ajax (the "Company") is a Virginia corporation with its principal office at 123 Main Street, McLean, Virginia, 22102.

2. A.   Exhibit 1A enclosed herewith is a copy of the Annual Report of Ajax for the fiscal year just ending, and included in said report under the same date, is a copy of the Certified Audit of the Company made by its current accounting firm for the above fiscal year. Also, Exhibit 1B enclosed herewith is a copy of the preliminary unaudited Financial Statements of Ajax of the one month just ended.
   B.   A list of Officers and Directors of the Company and their addresses is enclosed as Exhibit 2 hereof.

3. Joseph Entrepreneur, the President of the Company, is the sole owner owning 10 percent or more of record and beneficially of stock of the Company.

4. As of this date, Mr. Entrepreneur owns of record and beneficially 200,000 shares of stock of the Company.

5. The Company is not a holding Company and has no subsidiary corporations.

6. Ajax has 2,000,000 authorized shares of stock, all common, with a par value of $1.00 per share and presently issued and outstanding there are 300,000 shares of stock. In addition thereto, there are options to purchase 100,000 shares of stock issued to and held by existing employees. The company has a stock option plan with 100,000 remaining unissued shares.

7. See Exhibit 3 pertaining to a list of Stock Options outstanding that have been granted to employees of the Company.

8. The Company intends to sell not less than 250,000 shares of stock in this private placement at an offering price of $10.00 per share. The Company may sell additional shares of stock to a secured venture capital firm at a price of not less than $10.00 per share, which transaction would take place in the near future if consummated.

9. Proceeds of the private placement will be used as follows; $1,000,000 in research and development, $1,000,000 in plant expansion, and $500,000 in salaries and working capital.

10. For the year end period just ending, the Company paid salaries, bonuses, and director's fees to Joseph Entrepreneur in the amount of

$51,000.00. For the current fiscal year Mr. Entrepreneur is being paid a base salary of $50,000.00.

11. The net book value per share of Ajax is $5.00 as of the year just ended. The Company anticipates receiving the entire net proceeds, with the exception of commissions and legal expenses that might be incurred under 12 below, derived from the sale of the securities being offered at $10.00 per share.

12. Commissions being paid for services rendered in the sale will be $20,000.00 to the Venture Capital Corporation.

13. The Company has:

    A.   Employment Contract with Joseph Entrepreneur entered for a period of five years providing for annual compensation of not less than $50,000.00.

    B.   The other basic contracts that the Company has are for leases for office space where it maintains its offices in McLean, Virginia.

14. Enclosed herewith is Exhibit 4, a copy of the Articles of Incorporation together with all Amendments thereto of Ajax, and Exhibit 5, a copy of the existing Bylaws of the Company.

Appendix 2

Members of NVCA
and NASBIC

Who Should You Contact for Venture Capital?
Here Is The Best List.

The following pages contain a list of the most active venture capital companies. They are listed by states. You should seek funds from the venture capital
firms nearest your company. The cities with the most venture capital in the
United States are: New York, Boston, Chicago, Los Angeles, and San Francisco. Next are Denver, Houston, Dallas, and Washington, D.C.

While the list is accurate, you may wish to obtain a current list by writing
directly to the association as listed in Chapter 1.

Alabama

First SBIC of Alabama   (205) 476-0700
16 Midtown Park East
Mobile, Alabama 36606

Hickory Venture Capital Corp.   (205) 539-1931
699 Gallatin Street, Ste. A-2
Huntsville, Alabama 35801

Remington Fund, Inc., (The)   (205) 326-3509
P.O. Box 10686
Birmingham, Alabama 35202

Tuskegee Capital Corporation   (205) 281-8059
4453 Richardson Road
Montgomery, Alabama 36108

Alaska

Alaska Business Investment Corp.   (907) 278-2071
P.O. Box 600
Anchorage, Alaska 99510

Calista Business Investment Corp.   (901) 277-0425
516 Denali Street
Anchorage, Alaska 99501

Arizona

FBS Venture Capital Co.   (602) 941-2160
6900 E. Camelback Road, Ste. 452
Scottsdale, Arizona 85251

Greyhound Capital Management   (602) 222-8226
Greyhound Tower, 14th Floor
Phoenix, Arizona 85077

Norwest Growth Fund, Inc.   (602) 483-8940
8777 East Via de Ventura, Ste. 335
Scottsdale, Arizona 85258

Rocky Mountain Equity Corp.   (602) 274-7558
4530 N. Central Avenue, Ste. 3
Phoenix, Arizona 85012

Sun Belt Capital Corp.   (602) 253-7600
320 N. Central Avenue, Ste. 700
Phoenix, Arizona 85004

VNB Capital Corporation   (602) 261-1577
15 E. Monroe, Ste. 1200
Phoenix, Arizona 85004

Arkansas

Capital Management Services, Inc.   (501) 644-8613
1910 N. Grant, Ste. 200
Little Rock, Arkansas 72207

First SBIC of Arkansas, Inc.   (501) 378-1876
Worthen Bank Bldg.
200 W. Capitol Avenue, Ste. 700
Little Rock, Arkansas 72201

Independence Financial Service   (501) 793-4533
P.O. Box 3878
Batesville, Arkansas 72503

Kar-Mal Venture Capital, Inc.   (501) 661-0010
2821 Kavanaugh Blvd.
Little Rock, Arkansas 72205

Power Ventures, Inc.   (501) 332-3695
Hwy. 270N.
P.O. Box 518
Malvern, Arkansas 72104

Worthern Finance & Inv., Inc.   (501) 332-3695
P.O. Box 1681
Little Rock, Arkansas 72203

California

Accel Partners   (415) 989-5656
One Embarcadero Center, Ste. 2102
San Francisco, California 94111

Adler & Company   (408) 720-8700
1245 Oakmead Parkway
Sunnyvale, California 94086

Advanced Technology Ventures   (415) 321-8601
1000 El Camino Real, Ste. 210
Menlo Park, California 94025-4327

Alan Patricof Associates, Inc.   (408) 737-8788
1245 Oakmead Parkway
Sunnyvale, California 94806

Arscott, Norton & Associates   (415) 853-0766
375 Forest Avenue
Palo Alto, California 94301

Asset Management Company   (415) 494-7400
2275 East Bayshore Road
Palo Alto, California 94303

Atalanta Investment Co., Inc.   (213) 273-1730
141 El Camino Drive
Los Angeles, California 90212

Bancorp Venture Capital, Inc.   (714) 752-7220
2082 Michelson Drive, Ste. 302
Irvine, California 92715

BankAmerica Capital Corporation   (415) 622-2230
555 California Street, Ste. 2160
San Francisco, California 94104

BankAmerica Ventures, Inc.   (415) 622-2230
555 California Street, #3908, 42nd Floor
San Francisco, California 94104

Bay Partners   (408) 725-2444
10600 North DeAnza Blvd., Ste. 100
Cupertino, California 95014-2031

Bay Venture Group   (415) 989-7680
One Embarcadero Center, Ste. 3303
San Francisco, California 94111

Bessemer Venture Partners   (415) 854-2200
3000 Sand Hill Road, #3-225
Menlo Park, California 94025

Brentwood Associates   (213) 826-6581
11661 San Vicente Blvd., Ste. 707
Los Angeles, California 90049

Bryan & Edwards   (415) 854-1555
3000 Sand Hill Road
Bldg. Two, Ste. 215
Menlo Park, California 94025

Burr, Egan, Deleage & Co.   (415) 362-4022
Three Embarcadero Center, Ste. 2560
San Francisco, California 94111

Business Equity & Dev. Corp.   (213) 385-0351
1411 W. Olympic Blvd., Ste. 200
Los Angeles, California 90015

CFB Venture Capital Corp.   (619) 230-3304
530 B. Street, 2nd Floor
San Diego, California 92101

CIN Investment Co.   (415) 398-7677
444 Market Street, 25th Floor
San Francisco, California 94111

Cable & Howse Ventures   (415) 322-8400
435 Tasso Street, Ste. 115
Palo Alto, California 94301

California Capital Investors   (213) 820-7222
11812 San Vicente Blvd.
Los Angeles, California 90049

California Partners   (415) 854-7472
3000 Sand Hill Rd., Bldg. 4, Ste. 210
Menlo Park, California 94025

Camden Investments, Inc.   (213) 859-9738
9560 Wilshire Blvd., #310
Beverly Hills, California 90212

Charterway Investment Corp.   (213) 687-8534
222 S. Hill Street, Ste. 800
Los Angeles, California 90012

Citicorp Venture Capital, Ltd.   (415) 627-6472
One Sansome Street, Ste. 2410
San Francisco, California 94104

Citicorp Venture Capital, Ltd.   (415) 424-8000
2200 Geng Road, Ste. 203
Palo Alto, California 94303

Cogeneration Capital Fund   (415) 924-3525
300 Tamal Plaza, Ste. 190
Corte Madera, California 94925

Concord Partners   (415) 327-2600
435 Tasso Street, Ste. 305
Palo Alto, California 94301

Continental Capital Ventures   (415) 989-2020
555 California Street, Ste. 5070
San Francisco, California 94104

Continental Investors, Inc.   (714) 964-5207
8781 Seaspray Drive
Huntington Beach, California 90014

Crocker Ventures, Inc.   (415) 983-3636
One Montgomery Street
San Francisco, California 94104

Crosspoint Investment Corp.   (415) 964-3545
1951 Landings Drive
Mountain View, California 94043

Dime Investment Corp.   (213) 739-1847
2772 W. 8th Street
Los Angeles, California 90005

Dougery, Jones & Wilder   (415) 968-4820
2003 Landings Drive
Mountain View, California 94043

El Dorado Ventures   (818) 304-1980
2 North Lake Avenue, Ste. 480
Pasadena, California 91101

First American Cap. Funding, Inc.   (714) 638-7171
9872 Chapman Avenue, #216
Garden Grove, California 92641

First SBIC of California   (714) 556-1964
650 Town Center Drive, 17th Floor
Costa Mesa, California 92626

First SBIC of California   (818) 304-3451
155 N. Lake Avenue, Ste. 1010
Pasadena, California 91109

First SBIC of California   (415) 424-8011
5 Palo Alto Square, Ste. 938
Palo Alto, California 94304

Glenwood Management   (415) 854-8070
3000 Sand Hill Rd., Bldg. 1, Ste. 230
Menlo Park, California 94025

Frace Ventures Corp.   (408) 725-0774
20300 Stevens Creek Blvd., Ste. 330
Cupertino, California 95014

Hambert & Quist Venture Partners   (415) 393-9800
One Post Street, 4th Floor
San Francisco, California 94104

Hamco Capital Corp.   (415) 393-9813
One Post Street, 4th Floor
San Francisco, California 94104

Harvest Ventures, Inc.   (408) 996-3200
Bldg. SW3, 10080 N. Wolfe Rd., Ste. 365
Cupertino, California 95014

Hewlett-Parkard Company   (415) 857-7308
3000 Hanover Street
Palo Alto, California 94304

Inman & Bowman   (415) 253-1611
4 Orinda Way, Bldg. D, Ste. 150
Orinda, California 94563

Institutional Venture Partners   (415) 854-0132
3000 Sand Hill Rd., Bldg. 2, Ste. 290
Menlo Park, California 94025

Interscope Investments, Inc. (213) 208-8525
10900 Wilshire Blvd., #1400
Los Angeles, California 90024

InterVen Partners (213) 622-1922
445 A. Figueroa, Ste. 2940
Los Angeles, California 90071

InterWest Partners (415) 854-8585
3000 Sand Hill Rd., Bldg. 3, Ste. 255
Menlo Park, California 94025

IvanHoe Venture Capital, Led. (415) 854-8585
737 Pearl St., Ste. 201
La Jolla, California 92037

JeanJoo Finance, Inc. (213) 627-6660
700 So. Flower Street, Ste. 3305
Los Angeles, California 90017

Julian, Cole & Stein, (213) 826-8002
11777 San Vicente Blvd., Ste. 522
Los Angeles, California 90049

Kleiner Perkins Caufield & Byers (415) 421-3110
Four Embarcadero Center, Ste. 3520
San Francisco, California 94111

Lasung Investment & Finance Co. (213) 384-7548
3600 Wilshire Blvd., Ste. 1410
Los Angeles, California 90010

Latigo Capital Partners (213) 456-7024
23410 Civic Ctr. Way, Ste. E-2
Malibu, California 90265

Los Angeles Capital Corp. (213) 460-4646
606 N. Larchmont Blvd., Ste. 309
Los Angeles, California 90004

MBW Management, Inc. (415) 941-2392
350 Second Street, Ste. 7
Los Altos, California 94022

MCA New Ventures, Inc. (818) 777-2937
100 Universal City Plaza
Universal City, California 91608

Mayfield Fund (415) 854-5560
2200 Sand Hill Road
Menlo Park, California 94025

Menlo Ventures   (619) 454-8882
3000 Sand Hill Road
Menlo Park, California 94025

Merrill, Pickard, Anderson   (415) 856-8880
Two Palo Alto Square, Ste. 425
Palo Alto, California 94306

Montgomery Securities   (415) 627-2000
600 Montgomery Street
San Francisco, California 94111

Myraid Capital, Inc.   (818) 289-5689
2225 W. Commonwealth Avenue, #111
Alhambra, California 91801

Nelson Capital Corp.   (213) 556-1944
10000 Santa Monica Blvd.
Los Angeles, California 90067

New Kukje Investment Co.   (213) 389-8679
958 S. Vermont Ave., #C
Los Angeles, California 90006

New West Ventures   (619) 457-0722
4350 Executive Drive, #206
San Diego, California 92121

Orange Nassau Capital Corp.   (714) 752-7811
1500 Quail Street, Ste. 540
Newport Beach, California 92660

Opportunity Capital Corp.   (415) 421-5935
50 California Street, Ste. 2505
San Francisco, California 94111

PBC Venture Capital, Inc.   (805) 395-3206
P.O. Box 6008
Bakersfield, California 93386

PCF Venture Capital Corp.   (415) 574-4747
675 Mariner's Island Blvd., #103
San Mateo, California 94404

Paragon Partners   (415) 854-8000
3000 Sand Hill Road, Bldg. 2, Ste. 190
Menlo Park, California 94025

SAS Associates   (213) 624-4232
515 South Figueroa St., Ste. 600
Los Angeles, California 90071-3396

San Joaquin Capital Corp. (805) 323-7581
1675 Chester Ave., Ste. 330, P.O. 2538
Bakersfield, California 93303

San Jose SBIC, Inc. (408) 293-8052
100 Park Ctr. Pl., Ste. 427
San Jose, California 95113

Seaport Ventures, Inc. (619) 232-4069
525 B Street, Ste. 630
San Diego, California 92101

Security Pacific Capital (714) 556-1964
650 Town Ctr. Drive, 17th Floor
Costa Mesa, California 92626

Sequoia Capital (415) 854-3927
3000 Sand Hill Rd., Bldg. 4, Ste. 280
Menlo Park, California 94025

Sutter Hill Ventures (415) 493-5600
Two Palo Alto Square, Ste. 700
Palo Alto, California 94306-0910

Taylor & Turner (415) 398-6821
220 Montgomery Street, Penthouse 10
San Francisco, California 94104

Technology Venture Investors (415) 854-7472
3000 Sand Hill Road, Bldg. 4, #210
Menlo Park, California 94025

U.S. Venture Partners (415) 854-9080
2180 Sand Hill Road, Ste. 300
Menlo Park, California 94025

Union Venture Corp. (818) 304-1989
225 S. Lake Ave., #601
Pasadena, California 91101

Union Venture Corp. (714) 304-1989
18300 Von Karman
Irvine, California 92713

Unity Capital Corp. (619) 275-6030
4343 Morena Blvd., #3-A
San Diego, California 92117

VK Capital Co. (415) 391-5600
50 California Street, #2350
San Francisco, California 94111

Weiss, Peck & Greer Venture   (415) 622-6864
555 California Street, Ste. 4760
San Francisco, California 94104

Westamco Investment Co.   (213) 652-8288
8929 Wilshire Blvd., Ste. 400
Beverly Hills, California 90211

Wilshire Capital Inc.   (213) 388-1314
3932 Wilshire Blvd., Ste. 305
Los Angeles, California 90010

Wood River Capital Corp.   (415) 854-1000
3000 Sand Hill Rd., Ste. 280
Menlo Park, California 94025

Wothern Finance & Inv. Inc.   (213) 480-1908
3660 Wilshire Blvd.
Los Angeles, California 90010

Yosemite Capital Investment   (209) 485-2431
448 Fresno Street
Fresno, California 93706

Colorado

Colorado Growth Capital, Inc.   (303) 831-0205
1600 Broadway, Ste. 2125
Denver, Colorado 80202

Columbine Venture Fund, Ltd.   (303) 694-3222
5613 DTC Parkway, Ste. 510
Englewood, Colorado 80111

Enterprise Fin. Cap. Dev. Corp.   (303) 923-4144
P.O. Box 5840
Snowmass Village, Colorado 81615

FBS Venture Capital Co.   (303) 442-6885
3000 Pearl St., #206
Boulder, Colorado 80301

Hill & Kirby   (303) 442-5151
885 Arapahoe Avenue
Boulder, Colorado 80302

InterMountain Ventures, Ltd.   (303) 356-3229
1100 10th St., P.O. Box 1406
Greeley, Colorado 80632

Larimer & Co. 1999 Broadway, Ste. 2100 Denver, Colorado 80202	(303) 298-9066
Mile Hi SBIC 2505 W. 16th Avenue Denver, Colorado 80204	(303) 629-5339
Stephenson Merchant Banking 100 Garfield Street Denver, Colorado 80206	(303) 355-6000
UBD Caoutak Ubc. 1700 Broadway Denver, Colorado 80274	(303) 863-6329

Connecticut

Abacus Ventures 283 Greenwich Avenue Greenwich, Connecticut 06830	(203) 629-4991
Asset Capital & Management Corp. 608 Ferry Blvd. Stratford, Connecticut 06497	(203) 375-0299
Capital Impact 961 Main Street Bridgeport, Connecticut 06601	(203) 384-5670
Capital Resource Co. of CT L.P. 699 Bloomfield Avenue Bloomfield, Connecticut 06002	(203) 243-1114
DCS Growth Fund P.O. Box 740 Old Greenwich, Connecticut 06870	(203) 637-1704
ELF Technologies, Inc. P.O. Box 10037 High Ridge Park Stamford, Connecticut 06904-2037	(203) 358-5121
Fairfield Venture Partners 1275 Summer Street Stamford, Connecticut 06905	(203) 358-0255
First Connecticut SBIC (The) 177 State Street Bridgeport, Connecticut 06604	(203) 366-4726

General Electric Venture Company   (203) 373-3333
3135 Easton Turnpike
Fairfield, Connecticut 06431

Grayrock Capital Inc.   (203) 966-8392
36 Grove Street
New Canaan, Connecticut 06840

MIP Equity Fund   (203) 358-9950
1266 Main Street
Stamford, Connecticut 06902

Marcon Capital Corp.   (203) 226-6893
49 Riverside Avenue
Westport, Connecticut 06880

MarketCorp Venture Associates,   (203) 222-1000
Limited Partners
285 Riverside Avenue
Westport, Connecticut 06880

Northeastern Capital Corp.   (203) 469-7901
62 High Street
East Haven, Connecticut 06512

Oak Management Corporation   (203) 226-8346
257 Riverside Avenue
Westport, Connecticut 06880

Oxford Partners   (203) 964-0592
Soundview Plaza, 1266 Main Street
Stamford, Connecticut 06902

Prime Capital Management Co.   (203) 964-0642
One Landmark Square, Ste. 800
Stamford, Connecticut 06901

Regional Financial Enterprises   (203) 966-2800
36 Grove Street
New Canaan, Connecticut 06840

SBIC of Connecticut   (203) 367-3282
1115 Main Street, Ste. 610
Bridgeport, Connecticut 06604

Saugatuck Capital Company   (203) 348-6669
595 Summer Street
Stamford, Connecticut 06901

Technology Transitions, Inc.   (203) 246-8142
One State Street, Ste. 1950
Hartford, Connecticut 06103

Vista Ventures   (617) 972-3400
36 Grove Street
New Canaan, Connecticut 06840

Xerox Venture Capital   (203) 329-8711
800 Long Ridge Road
Stamford, Connecticut 06904

District of Columbia

Allied Capital Corporation   (202) 331-1112
1666 K. Street, N.W., Ste. 901
Washington, D.C. 20006

American Security Capital Corp.   (202) 624-4843
730 15th Street, N.W.
Washington, D.C. 20013

Broadcast Capital, Inc.   (202) 429-5393
1771 N. Street, N.W.
Washington, D.C. 20036

Continental Investors, Inc.   (202) 466-7609
2020 K. Street, N.W., Ste. 350
Washington, D.C. 20006

D.C. Bancorp Venture Capital Co.   (202) 955-6970
1801 K. Street, N.W.
Washington, D.C. 20006

Fulcrum Venture Capital Corp.   (202) 833-9590
2021 K. Street, N.W., Ste. 701
Washington, D.C. 20006

Syncom Capital Corporation   (202) 293-9428
1030 15th Street, N.W., Ste. 203
Washington, D.C. 20006

Washington Finance & Inc. Corp.   (202) 338-2900
2600 Virginia Avenue, N.W., Ste. 515
Washington, D.C. 20037

Worthen Finance & Inv., Inc.   (619) 454-8882
2121 K. Street, N.W., Ste. 830
Washington, D.C. 20037

Florida

Allied North-American   (305) 763-8484
111 E. Las Olas Boulevard
Fort Lauderdale, Florida 33301

Caribank Capital Corp. 255 E. Dania Beach Blvd. Dania, Florida 33004	(305) 925-2211
FAIC Capital Corp. 2701 S. Bayshore Dr., Ste. 402 Coconut Grove, Florida 33133	(305) 854-6840
First Tampa Capital Corp. 501 E. Kennedy Blvd., Ste. 806 Tampa, Florida 33602	(619) 454-8882
Ideal Financial Corp. 780 N.W. 42nd Avenue, Ste. 304 Miami, Florida 33126	(305) 442-4653
J&D Capital Corp. 12747 Biscayne Blvd. North Miami, Florida 33160	(305) 893-0303
Market Capital Corp. P.O. Box 22667 Tampa, Florida 33630	(813) 247-1357
Small Business Assistance Corp. 2612 W. 15th Street Panama City, Florida 32401	(904) 785-9577
South Atlantic Venture Fund 220 East Madison Street, Ste. 530 Tampa, Florida 33602-4825	(813) 229-7400
Southeast Venture Capital Ltd. I One Southeast Financial Ctr. Miami, Florida 33131	(305) 375-6470
Universal Financial Services 3550 Biscayne Blvd., Ste. 702 Miami, Florida 33137	(305) 538-5464
Venture Opportunities Corp. 444 Brickell Avenue, Ste. 650 Miami, Florida 33131	(305) 358-0359
Verde Capital Corp. 255 Alhambra Circle, #720 Coral Gables, Florida 33134	(305) 444-8938

Georgia

Mighty Capital Corp. 50 Technology Park, Atlanta, Ste. 100 Norcross, Georgia 30092	(404) 448-2232

North Riverside Capital Corp.   (404) 252-1076
5775-D Peachtree Dunwoody Road, Ste. 650
Atlanta, Georgia 30342

Hawaii

Bancorp Hawaii SBIC, Inc.   (808) 521-6411
P.O. Box 2900
Honolulu, Hawaii 96846

Idaho

First Idaho Venture Capital Corp.   (208) 345-3460
P.O. Box 1739
Boise, Idaho 83701

Illinois

Abbott Capital Corp.   (312) 982-0404
9933 Lawler Avenue, Ste. 125
Skokie, Illinois 60077

Alpha Capital Venture Partners   (312) 372-1556
3 First National Place, Ste. 1400
Chicago, Illinois 60602

Allstate Insurance Company   (312) 291-5681
E-2 Venture Capital Division
Northbrook, Illinois 60062

Ameritech Development Corporation   (312) 993-1900
233 South Wacker Drive, Ste. 9720
Chicago, Illinois 60606

Amoco Venture Capital Co.   (312) 856-6523
200 E. Randolph Drive
Chicago, Illinois 60601

William Blair Venture Partner   (312) 853-8250
135 South LaSalle Street
Chicago, Illinois 60603

Business Venture, Inc.   (312) 346-1580
20 N. Wacker Drive, Ste. 550
Chicago, Illinois 60606

Caterpillar Venture Capital, Inc.   (309) 675-5503
100 N.E. Adams Street
Peoria, Illinois 61629-6170

Chicago Community Ventures Inc. 104 S. Michigan, #215 Chicago, Illinois 60603	(312) 726-6084
Combined Fund, Inc. (The) 1525 E. 53rd Street, #908 Chicago, Illinois 60615	(312) 363-0300
Continental IL Venture Corp. 231 S. LaSalle Street Chicago, Illinois 60697	(312) 828-8021
First Capital Corp. of Chicago Three 1st National Place, Ste. 1330 Chicago, Illinois 60670-0501	(312) 732-5400
First Chicago Investment Advisors Three First National Plaza, Ste. 0140 Chicago, Illinois 60670	(312) 732-4171
First Chicago Venture Capital Three First National Plaza, Ste. 1330 Chicago, Illinois 60670	(312) 732-5400
Frontenac Capital Corp. 208 S. LaSalle Street, #1900 Chicago, Illinois 60604	(312) 368-0044
Golder, Thoma & Cressey 120 S. LaSalle Street, Ste. 630 Chicago, Illinois 60603	(312) 853-3322
Mesirow Venture Capital 350 N. Clark Chicago, Illinois 60610	(312) 670-6000
Northern Capital Corp. 50 S. LaSalle Street Chicago, Illinois 60675	(312) 444-5399
Prince Venture Partners One First National Plaza, Ste. 4950 Chicago, Illinois 60603	(312) 726-2232
Seidman Jackson Fisher & Co. 233 N. Michigan Avenue, Ste. 1812 Chicago, Illinois 60601	(312) 856-1812
Tower Ventures, Inc. Sears Tower, BSC 43-50 Chicago, Illinois 60684	(312) 875-0571

Walnut Capital Corp.   (312) 269-1732
Three First National Plaza
Chicago, Illinois 60602

Indiana

Circle Ventures, Inc.   (317) 636-7242
20 N. Meridian Street, 3rd Floor
Indianapolis, Indiana 46240

Equity Resource Co., Inc.   (219) 237-5255
202 S. Michigan Street
South Bend, Indiana 46601

1st Source Capital Corp.   (219) 236-2180
100 N. Michigan
South Bend, Indiana 46601

White River Capital Corp.   (812) 276-1759
500 Washington Street, P.O. Box 929
Columbus, Indiana 47202

Iowa

Allsop (R.W.) & Associates   (319) 363-8971
2750 First Avenue, Ste. 210
Cedar Rapids, Iowa 52402

MorAmerica Capital Corp.   (319) 363-8249
300 American Bldg.
Cedar Rapids, Iowa 52401

Kansas

Kansas Venture Capital, Inc.   (619) 454-8882
1030 First National Bank Towers
Topeka, Kansas 66603

Kentucky

Equal Opportunity Finance, Inc.   (502) 423-1943
420 Hurstbourne Lane, Ste. 201
Louisville, Kentucky 40222

Financial Opportunities, Inc.   (502) 584-8259
833 Starks Bldg.
Louisville, Kentucky 40202

Mountain Ventures, Inc.   (606) 864-5175
911 N. Main Street, P.O. Box 628
London, Kentucky 40741

Louisiana

Commercial Capital, Inc.   (504) 345-8820
P.O. Box 1776
Covington Lane, Louisiana 70434

Dixie Business Inv. Co., Inc.   (318) 559-1558
P.O. Box 588
Lake Providence, Louisiana 71254

First Southern Capital Corp.   (504) 769-3004
P.O. Box 14418
Baton Rouge, Louisiana 70898

Louisiana Equity Capital Corp.   (504) 389-4421
Louisiana Nat'l Bank, P.O. Box 1511
Baton Rouge, Louisiana 70821

Walnut Street Capital Co.   (504) 525-2112
231 Carondelet Street, #702
New Orleans, Louisiana 70130

Maine

Maine Capital Corp.   (207) 772-1001
70 Center Street
Portland, Maine 04101

Maryland

ABS Ventures Limited Partnerships   (301) 727-2154
135 E. Baltimore Street
Baltimore, Maryland 21202

Broventure Capital Management   (301) 727-4520
16 West Madison Street
Baltimore, Maryland 21201

First Maryland Capital, Inc.   (301) 251-6630
107 W. Jefferson Street
Rockville, Maryland 20850

Greater Washington Investors   (301) 656-0626
5454 Wisconsin Ave., Ste. 1315
Chevy Chase, Maryland 20815

T. Rowe Price Threshold Part.   (301) 547-2179
100 East Pratt Street
Baltimore, Maryland 21202

Suburban Capital Corp.   (301) 493-7025
6610 Rockledge Drive
Bethesda, Maryland 20817

Massachusetts

Advanced Technology Ventures   (617) 423-4050
10 Post Office Square, Ste. 1230
Boston, Massachusetts 02109

Aegis Fund (The)   (617) 862-0200
One Cranberry Hill
Lexington, Massachusetts 02173

American Research & Development   (617) 423-7500
45 Milk Street
Boston, Massachusetts 02109

Atlantic Energy Capital Corp.   (617) 451-6220
260 Franklin Street, Ste. 1501
Boston, Massachusetts 02110

BancBoston Ventures, Inc.   (617) 434-5700
100 Federal Street
Boston, Massachusetts 02110

Battery Ventures   (617) 542-7710
60 Batterymarch Street
Boston, Massachusetts 02110

Boston Capital Ventures   (619) 454-8882
One Devonshire Place, Ste. 2913
Boston, Massachusetts 02109

Boston Hambro Capital Co.   (617) 722-7055
One Boston Place, Ste. 723
Boston, Massachusetts 02106

Burr, Egan, Deleage & Co.   (617) 482-8020
One Post Office Square, Ste. 3800
Boston, Massachusetts 02109

Charles River Ventures   (617) 482-9370
67 Batterymarch Street
Boston, Massachusetts 02110

Churchill International   (617) 893-6555
9 Riverside Road
Weston, Massachusetts 02193

Commonwealth Partners   (619) 454-8882
Limited Partnership
881 Commonwealth Avenue, Rm. 540
Boston, Massachusetts 02215

Eastech Management Company, Inc.   (617) 338-0200
One Liberty Square, 9th Floor
Boston, Massachusetts 02109

Elrod Technologies, Inc.   (617) 275-9644
12 Oak Park Drive
Bedford, Massachusetts 01730

First SBIC of California   (617) 542-7601
50 Milk Street, 15th Floor
Boston, Massachusetts 02109

Fleet Venture Resources, Inc.   (617) 367-6700
60 State Street
Boston, Massachusetts 02100

Faneuil Hall Associates   (617) 723-1955
One Boston Place
Boston, Massachusetts 02108

Fidelity Venture Associates   (617) 570-6450
82 Devonshire Street
Boston, Massachusetts 02109

Greylock Management Corporation   (617) 423-5525
One Federal Street
Boston, Massachusetts 02110

John Hancock Venture Cap. Mngt.   (617) 350-4002
One Financial Center
Boston, Massachusetts 02111

Investments Orande Nassau, Inc.   (617) 439-6160
260 Franklin Street, Ste. 1501
Boston, Massachusetts 02110

Matrix Partners   (617) 482-7735
One Post Office Square
Boston, Massachusetts 02109

Memorial Drive Trust   (617) 864-5770
20 Acorn Park
Cambridge, Massachusetts 02140

Morgan Holland Ventures   (617) 423-1765
One Liberty Square
Boston, Massachusetts 02109

New England Capital Corp.   (617) 722-6400
One Washington Mall, 7th Floor
Boston, Massachusetts 02108

New England MESBIC, Inc.   (617) 449-2066
50 Kearney Road, Ste. 3
Needham, Massachusetts 02194

Orange Nassau Capital Corp.   (617) 451-6220
260 Franklin Street, Ste. 1501
Boston, Massachusetts 02110

PaineWebber Venture   (617) 439-8300
265 Franklin Street, Ste. 1501
Boston, Massachusetts 02110

Palmer Partners   (617) 933-5445
300 Unicorn Park Drive
Woburn, Massachusetts 01801

Plant Resources Venture Funds   (617) 492-3900
124 Mount Auburn Street, Ste. 310
Cambridge, Massachusetts 02138

TA Associates   (617) 338-0800
45 Milk Street
Boston, Massachusetts 02109

3i Capital Corp   (617) 542-8560
99 High Street, Ste. 1530
Boston, Massachusetts 02110

Transportation Capital Corp.   (617) 262-9701
566 Commonwealth Ave., Ste. 810
Boston, Massachusetts 02215

UST Capital Corp.   (617) 726-7138
30 Court Street
Boston, Massachusetts 02108

Vandus Capital Corp.   (617) 451-6220
260 Franklin Street, Ste. 1501
Boston, Massachusetts 02110

The Venture Capital Fund   (617) 451-2575
100 Franklin Street
Boston, Massachusetts 02110

Venture Founders Corporation   (617) 863-0900
One Cranberry Hill
Lexington, Massachusetts 02173

VIMAC Corp.   (617) 267-2785
12 Arlington Street
Boston, Massachusetts 02116

Worcester Capital Corp.   (617) 793-4508
446 Main Street
Worcester, Massachusetts 01608

Michigan

Accel Partners   (313) 971-4451
2020 Hogback Road
Ann Arbor, Michigan 48104

Comerica Capital Corp.   (313) 258-5800
30150 Telegraph Road, Ste. 245
Birmingham, Michigan 48010

Doan Resources, L.P.   (313) 971-3100
2000 Hogback Road, Ste. 2
Ann Arbor, Michigan 48105

Metro-Detroit Investment Co.   (313) 971-3100
30777 Northwestern Highway, Ste. 300
Farmington Hills, Michigan 48018

Michigan Cap. & Service, Inc.   (313) 663-0702
500 First Nat'l Bldg., 201 S. Main Street
Ann Arbor, Michigan 48104

Michigan Tech Capital Corp.   (909) 487-2643
P.O. Box 529
Hubbell, Michigan 49934

Motor Enterprises, Inc.   (313) 556-4273
3044 W. Grand Blvd., Rm 13-152
Detroit, Michigan 48202

Mutual Investment Co., Inc.   (313) 559-5210
21415 Civic Center Drive, Ste. 217
Southfield, Michigan 48076

Regional Financial Enterprises   (313) 769-0941
315 E. Eisenhower Parkway, Ste. 300
Ann Arbor, Michigan 48104

Minnesota

Cherry Tree Ventures   (612) 893-9012
1400 Northland Plaza, 3800 West 80th Street
Minneapolis, Minnesota 55431

Control Data Capital Corp.   (612) 921-4118
3601 W. 77th Street
Minneapolis, Minnesota 55435

Control Data Community Venture   (612) 921-4352
3601 W. 77th Street
Minneapolis, Minnesota 55435

DGC Capital Co.   (218) 722-0058
603 Alworth Bldg.
Duluth, Minnesota 55802

FBS Venture Capital Company   (612) 544-2754
7515 Wayzata Blvd., Ste. 110
Minneapolis, Minnesota 55426

Northland Capital Corp.   (218) 722-0545
613 Missabe Bldg., 277 W. 1st Street
Duluth, Minnesota 55802

North Star Ventures, Inc.   (612) 333-1133
100 S. Fifth Street, #2200
Minneapolis, Minnesota 55402

Northwest Venture Partners   (612) 372-8770
222 S. Ninth Street, #2800
Minneapolis, Minnesota 55402

Norwest Growth Fund, Inc.   (612) 372-8770
222 S. Ninth Street, #2800
Minneapolis, Minnesota 55402

Pathfinder Venture Capital Funds   (612) 835-1121
7300 Metro Blvd., Ste. 585
Minneapolis, Minnesota 55435

Piper Jaffray Ventures Inc.   (612) 342-6310
Piper Tower
Minneapolis, Minnesota 55402

Retailers Growth Fund, Inc.   (612) 872-4929
2318 Park Avenue
Minneapolis, Minnesota 55404

Shared Ventures, Inc.   (612) 925-3411
6550 York Avenue South, Ste. 419
Minneapolis, Minnesota 55435

Threshold Ventures, Inc.   (612) 874-7199
430 Oak Grove Street, Ste. 303
Minneapolis, Minnesota 55403

Mississippi

Columbia Ventures, Inc.   (601) 354-1453
P.O. Box 1066
Jackson, Mississippi 39215

Invest Capital Corp.   (601) 969-3242
P.O. Box 1066
Jackson, Mississippi 39207

Vicksburg SBIC   (601) 636-4762
P.O. Box 852
Vicksburg, Mississippi 39180

Missouri

Bankers Capital Corp.   (816) 531-1600
3100 Gillham Road
Kansas City, Missouri 64109

Capital for Business, Inc.   (314) 854-7427
11 S. Meramec, #800
St. Louis, Missouri 63105

Capital for Business, Inc.   (816) 234-2357
120 Main Street, Ste. 700
Kansas City, Missouri 64105

Intercapco, Inc.   (314) 863-0600
7800 Bonhomme Avenue
Clayton, Missouri 63105

Intercapco West, Inc.   (314) 863-0600
7800 Bonhomme Avenue
Clayton, Missouri 63105

MorAmerica Capital Corp.   (816) 842-0114
Commerce Tower Bldg., Ste. 2724
911 Main Street
Kansas City, Missouri 64105

United Missouri Capital Corp.   (816) 556-7115
928 Grand Avenue, 1st Floor
Kansas City, Missouri 64106

New Hampshire

Granite State Capital, Inc.   (603) 228-9090
10 Fort Eddy Road
Concord, New Hampshire 03301

Harvard Venture Capital (603) 429-0858
27 Loop Road, P.O. Box 746
Merrimack, New Hampshire 03054

Lotus Capital Corp. (603) 668-8617
875 Elm Street
Manchester, New Hampshire 03101

New Jersey

Accel Partners (609) 683-4500
One Palmer Square
Princeton, New Jersey 08542

Bradford Associates (609) 921-3880
22 Chambers Street
Princeton, New Jersey 08540

Capital Circulation Corp. (201) 947-8637
208 Main Street
Ft. Lee, New Jersey 07024

DSV Partners (609) 454-8882
221 Nassau Street
Princeton, New Jersey 08542

Domain Associates (609) 454-8882
One Palmer Square
Princeton, New Jersey 08542

ESLO Capital Corp. (201) 687-4920
2401 Morris Avenue, Ste. 220EW
Union, New Jersey 07083

Edelson Technology Partners (201) 843-4474
Park 80 West, Plaza II
Saddle Brook, New Jersey 07662

First Princeton Capital Corp. (201) 831-0330
227 Hamburg Turnpike
Pompton Lakes, New Jersey 07442

InnoVen Group (201) 845-4900
Park 80 Plaza West-One
Saddle Brook, New Jersey 07662

Johnston Associates (609) 924-3131
181 Cherry Valley Road
Princeton, New Jersey 08540

Monmouth Capital Corp. (201) 542-4927
P.O. Box 335, 125 Wyckoff Road
Eatontown, New Jersey 07724

MBW Management, Inc.   (201) 285-5533
365 South Street, 2nd Floor
Morristown, New Jersey 07960

Rutgers Minority Investment Co.   (201) 648-5627
180 University Avenue, 3rd Floor
Newark, New Jersey 07102

Tappan Zee Capital Corp.   (201) 256-8280
201 Lower North Road
Little Falls, New Jersey 07424

Unicorn Ventures, Ltd.   (201) 276-7880
6 Commerce Drive
Cranford, New Jersey 07016

Unicorn Ventures II, L.P.   (201) 276-7880
6 Commerce Drive
Cranford, New Jersey 07016

New Mexico

Albuquerque SBIC   (505) 247-0145
P.O. Box 487
Albuquerque, New Mexico 87103

Associated SW Investors, Inc.   (505) 881-0066
2400 Louisiana, N.E., #4
Albuquerque, New Mexico 87110

Equity Capital Corporation   (505) 988-4273
231 Washington Avenue, Ste. 2
Santa Fe, New Mexico 87501

Fluid Capital Corp.   (505) 292-4747
8421 B. Montgomery Blvd., N.E.
Albuquerque, New Mexico 87111

Meadows Ventures   (505) 768-6267
1650 University Blvd., N.E., Ste. 500
Albuquerque, New Mexico 87102

Southwest Capital Inc.   (505) 884-7161
3500-E Commanche Rd., N.E.
Albuquerque, New Mexico 87107

New York

Adler & Company   (212) 759-2800
375 Park Avenue, Ste. 3303
New York, New York 10152

Adler & Shaykin
375 Park Avenue, Ste. 1401
New York, New York 10152

(212) 319-2800

Alan Patricof Associates, Inc.
545 Madison Avenue
New York, New York 10022

(212) 753-6300

American Commercial Capital Corp.
310 Madison Ave., Ste. 1304
New York, New York 10017

(212) 986-3305

AMEV Capital Corp.
One World Trade Ctr, Ste. 5001
New York, New York 10048

(212) 775-9100

Atalanta Investment Co., Inv.
450 Park Avenue, Ste. 2102
New York, New York 10022

(212) 832-1104

Atlantic Capital Corp.
40 Wall Street
New York, New York 10005

(212) 612-0616

BT Capital Corporation
280 Park Avenue
New York, New York 10017

(619) 454-8882

Bessemer Venture Partners
630 Fifth Avenue
New York, New York 10111

(212) 708-9300

Boston Hambro Capital Co.
17 E. 71st Street
New York, New York 10021

(212) 288-7778

BY Capital Corp.
280 Park Avenue
New York, New York 10017

(212) 850-1916

CW Group Inc.
1041 Third Avenue
New York, New York 10021

(212) 308-5266

The Central New York SBIC, Inc.
351 S. Warren Street, Ste. 600
Syracuse, New York 13202

(315) 478-5026

Chase Manhattan Capital Corp.
One Chase Manhattan Plaza, 23rd Floor
New York, New York 10081

(212) 552-6275

Chemical Venture Capital Corp.   (212) 310-4949
277 Park Avenue, 10th Floor
New York, New York 10172

Citicorp Venture Capital Ltd.   (212) 559-1127
153 East 53rd Street, 28th Floor
New York, New York 10043

Clinton Capital Corp.   (212) 696-4334
419 Park Avenue, South
New York, New York 10016

CMNY Capital Co., Inc.   (212) 437-7078
77 Water Street
New York, New York 10005

College Venture Equity Corp.   (813) 248-3878
256 Third Street, P.O. Box 135
Niagara Falls, New York 14303

Concord Partners   (212) 906-7000
535 Madison Avenue
New York, New York 10022

Croyden Capital Corp.   (212) 974-0184
45 Rockefeller Place, Ste. 2165
New York, New York 10111

DeMuth, Folger & Terhune   (212) 509-5580
One Exchange Plaza at 55 Broadway
New York, New York 10006

Drexel Burnham Lambert Inc.   (212) 480-5160
55 Broad Street, 15th Floor
New York, New York 10004

Edwards Capital Co.   (212) 686-2568
215 Lexington Avenue, #805
New York, New York 10016

Elk Associates Funding Corp.   (212) 972-8550
600 Third Avenue, #3810
New York, New York 10016

Equico Capital Corp.   (212) 397-8660
1290 Avenue of the Americas, Ste. 3400
New York, New York 10019

Elrod Technologies, Inc.   (212) 819-1644
1211 Avenue of the Americas
New York, New York 10036

Euclid Partners Corporation   (212) 489-1770
50 Rockefeller Plaza
New York, New York 10020

Everlast Capital Corp.   (212) 695-3910
350 Fifth Avenue, Ste. 2805
New York, New York 10118

Fairfield Equity Corp.   (212) 867-0150
200 E. 42nd Street
New York, New York 10017-5893

Ferranti High Technology, Inc.   (212) 688-9828
515 Madison Avenue, #1225
New York, New York 10022

Fifty-Third Street Ventures, L.P.   (212) 752-8010
420 Madison Ave., #1101
New York, New York 10017

The First Boston Corporation   (212) 909-2000
12 East 49th Street
New York, New York 10017

First Century Partners   (212) 698-6388
1345 Avenue of the Americas
New York, New York 10105

J. H. Foster & Co., Ltd   (212) 753-4810
437 Madison Avenue
New York, New York 10024

Foster Management Company   (212) 753-4810
437 Madison Avenue
New York, New York 10022

Franklin Corp. (The)   (212) 719-4844
1185 Avenue of the Americas, 27th Floor
New York, New York 10036

Fredericks Michael & Co.   (619) 454-8882
1 World Trade Ctr., 15th Floor, Ste. 1509
New York, New York 10048

Fundex Capital Corp.   (619) 454-8882
525 Northern Blvd.
Great Neck, New York 11021

GHW Capital Corp.   (619) 454-8882
489 Fifth Avenue, 2nd Floor
New York, New York 10017

Hambro International Venture Fund   (212) 288-7778
17 East 71st Street
New York, New York 10021

The Hanover Capital Corp.   (212) 687-7083
150 E. 58th Street, Ste. 2710
New York, New York 10155

Harvest Ventures   (212) 838-7776
767 Third Avenue
New York, New York 10017

Hutton Venture Investment   (212) 742-3722
One Battery Park Plaza, Ste. 1801
New York, New York 10004

Hycliff Partners   (212) 921-7755
1211 Avenue of the Americas, Ste. 2905
New York, New York 10036

Ibero-American Investors Corp.   (716) 262-3440
55 St. Paul Street
Rochester, New York

Instoria, Inc./Providentia, Ltd.   (212) 687-7525
140 East 45th Street, 34th Floor
New York, New York 10017

Intergroup Venture Capital Corp.   (212) 661-5428
230 Park Avenue, Ste. 206
New York, New York 10169

Irving Capital Corp.   (212) 408-4800
1290 Avenue of the Americas, 3rd Floor
New York, New York 10104

Key Venture Capital Corp.   (518) 447-3227
60 State Street
Albany, New York 12207

Kwiat Capital Corp.   (212) 391-2461
576 Fifth Avenue
New York, New York 10036

Lawrence Venture Associates   (212) 826-9080
515 Madison Avenue, 29th Floor
New York, New York 10022

ML Technology Ventures, L.P.   (212) 766-6246
165 Broadway
New York, New York 10080

ML Venture Partners 1, L.P.　　　　(212) 980-0410
717 Fifth Avenue
New York, New York 10022

M&T Capital Corp.　　　　　　　　(716) 842-5881
One M&T Place, 5th Floor
Buffalo, New York 14240

Medallion Funding Corp.　　　　　(212) 682-3300
205 E. 42nd Street, Ste. 2020
New York, New York 10017

Minority Equity Capital Co., Inc.　(212) 686-9710
275 Madison Avenue, Ste. 1901
New York, New York 10016

Morgan Stanley Venture Partners　(212) 703-8485
1251 Avenue of the Americas
New York, New York 10020

Multi-Purpose Capital Corp.　　　(914) 963-2733
31 S. Broadway
Yonkers, New York 10701

NAB Nordic Investors Ltd.　　　　(212) 315-6500
600 Fifth Avenue
New York, New York 10020

NatWest USA Capital Corp.　　　　(212) 602-1200
175 Water Street
New York, New York 10038

Nelson Capital Corp.　　　　　　(516) 222-2555
591 Stewart Avenue
Garden City, New York 11530

Norstar Bancorp　　　　　　　　(518) 447-4492
1450 Western Avenue
Albany, New York 12203

Norstar Venture Capital Corp.　　(518) 447-4050
One Norstar Plaza
Albany, New York 12207-2796

North American Funding Corp.　　(212) 226-0080
177 Canal Street
New York, New York 10013

North Street Capital Corp.　　　　(914) 335-7901
250 North Street, RA-6S
White Plains, New York 10625

Northwood Ventures 420 Madison Avenue, 13th Floor New York, New York 10017	(212) 935-4625
NYBDC Capital Corp. 41 State Street Albany, New York 12207	(518) 463-2268
Alan Patricof Associates, Inc. 545 Madison Avenue New York, New York 10022	(212) 753-6300
Pan Pac Capital Corp. 19 Rector Street, 35th Floor New York, New York 10006	(212) 344-6680
Pioneer Ventures 113 East 55th Street New York, New York 10022	(212) 980-9094
Questech Capital Corp. 600 Madison Avenue New York, New York 10022	(619) 454-8882
Rand SBIC, Inc. 1300 Rand Bldg. Buffalo, New York 14203	(716) 853-0802
Rothschild Ventures Inc. One Rockefeller Plaza New York, New York 10020	(212) 757-6000
Salomon Brothers Venture Capital One New York Plaza New York, New York 10004	(212) 747-6293
Peter J. Schmitt Co., Inc. P.O. Box 2 Buffalo, New York 14240	(716) 821-1400
Schroder Ventures One State Street New York, New York 10004	(212) 269-6500
Small Bus. Electronics Co., Inc. 1220 Peninsula Blvd. Hewlett, New York 11557	(516) 374-0743
Southern Tier Capital Corp. 55 S. Main Street Liberty, New York 12754	(914) 292-3030

Sprout Group
140 Broadway
New York, New York 10005

(408) 554-1515

Tappan Zee Capital Corp.
120 N. Main Street
New City, New York 10956

(914) 634-8890

TLC Funding Corp.
141 S. Central Avenue
Hartsdale, New York 10530

(914) 683-1144

Transportation Capital Corp.
60 E. 42nd Street, Ste. 3126
New York, New York 10023

(212) 496-1010

Triad Capital Corp. of NY
960 Southern Blvd.
Bronx, New York 10459

(212) 589-6541

Vega Capital Corp.
720 White Plains Road
Scarsdale, New York 10583

(914) 472-8550

Venrock Associates
30 Rockefeller Plaza, Rm. 5508
New York, New York 10112

(212) 247-3700

Venture SBIC, Inc.
249-12 Jericho Tpke.
Floral Park, New York 1101

(516) 352-0068

Walnut Capital Corp.
110 E. 59th Street, 37th Floor
New York, New York 10016

(212) 750-1000

Warburg, Pincus Ventures, Inc.
466 Lexington Avenue
New York, New York 10017

(212) 878-0600

Welsh, Carson, Anderson & Stowe
One World Financial Center, Ste. 3601
New York, New York 10281

(212) 945-2000

J. H. Whitney & Co.
630 Fifth Avenue, Rm. 3200
New York, New York 10111

(212) 757-0500

Winfield Capital Corp.
237 Mamaroneck Avenue
White Plains, New York 10605

(914) 949-2600

Wood River Capital Corp.   (212) 750-9420
645 Madison Avenue
New York, New York 10022

Worthen Finance & Inv.   (212) 750-9100
17th Floor
New York, New York 10022

North Carolina

Carolina Venture Capital Corp.
P.O. Box 646
Chapel Hill, North Carolina 27514

Delta Capital Inc.   (704) 372-1410
227 N. Tryon Street, Suite 201
Charlotte, North Carolina 28202

Falcon Capital Corp.   (619) 454-8882
400 W. 5th Street
Greenville, North Carolina 27834

Heritage Capital Corp.   (704) 334-2867
2290 First Union Plaza
Charlotte, North Carolina 28282

Kitty Hawk Capital, Ltd.   (704) 333-3777
One Tryon Ctr., Ste. 2030
Charlotte, North Carolina 28284

NCNB SBIC Corp.   (704) 374-5000
One NCNB Plaza, T05-2
Charlotte, North Carolina 28255

NCNB Venture Corp.   (704) 374-0435
One NCNB Plaza
Charlotte, North Carolina 28255

Venture First Associates   (919) 722-9600
2422 Reynolds Road
Winston-Salem, North Carolina 27106

Ohio

A.T. Capital Corp.   (216) 687-4970
900 Euclid Avenue, T-18
Cleveland, Ohio 44101

Capital Funds Corp.   (216) 622-8628
127 Public Square
Cleveland, Ohio 44114

Cardinal Development   (614) 464-5557
40 South 3rd St., Ste. 460
Columbus, Ohio 43215

Clarion Capital Corp.   (216) 953-0555
3555 Curtis Boulevard
Eastlake, Ohio 44114

First Ohio Capital Corp.   (419) 259-7146
606 Madison Avenue
Toledo, Ohio 43604

Gries Investment Co.   (216) 861-1146
720 Statler Office Tower
Cleveland, Ohio 44115

Lubrizol Enterprises, Inc.   (216) 943-4200
28400 Lakeland Blvd.
Wickliffe, Ohio 44092

Morgenthaler Ventures   (216) 621-3070
700 National City Bank Bldg.
Cleveland, Ohio 44114

National City Capital Corp.   (216) 575-2491
623 Euclid Avenue
Cleveland, Ohio 44114

Primus Capital Fund   (216) 621-2185
1375 E. 9th Street, Ste. 2140
Cleveland, Ohio 44114

River Capital Corp.   (216) 781-3655
796 Huntington Building
Cleveland, Ohio 44115

Scientific Advances, Inc.   (614) 294-5541
601 West Fifth Avenue
Columbus, Ohio 43201-3195

SeaGate SBIC   (419) 259-8397
245 Summit Street, #1403
Toledo, Ohio 43603

Oklahoma

Alliance Business Investment Co.   (918) 584-3581
One Williams Ctr., Ste. 2000
Tulsa, Oklahoma 74172

Southwest Venture Capital, Inc.   (918) 742-3177
2700 E. 51st Street, Ste. 340
Tulsa, Oklahoma 74105

Western Venture Capital Corp.   (918) 749-7981
4900 S. Lewis
Tulsa, Oklahoma 74105

Oregon

Cable & Howse Ventures   (503) 248-9646
1800 One Main Place, 101 SW Main
Portland, Oregon 97204

InterVen Partners   (503) 223-4334
227 SW Pine Street, Ste. 200
Portland, Oregon 97204

Northern Pacific Capital Corp.   (503) 241-1255
1201 SW 12th Avenue
Portland, Oregon 97205

Norwest Growth Fund, Inc.   (503) 223-6622
1300 SW Fifth Ave., Ste. 3018
Portland, Oregon 97201

Trendwest Capital Corp.   (503) 882-8059
P.O. Box 5106
Klamath Falls, Oregon 97601

Pennsylvania

Adler & Shaykin   (215) 985-9999
1632 Locust Street
Philadelphia, Pennsylvania 19103

Alliance Enterprise Corp.   (215) 977-3925
1801 Market Street, 3rd Floor
Philadelphia, Pennsylvania 19103

Century IV Partners   (215) 751-9444
1760 Market Street
Philadelphia, Pennsylvania 19103

Enterprice Vent. Cap. Corp of PA   (814) 535-7597
227 Franklin Street, #215
Johnstown, Pennsylvania 15901

First SBIC of California   (412) 223-0707
P.O. Box 512
Washington, Pennsylvania 15901

First Valley Capital Corp.   (215) 732-6760
One Center Square, Ste. 201
Allentown, Pennsylvania 18101

Fostin Capital Corp.   (412) 928-8900
P.O. Box 67
Pittsburgh, Pennsylvania 15230

Gtr. Phil. Ven. Cap. Corp., Inc.   (215) 732-1666
225 S. 15th Street, Ste. 920
Philadelphia, Pennsylvania 19102

Genesis Seed Management Company   (215) 648-3950
5 Great Valley Parkway, Ste. 227
Malvern, Pennsylvania 19102

Hillman Ventures, Inc.   (412) 281-2620
2000 Grant Building
Pittsburgh, Pennsylvania 15219

Meridian Capital Corp.   (215) 278-8907
Blue Bell West, Ste. 122
Blue Bell, Pennsylvania 19422

PNC Capital Corp.   (412) 355-2245
5th Avenue & Wood Street, 19th Floor
Pittsburgh, Pennsylvania 15222

Puerto Rico

First Puerto Rico Capital, Inc.   (809) 832-9171
P.O. Box 816
Mayaguez, Puerto Rico 00709

North America Investment Corp.   (809) 754-6177
Banco Popular Center, Ste. 1710
Hato Rey, Puerto Rico 00919

Rhode Island

Domestic Capital Corp.   (401) 946-3310
814 Reservoir Avenue
Cranston, Rhode Island 02910

Fleet Venture Resources, Inc.   (401) 278-6770
111 Westminster Street
Providence, Rhode Island 02920

Narragansett Capital Corp.   (401) 751-1000
40 Westminster Street
Providence, Rhode Island 02903

Old Stone Capital Corp.   (401) 278-2559
One Old Stone Square, 11th Floor
Providence, Rhode Island 02901

River Capital Corp.   (401) 278-8819
One Hospital Trust Plaza
Providence, Rhode Island 02903

South Carolina

Carolina Venture Capital Corp.   (803) 842-3101
14 Archer Road
Hilton Head Island, South Carolina 29928

Reedy River Ventures   (803) 297-9198
P.O. Box 17529
Greenville, South Carolina 29606

Tennessee

Checkasaw Capital Corp.   (901) 523-6470
P.O. Box 387
Memphis, Tennessee 38147

Financial Resources, Inc.   (901) 527-9411
2800 Sterick Building
Memphis, Tennessee 38103

Leader Capital Corp.   (901) 578-2405
158 Madison Avenue, P.O. Box 708
Memphis, Tennessee 38101-0708

Suwannee Capital Corp.   (901) 345-4200
3030 Poplar Avenue
Memphis, Tennessee 38111

Tennessee Equity Capital Corp.   (615) 373-4502
1102 Stonewall Jackson
Nashville, Tennessee 37220

Valley Capital Corp.   (615) 265-1557
100 W. Martin L. King Blvd., #806
Chattanooga, Tennessee 37402

West Tennessee Venture Cap. Corp.   (901) 527-6091
152 Beale Street, P.O. Box 300
Memphis, Tennessee 38101

Texas

Acorn Ventures, Inc.   (713) 977-7421
2401 Fountainview, Ste. 950
Houston, Texas 77057

Alliance Business Investment Co.   (713) 224-8224
3990 One Shell Place
Houston, Texas 77002

Allied Bancshares Capital Corp.   (713) 226-1625
P.O. Box 3326
Houston, Texas 77253

Americap Corp.   (713) 780-8084
7575 San Felipe, #160
Houston, Texas 77063

Brittany Capital Co.   (214) 954-1515
2424 LTV Tower, 1525 Elm Street
Dallas, Texas 75201

Business Cap. Corp. of Arlington   (817) 656-7380
1112 Copeland Road, Ste. 420
Arlington, Texas 76011-4994

Capital Southwest Venture Corp.   (214) 233-8242
12900 Preston Road, Ste. 700
Dallas, Texas 75230

Central Texas SBIC   (817) 753-6461
514 Austin Avenue, P.O. Box 2600
Waco, Texas 76702-2600

Charter Venture Group, Inc.   (713) 863-0704
2600 Citadel Plaza Dr., 6th Floor
Houston, Texas 77008

Citicorp Venture Capital Ltd.   (214) 880-9670
717 Harwood
Dallas, Texas 75221

Criterion Venture Partners   (713) 751-2400
333 Clay, Ste. 4300
Houston, Texas 77002

Curtin & Co., Inc.   (713) 658-9806
2050 Houston Natural Gas Bldg.
Houston, Texas 77002

Dougery, Jones & Wilder   (214) 960-0077
Two Lincoln Centre, Ste. 1100
5420 LBJ Freeway
Dallas, Texas 75240

Energy Capital Corp.   (713) 236-0006
953 Esperson Bldg.
Houston, Texas 77002

Enterprise Capital Corp. 3501 Allen Pkwy. Houston, Texas 77019	(713) 521-4401
FCA Investment Co. 30900 Post Oak Blvd., #1790 Houston, Texas 77056	(713) 965-0077
The First Dallas Group, Ltd. 5659 Sherry Lane, Ste. 1902 Dallas, Texas 75225	(214) 692-9300
The Grocers SBI Corp. 3131 E. Holcombe Blvd., #101 Houston, Texas 77021	(713) 747-7913
Hickory Venture Capital Corp. 3811 Turtle Creek Blvd., #1000, LB33 Dallas, Texas 75219	(214) 522-1892
Idanta Partners 201 Main Street, Ste. 3200 Ft. Worth, Texas 76102	(817) 338-2020
InterFirst Venture Corp. 901 Main Street, 10th Floor Dallas, Texas 75283	(214) 977-3164
Livingston Capital Ltd. P.O. Box 2507 Houston, Texas 77252	(713) 872-3213
Lone Star Capital, Ltd. 2401 Fountainview, Ste. 950 Houston, Texas 77057	(713) 880-4494
MSI Capitals Corporation 6510 Abrams Road, Ste. 650 Dallas, Texas 75231	(214) 341-1553
Mapleleaf Capital Corp. 55 Waugh Drive, #170 Houston, Texas 77007	(713) 880-4494
MESBIC Financial Corp. of Dallas 12655 North Central Expwy., #814 Dallas, Texas 75243	(213) 637-1597
MESBIC Financial Corp. of Houston 1801 Main Street, Ste. 320 Houston, Texas 77002	(713) 228-8321

Mid-State Capital Corp.   (817) 776-9500
P.O. Box 7554
Waco, Texas 76714

MVenture Corp.   (214) 741-1469
P.O. Box 662090
Dallas, Texas 75266-2090

Omega Capital Corp.   (409) 832-0221
755 S. 11th Street, #250
Beaumont, Texas 77701

Orange Nassau Capital Corp.   (214) 385-9685
13355 Noel Road, Ste. 635
Dallas, Texas 75240

Red River Ventures, Inc.   (214) 422-4999
777 E. 15th Street
Plano, Texas 75074

Republic Venture Group, Inc.   (214) 922-5078
P.O. Box 225961
Dallas, Texas 75265

Retzloff Capital Corp.   (713) 466-4633
P.O. Box 41250
Houston, Texas 77240

Rust Ventures, L.P.   (512) 479-0055
114 West 7th Street
Austin, Texas 78701

San Antonio Venture Grp., Inc.   (512) 223-3633
2300 W. Commerce
San Antonio, Texas 78207

SBI Capital Corp.   (713) 975-1188
P.O. Box 771668
Houston, Texas 77215-1668

Southwest Venture Partnerships   (512) 227-1010
300 Convent, Ste. 1400
San Antonio, Texas 78205

Southern Orient Capital Corp.   (619) 454-8882
2419 Fannin, Ste. 200
Houston, Texas 77002

Southwestern Ven. Cap. TX, Inc.   (512) 379-0380
P.O. Box 1719
Sequin, Texas 78155

Southwestern Ven. Cap. of TX   (512) 822-9949
N. Frost Ctr. Ste. 700
1250 NE Loop 410
San Antonio, Texas 78209

Sunwestern Capital Corp.   (214) 239-5650
12221 Merit Drive, #1680
Dallas, Texas 75251

Sunwestern Management Inc.   (214) 239-5650
3 Forest Plaza, Ste. 1680
12221 Merit Drive
Dallas, Texas 75251

Tenneco Ventures Inc.   (713) 757-8776
1010 Milam, Ste. T2919
Houston, Texas 77001

Texas Capital Corp.   (214) 638-0638
1341 W. Mockingbird, #1250E
Dallas, Texas 75347

United Mercantile Capital Corp.   (915) 533-6375
P.O. Box 66
El Paso, Texas 79940

United Oriental Cap. Co.   (713) 461-3909
908 Town & Country Blvd., #310
Houston, Texas 77024

Wesbanc Ventures, Ltd.   (713) 977-7421
2401 Fountainview, #950
Houston, Texas 77057

Virginia

East West United Investment Co.   (713) 821-6616
6723 Whittier Avenue, Ste. 206B
McLean, Virginia 22101

Hillcrest Group   (804) 643-7358
9 S. 12th Street, P.O. Box 1776
Richmond, Virginia 23219

Metropolitan Capital Corp.   (703) 960-4698
2550 Huntington Avenue
Alexandria, Virginia 22303

River Capital Corp.   (703) 739-2100
1033 N. Fairfax Street
Alexandria, Virginia 22314

Sovran Funding Corp.   (804) 441-4041
One Commercial Place
Norfolk, Virginia 23510

Washington

Cable & Howse Ventures   (206) 646-3030
777 107th Avenue, N.E., Ste. 2300
Bellevue, Washington 98004

Peoples Capital Corp.   (206) 344-8105
2411 4th Avenue, Ste. 400
Seattle, Washington 98121

The Phoenix Partners   (206) 624-8968
2125 One Union Square
Seattle, Washington 98101

Seafirst Capital Corp.   (206) 442-3501
Columbia Seafirst Ctr, 14th Floor
P.O. Box C-34103
Seattle, Washington 98124-1103

Wisconsin

Bando-McGlocklin Inv. Co., Inc.   (414) 784-9010
13555 Bishops Ct., Ste. 205
Brookfield, Wisconsin 53005

Capital Investments, Inc.   (414) 273-6560
744 N. 4th Street
Milwaukee, Wisconsin 53203

Lubar & Co. Incorporated   (414) 291-9000
777 E. Wisconsin Avenue, Ste. 3060
Milwaukee, Wisconsin 53202

M&I Ventures Corp.   (414) 765-7910
770 N. Water Street
Milwaukee, Wisconsin 53203

Madison Capital Corp.   (608) 256-8185
102 State Street
Madison, Wisconsin 53703

Marine Venture Capital, Inc.   (414) 765-2274
111 E. Wisconsin Avenue
Milwaukee, Wisconsin 53202

MorAmerica Capital Corp.   (414) 276-3839
600 East Mason Street
Milwaukee, Wisconsin 53202

Super Market Investors, Inc.   (414) 547-7999
P.O. Box 473
Milwaukee, Wisconsin 53201

Twin Ports Capital Co.   (715) 392-5525
1230 Poplar Avenue, P.O. Box 849
Superior, Wisconsin 54880

Wind Point Partners, L.P.   (414) 631-4030
1525 Howe Street
Racine, Wisconsin 53403

Wisconsin Community Capital Inc.   (608) 256-3441
14 W. Mifflin Street, #314
Madison, Wisconsin 53703

Wisconsin MESBIC, Inc. (The)   (414) 278-0377
622 N. Water Street, Ste. 500
Milwaukee, Wisconsin 53202

Wyoming

Capital Corp. of Wyoming, Inc.   (307) 234-5438
P.O. Box 3599
Casper, Wyoming 82602

——— Glossary ———

The Words

What Terms Should You Know?
Here Are a Few.

This glossary contains some of the more colorful terms used by venture capitalists. It does not include a large number of standard accounting or business terms that you should know. If you find that you do not recognize some of the terms in this book and they are not covered in the glossary, you should refer to a standard business text or your accounting book in order to find definitions of the words being used.

Arm's length   Refers to business transactions where neither the buyer nor the seller is influenced by the other. In a non-arm's length transaction you might sell a family member some assets of the business at a low price to move assets out of the business.

Board   Meaning board of directors of a corporation. These are the individuals who control a corporation for the benefit of the stockholders. They listen to management's recommendations and set policy for the corporation.

Boiler plate   Boiler plate paragraphs are the standard paragraphs in most venture capital and investment documents.

Bricks and mortar   The assets of your company. The term is derived from a building that is built of bricks and mortar.

Buy-Sell   A buy-sell agreement is one in which, under certain circumstances, the first party in a partnership must agree to buy out the second party, or the second party must agree to buy out the first party. Buy-sell arrangements usually are negotiated between two partners such as an entrepreneur and a venture capitalist.

Buy out   The term refers to the sale of a business; for example, when the buyer of a business buys it, he "buys out" the seller.

Cash flow   The most important aspect of any small business is the cash flow. The money coming in and the money going out is the flow of cash that determines whether a business will survive.

Cash in   When you sell all or part of your stock for cash. Cashing in is an extremely exciting moment because it usually means you are rich.

Closing   The event that occurs when you sign legal documents binding your company and transferring cash from the venture capitalist to your company.

Collateral   The assets you pledge for a loan made to your company. If you do not repay the loan, the collateral can be sold.

Control   Owning 51 percent of the stock of a company or, from another perspective, owning enough stock in the company to control what management will do.

Convertible   Usually refers to debt or preferred stock, each of which is convertible into common stock of the company. Obviously, it is possible to have debt convertible into preferred stock and it is even possible to have preferred stock convertible into debt, although the latter is unusual.

Covenant   Paragraphs in the legal documents stating the things you agree you will do and paragraphs stating what you will not do.

Deal   The bargain struck between the venture capitalist and the entrepreneur. In more general terms, any agreement between two individuals, especially a buyer and a seller.

Debenture   Another word for a debt, note, or loan.

Debt service   The amount of money you have to pay on a debt in order to keep it from being in default. If you make the payments that are called for under a note or loan, then you are servicing the debt.

Default   When you have done something you told your investor you would not do, which is written down in the investment agreement, then it is a default.

Downside   The amount of risk an investor takes in any venture is called the downside. If you stand to lose half your money if a business goes under, the downside risk is said to be 50 percent.

Due diligence   The process of investigating a business venture to determine its feasibility.

Earn out The contract between the entrepreneur and the buying corporation that provides for the entrepreneur to earn additional money on the sale of his company, if operating earnings are in excess of a specified amount during the future years.

Equity Normally it describes the preferred and common stock of a business. Also, it is frequently used to describe the amount of ownership of one person or a venture capitalist in a business.

Exit The sale of equity or ownership in the business for cash or notes.

Good idea A good idea is one that makes a large amount of money.

Good people The supreme compliment to an entrepreneur by a venture capitalist. It means the entrepreneur is honest, loyal, and a straight shooter.

Grace period The period of time you have to correct a default. *See* Default, above.

Lead investor The investor who leads a group of investors into an investment. Usually one venture capitalist will be the lead investor when a group of venture capitalists invest in a single business. *See* Syndication, below.

Leverage Another term for debt. Debt is usually referred to as leverage because in using debt, one does not have to give up equity. So for a very small amount of equity and a large amount of debt, one can leverage a business on the basis of its assets.

Leverage buy-out An acquisition of a business using mostly debt and a small amount of equity. The debt is secured by the assets of the business.

Options The right given to someone, say the venture capitalist, to buy stock in your company. *See also* Warrants, below.

Paper The notes you receive for the sale of your stock or the assets in your company. These are called paper because paper is fairly worthless. Many of the notes received by entrepreneurs from the sale of their company to someone else have turned into worthless paper.

PE *See* Price-earnings ratio, below.

Pool Usually a venture capital limited partnership in which each investor has "pooled" his resources by purchasing a limited partnership interest in the venture capital partnership. The partnership then invests in small businesses.

Price-earnings ratio The number you multiply times the earnings per share number in order to determine a fair price for a stock. For example, if a stock is earning $.50 a share and a price-earnings ratio of eight is used, then the stock is worth $4 per share.

Pricing The determination as to the price that an investor will pay to purchase shares of stock in the business. Pricing is determined on the basis of the full value of the company. Every time one share of stock is sold, the sale determines the value of the company and in this way, pricing occurs.

Proposal   The document that must be put together by an entrepreneur in order to propose an investment to a venture capitalist or other investors.

Public offering   The selling of shares to the general public through the registration of shares with the Securities and Exchange Commission.

Raising capital   Raising capital refers to obtaining capital from investors or venture capital sources.

Reality   What every individual should make sure he understands before jumping into the small business arena.

Representations   These are the facts about your company that you represent to the investor to be true.

Situation   General term used to refer to any business deal. It is common to refer to a business opportunity as a "situation."

Structure   Term referring to the type of financing that will be used to finance a small business. The structure might be $100,000 in common stock and $500,000 in debt at 15 percent interest for ten years.

Syndication   The process whereby a group of venture capitalists will each put in a portion of the amount of money needed to finance a small business.

Take back   Term referring to the situation where the seller of a business must take back something rather than cash. The take back usually refers to a note with reasonable terms and conditions.

Turnaround   This word is used to describe businesses that are in trouble and whose management will cause the business to become profitable so they are no longer in trouble.

Underwriter   The stockbrokerage house used to raise funds for a small business in a public offering. In a public offering the stockbrokerage house that underwrites the small business is the one that buys the shares from the small business and sells them to the general public.

Unlocking agreement   A legal agreement between two parties meaning that one party may require the other to buy it out under certain circumstances; thus, the so-called unlocking of the partnership.

Upside   The amount of money that one can make by investing in a certain deal is called the upside potential.

Warrant   A stock option given to someone else that entitles them to purchase stock in your company.

Warranties   These are items concerning your company that you have told the venture capitalist or investor are true.

Index